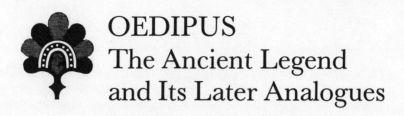

OEDIPUS
The Ancient Legend
and Its Later Analogues

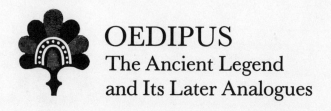

OEDIPUS
The Ancient Legend
and Its Later Analogues

Lowell Edmunds

THE JOHNS HOPKINS UNIVERSITY PRESS
Baltimore and London

The original edition of this book was brought to publication with
the generous assistance of the Andrew W. Mellon Foundation.

Johns Hopkins Paperbacks edition, 1996
05 04 03 02 01 00 99 98 97 96   5 4 3 2 1

The Johns Hopkins University Press
2715 North Charles Street
Baltimore, Maryland 21218-4319
The Johns Hopkins Press Ltd., London

Library of Congress Cataloging in Publication Data

Edmunds, Lowell.
    Oedipus: the ancient legend and its later analogues.

    Includes bibliographies and index.
    1. Oedipus (Tale)—History and criticism.   I. Title.
GR75.03E36   1984   398.2´2   84-47948
ISBN 0-8018-2490-7
ISBN 0-8018-5490-3 (pbk.: acid-free paper)

A catalog record for this book is available from the British Library.

Contents

Preface

It is odd that the Oedipus legend, perhaps the most famous story from classical antiquity, is almost never studied as a narrative. Classicists usually study it in the form of tragedy and thus from the point of view of literary history and literary criticism. Freud took the legend as confirmation of a universal psychic complex and named the complex after Oedipus. Although Lévi-Strauss discussed the Oedipus legend apropos of a theory of mythology, this theory entailed the systematic neglect of narrative sequence. Vladimir Propp wrote at length on Oedipus folklore in relation to the ancient legend, but his goal was to show that the narrative contained traces of prehistorical stages of human society. The interpretation, therefore, of the ancient legend as such (and not as tragedy or as symbolic of universal psychic experience or as whatever) can still be attempted; and the medieval and modern analogues are an intriguing, useful, and heretofore largely unexplored body of comparative material.

The Introduction represents an attempt to apply this comparative material to interpretation of the ancient legend (for my use of the term *legend*, see note 9 to the Introduction). The Introduction is not, therefore, a folkloristic analysis of the analogues, a task that a classicist must leave to folklorists. The geographical-historical problem, for example, receives short shrift. Although I discuss the historical relation of the analogues to the ancient Oedipus legend, I have not dealt with the problem of geographical diffusion except in passing. The geographical problem arises especially in connection with "Sikhalòl and His Mother" (UL1), collected by William Lessa on Ulithi Atoll, in the western Carolines, and with "The Boy and the Chief" (PO1). I agree in principle with Lessa that the tale's appearance in that remote place must be the result of geographical-historical diffusion (and thus I disagree with Roger E. Mitchell, cited in Bibliography 3) but I do not see that he has been able to trace this diffusion. Thanks to the kindness of Mrs. Judith Reed of the Bernice B. Bishop Museum, Honolulu, I was able to read some of the unpublished tales collected by Drs. J. L. Fischer and Samuel Elbert on Ponape, and of these only "The Boy and The Chief" (PO1) seemed to be germane to the problem, but it does not bring us much closer to the Near Eastern and European tales.

Despite these demurrals concerning the problem of diffusion, the analogues, after the first seven in the collection, which come from the medieval period, are arranged in broad geographic categories and are provided with sigla that indicate the language in which the story was originally told (see Sigla, below). The geographic categories and the number of analogues for each are as follows: Modern Europe, exclusive of Slavic (45), Slavic (11), Near East, Asia, Africa, Western Hemisphere (13). It will be immediately obvious that these figures are statistically meaningless, and, in any case, they are affected by intensity of collecting. Yet it is perhaps salutary to gain a sense of how few analogues we are working with, especially when the "world-wide occurrence of the Oedipus story" is sometimes invoked in discussion of the universality of the Oedipus complex and the folklorist sometimes gets the impression that a study of the Oedipus folktale on the model of Warren Roberts's *The Kind and the Unkind Girls* would be possible. Such a study of the Oedipus folktale is impossible. Even the usually modest figures given by Thompson in *The Types of the Folktale* (see Bibliography 1) under 931 (Oedipus) are sometimes exaggerated, especially in the case of Ireland.

Huge areas of the world, the Asian subcontinent, the Malay archipelago, and China and Japan may seem to have gone unnoticed, and some word of apology is called for. I read all the Indonesian tales cited by Lessa, and many more besides, and I should like to record here my gratitude to Mrs. Stella Admiraal Lubsen for her translations from the Dutch, the language in which much Indonesian mythology has come to the Western world. For a large amount of material on the *babad*, Serat Kanda, and related matters, I am grateful to Mr. F. Deeleman of the Koninklijk Instituut voor de Tropen, Amsterdam, and to Miss L. K. N. Tjoa of the Bibliotheck der Rijksuniversiteit, Leiden. Unfortunately, it was not possible to include any of the Indonesian material. I have also had to leave out the Japanese and Chinese folktales translated for me by Dr. Victor Mair, who did valuable research on them. Professors Indira Shetterley and George L. Hart III provided me with translations of interesting and perhaps relevant Sanskrit and Tamil folktales that have also gone undiscussed. I should mention here three Indian folktales that I could not persuade myself to add to what had to be a minimal collection: see Karve, d'Penha, and Ramanujan in Bibliography 3. These folktales are now well analyzed in the new version of Ramanujan's article.

My collection is far from including everything that one will find cited under 931 (Oedipus) in Thompson and in other type-indexes. As for Thompson, my experiences with this source are recorded in the Appendix to *The Sphinx in the Oedipus Legend* (see Bibliography 1). In any case, I have not limited the collection of analogues to tales that conform to 931, nor is my essay a discussion of this type or of any other type. As for other type-indexes and archives, because 931 is widely held to be a "tale of fate," practically any folktale reflecting the inevitability of fate may be listed under it, and one spends a great deal of time tracking down references to folktales that bear no resemblance to the Oedipus folktale—not only one's own time but also that of others. I put Professor Blaise Nagy to the trouble of locating and translating a Hungarian folktale that turned out to be a descendant of the medieval St. Julian legend.

Each of the analogues in the collection has headnotes containing all available information concerning the sources. Material from archives and from older ethnographical works is often unaccompanied by the sort of information that folklorists and anthropologists would like to have.

In my mind, the research for this book is closely connected with a time and a place. The time is the summer and fall of 1974 and the place is the Widener Library at Harvard University. The center of my activity was a study in Widener graciously lent me by the late Professor Cedric Whitman, but the quest for folktales led me to many parts of the library and brought me into contact with more, perhaps, of the staff than a scholar would ordinarily have occasion to meet. It is a pleasure to mention those who were especially helpful to me. The Reference Librarians, Pawel Depta (now Associate Librarian of the Cambridge Public Library), Sheila K. Hart (now Head of Public Services), Marion Schoon, and Heather Cole (now Librarian of Hilles and Lamont Libraries at Harvard) often performed feats of what seemed like serendipity to an ordinary researcher. In the Circulation Division, I was treated kindly by Mr. Edward B. Doctoroff, now Head of Circulation Services, then in charge of tracing lost books, by his associates, Messrs. Gerald Schwertfeger (now Head of Tracing), Francis Cox, Jeffrey Beuchner, and William Hanify (now Pension Accountant at Harvard), and by David Buxton, then Circulation Librarian, now of the University of Virginia Library. Barbara Dames, the Interlibrary Loan Librarian, often found works that I thought were not in the Harvard University Library's collection, and procured from elsewhere those that in fact were not. Dr. Charles Berlin,

Lee M. Friedman Bibliographer in Judaica, helped me locate HE1 proceeding from an almost impossibly vague reference. A similar service in the case of a Chinese tale was provided me by Yung-hsiang Lai, Assistant Librarian in the Harvard-Yenching Library. The following members of the Widener staff have contributed translations to this collection: Grazyna Slanda, Slavic Librarian; Emel Tekin, Turkish Specialist in the Middle Eastern Department; Annette Voth, formerly Book Selector for Scandinavian Languages. Milada Součkova (now deceased) of the Slavic Department in Widener Library at Harvard, and Helen Beneš, formerly of the Catalogue Division, helped me with Czech tales.

Those in other places who were especially helpful to me in making this collection were: Dr. P. N. Boratav, Paris; Mr. William Brisk, formerly Director of the Latin American Scholarship Program of American Universities, Cambridge; Mr. Ronald Grambo, Lektor, Kungsvinger; Ms. Polly Grimshaw, Librarian for Sociology, Anthropology, and Folklore, University Libraries, Indiana University; Professor A. M. Mehendale, Deccan College, Poona; Ms. Pirkko-Liisa Rausma, Suomalaisen Kirjallisuuden Seura, Helsinki; Max Rodriquez, Sub-Director, Ministerio de Educación Nacional, Bogota; Sean Ó Súilleabháin, Archivist and Lecturer, Department of Irish Folklore, University College, Belfield, Dublin; Professor Ahmet E. Uysal, Ankara; Professor Warren S. Walker, Texas Tech University.

There are some folktales that I should have liked to include, but could not find. Three of these are folktales to which scholars have alluded without giving references. One is the Oedipus folktale collected from the Cape Verde Islanders of Massachusetts that Stith Thompson mentions in *The Folktale* (New York, 1951), p. 141. Another is the Oedipus story told by the Shilluk, mentioned by William Bascom, in "The Forms of Folklore," *JAF* 70 (1957) 111. A third is a story of parricide and sexual rivalry for the mother told by the Lambda, a central Bantu tribe. Kluckhohn mentions this story in "Recurrent Themes in Myths and Mythmaking" (see Bibliography 3). Undoubtedly there are other stories, too, that should have been included and, although the collection may be the worse for their absence, perhaps it will at least serve as a magnet to draw them out of their present obscurity.

It remains for me to thank Professor William Hansen of Indiana University and my former colleague at Boston College Janis Kreslins for their careful reading of various drafts of the Introduction; Dr. Richard Ingber for his willingness to share his enormous learning with me; Professor Alan Dundes, whom I was fortunate to meet in the summer of 1974 and who has encouraged and helped me ever since; and Professor Froma Zeitlin for very useful comments on the final draft of the Introduction.

The folktales designated AR1, FI14, RS1, and ZL1 originally appeared in *The Sphinx in the Oedipus Legend,* Beiträge zur klassischen Philologie 127 (Königstein/Ts., 1981). I am grateful to Verlag Anton Hain for permission to reprint.

I also thank Harvard University Press, publishers of the Loeb Classical Library, for permission to quote from translations contained in the following: *Apollodorus: The Library,* trans. J. G. Frazer (1921); *Diodorus of Sicily,* trans. C. H. Oldfather, vol. 3 (1939); *Pausanias: Description of Greece,* trans. W. H. S. Jones, vol. 4 (1935); and *Athenaeus: The Deipnosophists,* trans. C. B. Gulick, vol. 5 (1933).

Sigla

Parentheses indicate the language from which the present translation was made, if it was not made from the language in which the folktale was originally told. A question mark indicates uncertainty concerning the language or dialect in which the folktale was told. An asterisk indicates that the source gave no title for the tale, and the title was therefore assigned by me.

AL	Albanian	LI	Lithuanian
AR	Arabic	LP	Lappish
BL	Bulgarian	ML	Malagasy
FI	Finnish	NG	Norwegian
FC	French Creole	OR	Old Russian
GK	Medieval Greek	PL	Polish
GR	Modern Greek	PO	Ponapean
GM	German	RM	Romanian
HE	Hebrew	RS	Russian
HU	Hungarian	SC	Serbo-Croatian
IR	Irish	SP	Spanish
IT	Italian	TK	Turkish
KR	Karelian	UK	Ukrainian
KV	Koutslovach	UL	Ulithian
LA	Latvian	ZL	Zulu
LT	Latin		

List of Analogues

Abbreviations

Abb. Abbildung = illustration.

Aesch. Aeschylus. 5th century B.C. Tragedian. *Sept.* = *Septem Contra Thebas* = *The Seven Against Thebes.* Text: Denys Page (Oxford, 1972). Translation: Christopher M. Dawson, *The Seven Against Thebes,* by Aeschylus (Englewood Cliffs, N.J., 1970).

Androtion Androtion. ca. 410–340 B.C. Athenian statesman and author of an Atthis, Athenian history. Fragments in *FGrH* (q.v.).

AP *Anthologia Palatina* = *The Palatine Anthology,* often called "The Greek Anthology." It is, in the form in which we have it, a Byzantine compilation of the 10th century A.D. Most recent text: H. Beckby, *Anthologia Graeca,* 4 vols. (Munich, 1957–58). No complete translation into English.

Antimachus Antimachus of Colophon. Born probably ca. 444 B.C. Poet and scholar. Five poems by him are mentioned. One is a Thebaid on the first expedition against Thebes. Another is the *Lyde,* a narrative elegy, two lines of which are preserved in schol. Eur. *Phoen.* 44. Text: Ernest Diehl, *Fragmenta Lyrica Graeca,* vol. 1, 3d ed. (Leipzig, 1949), pp. 110–11. No English translation.

Apollod. Apollodorus. 2nd century B.C. Scholar. The *Library,* a summary of Greek mythology, is attributed to him; but internal evidence shows that the work cannot be earlier than the middle of the first century B.C. Trans-

lation and text: *Apollodorus: The Library,* trans.
J. G. Frazer, 2 vols. (Loeb Classical Library, 1921).

Asclepiades   Asclepiades. 4th century B.C. Pupil of Isocrates. Wrote
Tragodoumena, "Stories from Greek Tragedy," which
became a source for the mythographers.

Athen.   Athenaeus. 2nd–3rd century A.D. Polyhistor. *The
Learned Banquet* is a symposium at which the guests
represent many fields of knowledge. Text and translation: C. B. Gulick, 7 vols. (Loeb Classical Library,
1927–41).

Cedrenus   Georgius Cedrenus. ca. A.D. 1100. Like Malalas (q.v.), a
Byzantine chronicler. Author of *Universal Chronicle.*
Text: A. I. Becker, *Georgius Cedrenus,* 2 vols., in *CSHB*
(1838). No English translation.

CSHB   B. G. Niehbuhr, ed. *Corpus Scriptorum Historiae Byzan-
tinae* (Bonn, 1828–97). The volumes of the collection
as a whole are not numbered; they are cited by year of
publication.

CVA   *Corpus Vasorum Anticorum.* Published by Union
Académique Internationale. Brussels, 1925– .

Dio Chrys.   Dio Chrysostomus. 1st–2nd century A.D. Rhetorician.
Or. = Orationes = Orations. Text and translation: J. W.
Cohoon and H. L. Crosby, *Dio Chrysostom,* 5 vols.
(Loeb Classical Library, 1932–51).

Diod.   Diodorus Siculus. 1st century B.C. Historian. Wrote
Library of History. Text and translation: C. H. Oldfather
and others, 12 vols. (Loeb Classical Library, 1933–67).

Eur.   Euripides. 5th century B.C. Tragedian. *Phoen. = Phoenissae = The Phoenician Women* (sometimes *The Phoenician Maidens*). Text and translation in A. S. Way,
Euripides, 4 vols. (Loeb Classical Library, 1962–66).
Oed. = Oedipus. Fragments in August Nauck, *Trag-
icorum Graecorum Fragmenta,* 2d ed. (repr. Hildesheim,
1964), pp. 404-10. No translation.

FGrH   Felix Jacoby, *Die Fragmente der griechischen Historiker*
(Berlin and Leiden, 1923–). No translation.

FHG   Carl Mueller, *Fragmenta Historicorum Graecorum*
(Paris, 1851). No translation.

fr. Fragment.

Hes. Hesiod. 8th and/or 7th century B.C. Poet. *Theog.* = *Theogony*. Text and translation: H. G. Evelyn-White, *Hesiod, The Homeric Hymns and Homerica* (Loeb Classical Library, 1964), including translations of the longer fragments. Text of fragments: R. Merkelbach and M. L. West, *Fragmenta Hesiodea* (Oxford, 1967).

Hom. Homer. 8th century B.C.(?) Epic poet. *Il.* = *Iliad. Od.* = *Odyssey*. Translations widely available.

Hyg. Hyginus. Date unknown. *Fab.* = *Fabulae,* a handbook of mythology. Text: H. J. Rose, *Hygini Fabulae* (Leiden, 1934). Translation: Mary Grant, *The Myths of Hyginus* (Lawrence, Kans., 1960).

hypoth. Hypothesis. Most Greek plays are prefaced by an intro-ductory note giving an outline of the play and some-times information concerning the original production, other treatments of the same theme, etc. The sources of information in the hypotheses cannot usually be ascertained. See "Hypothesis" in *The Oxford Classical Dictionary,* 2d ed. (1970).

Joh. Antioch. Johannes Antiochenus = John of Antioch. Probably 7th century A.D. Chronicler. Text: *FHG,* vol. 4. (See *FHG* above.) No translation. For problems related to the identity of this author, see Wolfgang Buchwald, Armin Hohlweg, and Otto Prinz, *Tusculum-Lexikon* (Munich, 1963), s.vv. Johannes von Antiocheia and Pseudo-Johannes von Antiocheia.

Lyc. Lycophron. 4th–3rd century B.C. Scholar and poet. See Tz., below.

Malalas Johannes Malalas. 6th century A.D. Greek rhetorician and historian. *Chronographia,* a universal history. Text: Ludwig Dindorf, *Ioannis Malalae Chronographia,* in *CSHB* (1831). No English translation of pertinent sec-tions. Dindorf gives a Latin translation.

MS Manuscript.

Myth. Vat. Mythographi Vaticani = Vatican Mythographers. This name is given to the anonymous authors of three miscellaneous collections of mythology, after the fact

that their first editor used only Vatican manuscripts.
On problems connected with these collections, see K. O.
Elliot and J. P. Elder, "A Critical Edition of the Vatican
Mythographers," *TAPA* 78 (1947): 189-207. Text:
George Bode, *Scriptores Rerum Mythicarum Latini Tres
Romae Nuper Reperti,* 2 vols. (Celle, 1834). No English
translation.

Nic. Dam. Nicolaus Damascenus = Nicholas of Damascus. 1st
century B.C. Dramatist, philosopher, biographer, historian. Fragments of his historical writing in *FGrH* (see
above), Pt. 2A, pp. 324-430. No English translation.

Ov. Ovid. 43 B.C.-A.D. 17 Poet. *Ib.* = *Ibis,* a poem full of
mythological learning putting a curse upon an unnamed
enemy. Text: Antonio La Penna, *Ibis: Prolegomeni,
etc.* (Florence, 1957). Translation: J. H. Mozley, *Ovid:
The Art of Love and Other Poems* (Loeb Classical
Library, 1962), pp. 251-307.

Palaeph. Palaephatus. 4th century B.C. Author of *On Incredible
Things,* a rationalizing study of myths. Text: Nicolaus
Festa, *Palaephati Peri Apistōn* . . . (in *Mythographi
Graeci,* vol. 3, fasc. 2 [Leipzig, 1902]). No translation.

Paus. Pausanias. 2nd century A.D. Traveler and geographer.
Description of Greece. Translation: J. G. Frazer,
Pausanias's Description of Greece (Biblo and Tannen:
New York, 1965), 6 vols. Text and translation:
W. H. S. Jones and R. E. Wycherley, 5 vols. (Loeb
Classical Library, 1918-35).

Peisander Peisander. The identity of this writer is uncertain. Fragments in *FGrH,* Pt. 1. Translation of the pertinent
fragment in E. L. de Kock (see Bibliography 1).

Pherecydes Pherecydes. 5th century B.C. Athenian author of gene-
alogical and mythological treatises. Fragments in *FGrH,*
Pt. 1. No translation.

Pind. Pindar. 5th century B.C. Lyric poet. *Ol.* = *Olympian
Odes.* Text: B. Snell, *Pindarus* (Leipzig, 1959), Pt. 1
(Epinician Odes), 3d ed. Translations: Sir John Sandys,
Pindarus (Loeb Classical Library, 1915), with text;
Sir Maurice Bowra, *The Odes of Pindar* (Harmonds-
worth, 1969).

Ps.-Plut. Pseudo-Plutarch. The designation for the unknown
author of works definitely not by Plutarch that have
come down to us in the manuscripts of Plutarch.
parall. min. = parallela minora (Minor Parallels), a short
collection of investigations into various matters, Greek
and Roman. Text: W. Nachstaedt, W. Sieveking, and
J. B. Titchener, *Plutarchi Moralia,* vol. 2 (Leipzig, 1971),
305A ff. Text and translation: F. C. Babbitt, *Plutarch's
Moralia,* vol. 4 (Loeb Classical Library, 1936), pp. 253–
317.

schol. scholium, scholia, or scholiast. Scholia are interpretive
or critical comments found in the margins of manuscripts. The sources of scholia are usually lost com-
mentaries. The scholia on ancient authors have been
collected and published by modern scholars. The
collections cited in this book are:
Eduard Schwartz, *Scholia in Euripidem,* vol. 1 (Berlin,
1887).
William Dindorf, *Scholia Graeca in Euripidis Tragoedia,*
vol. 3 (Oxford, 1863).
Harmut Erbse, *Scholia Graeca in Homeri Iliadem
(Scholia Vetera),* 3 vols. (Berlin, 1969–). William Din-
dorf and Ernest Maass, *Scholia Graeca in Homeri
Iliadem ex Codicibus Aucta et Emendata,* 6 vols. (Ox-
ford, 1875–88).
The scholia on Stat. (q.v.) *Theb.* are attributed to
Lactantius Placidus, but are not likely to be his. Text:
R. Jahnke, *Lactantii Placidi Qui Dicitur Commentarios
in Statii Thebaida et Commentarium in Achilleida*
(Leipzig, 1898).
Hans Flach, *Glossen und Scholien zur hesiodischen
Theogonie mit Prolegomena* (Leipzig, 1876).

Sen. Seneca. ca. A.D. 1–65. Roman orator, writer in various
genres, tutor and advisor to Nero. *Phoen. = Phoenissae
= Phoenician Women. Oed. = Oedipus.* Texts and
translations in F. J. Miller, *Seneca's Tragedies,* 2 vols.
(Loeb Classical Library, 1953).

Soph. Sophocles. 5th century B.C. Tragedian. *Ant. = Antigone.
OC = Oedipus Coloneus = Oedipus at Colonus. OT =
Oedipus Tyrannus = Oedipus the King.* Translations

everywhere, so to speak. E.g., D. Fitts and R. Fitzgerald, *The Oedipus Cycle* (New York, 1949).

Stat.   Statius. 1st century A.D. Poet. *Theb.* = *Thebaid,* an epic poem. Text and translation: J. H. Mozley, *Statius,* 2 vols. (Loeb Classical Library, 1955).

Stesichorus   Stesichorus. 7th–6th century B.C. Lyric poet. Text of the pertinent fragment cited in the notes.

Thebaid   *Thebaid,* the name of an epic by Stat. (q.v.) and also of a lost Greek epic belonging to the Epic Cycle (see "Epic Cycle" in *The Oxford Classical Dictionary,* 2d ed.). Text and translation of surviving fragments: H. G. Evelyn-White, *Hesiod, The Homeric Hymns and Homerica* (Loeb Classical Library, 1964), pp. 485–87.

Tz.   Tzetzes. 12th century A.D. Byzantine scholar. His scholia on Lycophron's *Alexandra* and the text of that poem in E. Scheer, *Lycophronis Alexandra,* vol. 1 (1881) and vol. 2 (1908).

Vat.   Vatican.

Zen.   Zenobius. 2nd century A.D. Proverbialist. Text: E. L. von Leutsch and F. G. Schneidewin, *Paroemiographi Graeci,* 2 vols. (Göttingen, 1839–51).

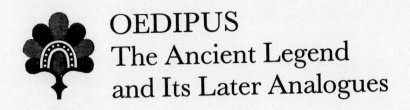

OEDIPUS
The Ancient Legend
and Its Later Analogues

Introduction

1. THE OEDIPUS LEGEND IN THE TWENTIETH CENTURY

Oedipus? Never heard of it." A remark, one must agree, that could be made only in a completely new order of things.[1] This side of the revolution, Oedipus continues to reign, as he has done since the rediscovery of Sophocles and Aristotle in the early sixteenth century. At that time, its own merits and the authority of Aristotle, who praised the perfection of its plot in the *Poetics,* combined to confer on *Oedipus the King* a unique and lasting prestige. Translations, adaptations, and performances still come forth in a never-ending stream. Again and again, playwrights have tried their hand at new shapings of the Sophoclean material. The literatures of England and of most of the countries of Western Europe have their Oedipuses, and often a country's Oedipus forms a whole chapter in the history of its literature.[2] Oedipus has been taken up in modern art forms too. The Sophoclean plot became the basis of librettos for Leoncavallo, for Orff, and for Stravinsky. In cinema, there have been the filmed stage performances directed by Sir Tyrone Guthrie (1956) and by Philip Saville (1969), the one invoking the mood of ritual, with masks, slow movement, and stationary camera, the other more immediate, emotional, and "human." Pier Paolo Pasolini's *Edipo Re* (1969) is a free adaptation of the material, with Freudian and Marxist themes, in a contemporary primitive setting.

One of the results of the vast and endless influence of Sophocles has

1. Gilles Deleuze and Félix Guattari, *Anti-Oedipus: Capitalism and Schizophrenia,* trans. Robert Hurley, Mark Seem, and Helen R. Lane (New York, 1977), p. 96.
2. See Frenzel and Schenkeveld (Bibliography 3).

been that Oedipus has attained an exemplary status. He may be the figure of the criminal, as in Dürrenmatt's *Monstervortrag über Gerechtigkeit und Recht*, or he may represent the problem of fate, as in Pavese's dialogue, "La Strada."[3] For Hegel and Nietzsche, Oedipus, the solver of the Sphinx's riddle, stood for the human intellect,[4] and, in this century, one distinguished classicist has seen in Oedipus "the working of a great intelligence," and another has said, "To me personally Oedipus is a kind of symbol of human intelligence which cannot rest until it has solved all the riddles."[5]

The tragedy to which Oedipus owes his exemplary stature has not, however, always impressed twentieth-century thinkers. The renowned classicist Gilbert Murray wrote to Yeats in 1904 concerning *Oedipus the King:* "Even the good things that have to be done in order to make the plot work are done through mere loss of temper. The spiritual tragedy is never faced or understood: all stress is laid on the mere external uncleanness." In a postscript to a letter to Iris Barry in 1916, Ezra Pound wrote: "Have looked at a bad translation of Sophocles. Certainly the whole Oedipus story is a darn silly lot of buncombe—used as a peg for some very magnificent phrases. Superbly used."[6]

Another refusal to admire is found in Walter Benjamin's review of Gide's *Oedipe*. The difference between the Gidean and the Sophoclean Oedipus, Benjamin says, is that the former has "won speech. The Sophoclean Oedipus is, in fact, dumb, almost dumb."[7] On the one hand, this remark seems to miss the point. It is precisely speech that Oedipus wins when he becomes the hero of a Greek tragedy. In the now lost Theban epics, Oedipus of course had speeches; but in tragedy he speaks for himself, not for a narrator, and in tragedy he is represented as speaking spontaneously and adequately, within necessary limitations, to every demand and event. He is anything but dumb. On the other hand, Benjamin's remark has a certain justice. In comparison with the Oedipuses of modern drama, the Sophoclean Oedipus is dumb above all

3. Friedrich Dürrenmatt, *Monstervortrag über Gerechtigkeit und Recht* (Zurich, 1969), p. 8. Cesare Pavese, *Dialoghi con Leucò* (Turin, 1947), pp. 72-77. Translation: W. Arrowsmith and D. S. Carne-Ross, *Dialogues with Leucò* (Ann Arbor, 1965), pp. 58-63.

4. See the last section of this Introduction for discussion and references.

5. Bernard Knox, *Oedipus at Thebes* (New York, 1971), p. 18; E. R. Dodds, "On Misunderstanding the *Oedipus Rex*," *Greece and Rome*, 2d ser., 13 (1966): 48.

6. Murray quoted in Joseph Hone, *W. B. Yeats, 1865-1939* (London, 1942), p. 256; Ezra Pound, *Selected Letters, 1907-1941* (New York, 1971), p. 95.

7. Walter Benjamin, "*Oedipus hat die Sprache gewonnen:* Der sophokleische Oedipus nämlich ist stumm, fast stumm," *Ausgewählte Schriften*, vol. 2 (Angelus Novus) (Frankfurt am Main, 1966), p. 464. The review appeared originally in *Blätter des hessischen Landestheaters* (1931-32): 157-62.

at the realization of his guilt. As Benjamin observes, the self-blinding of the Sophoclean Oedipus is even a flight from the realization.[8] The modern Oedipus, however, can reflect upon, can in one way or another appropriate, his guilt and see something beyond it. In short, the speech of the ancient Oedipus ends at the point at which the legend becomes a matter of consciousness. For the ancient Oedipus, the legend[9] can only become a bare fact of consciousness, from which consciousness then retreats. The speech of the modern Oedipus, on the other hand, becomes fuller at the same point, as the legend is appropriated by and for consciousness. The modern Oedipus not only knows the facts of his own case but wishes to reflect on them, to reach a full awareness of all that they might mean. The whole history of Oedipus drama from the sixteenth century to the present could be written in terms of this relation between legend and consciousness.

Freud and Lévi-Strauss represent radical solutions to this problem. Freud in effect abolishes the problem by transposing the legend, or at least its main events, into the unconscious. Oedipus is no longer the hero of a legend but the name of a complex. In relation to this complex, the self-blinding of Oedipus appears a deliberate refusal of consciousness. In his first major statement of the Oedipus complex, in *The Interpretation of Dreams* of 1900, Freud wrote: "Like Oedipus, we live in ignorance of these wishes, . . . and after their revelation we may all of us well seek to close our eyes to the scenes of our childhood."[10] Although Lévi-Strauss might admit that the problem of consciousness is raised in tragedy, for him the more fundamental problem reflected in the legend is one that attaches to the whole mentality of the ancient

---

8. Ibid., p. 465. Cf. M. Davies, "The End of Sophocles' O.T.," *Hermes* 110 (1982): 277, n. 24: "Why not say Oedipus loses his eyes to symbolise his lack of insight?"

9. In speaking of the ancient Oedipus "legend," I am following William Bascom, "The Forms of Folklore," *Journal of American Folklore* 78 (1965): 3–20, who distinguishes between myth, legend, and folktale with respect to characters (divine vs. human), time, setting, etc. Legends are set in a time less remote than that of myths, in a world much like that of the narrator and his audience, and the characters are humans, not gods. In the field of classics, the terminology appears to be relatively unfixed. Bascom's three categories correspond roughly, however, to H.J. Rose's myth, saga, and märchen in *A Handbook of Greek Mythology*, 5th ed. (London 1955), pp. 10–14. See also L. Edmunds, "The Cults and the Legend of Oedipus" (Bibliography 1), p. 221, n. 1. On the distinction between myth and folktale, see further Eleazar Melitinsky, "Problème de la morphologie historique du conte populaire," *Semiotica* 2 (1970): 128–34 = "Problem of the Historical Morphology of the Folktale," in P. Maranda, ed., *Soviet Structural Folkloristics*, vol. 1 (The Hague and Paris, 1974), pp. 53–59.

10. *The Standard Edition of the Complete Psychological Works of Sigmund Freud*, vol. 4, ed. James Strachey (London 1953; repr., 1968), p. 263.

Greeks.[11] This is the problem of reconciling the belief that man is au-
tochthonous with the knowledge that humans are born from the union
of man and woman. For Lévi-Strauss, then, the problem of consciousness would be specific to the literary treatment of the legend; the legend
itself is concerned with a quite different problem. In short, Freud solves
the problem of the relation between legend and consciousness by transposing the myth into the unconscious of the individual; Lévi-Strauss
solves this problem by removing the legend altogether from any necessary connection with the consciousness of the protagonist.

No matter how their interpretations are judged, Freud and Lévi-
Strauss have both stirred up a renewed concern with the legend itself,
with the foundations of the famous tragedy—which they claim to have
laid bare. The study of folklore has been another, though less famous,
means of reaching those foundations.

Vladimir Propp wrote at length and with characteristic skill on the
handful of Oedipus folktales that were known to him, but his thesis was
a historical one: the Oedipus legend contained traces of the passage from
a matriarchal to a patriarchal organization of society.[12] After all his
interesting observations on the various motifs of the folktales, one has
to ask why he could not have made the same historical reflections on
the basis of the ancient legend by itself, as, in fact, had already been
done by M. P. Nilsson, the historian of Greek religion, not to mention
Bachofen.[13] The approach to the ancient legend through folklore remains
open then, and should be taken again in any case with the aid of a
reasonably complete collection of texts.

But in order to institute a comparison between folktales and ancient
legend, it is necessary to come to a fuller sense of that legend by studying its variants, to the extent that these can be recovered. Indeed, much
of what can be learned about the ancient legend from the folktale
analogues depends upon the comparison of the folktales with rather un-
familiar variants of the legend, which will be presented in the following
section of this Introduction. The prestige of the Sophoclean tragedy is
all the more reason for a survey of the variants. Even though Freud re-
created, as it were, the figure of Oedipus outside of his centuries-old
role as the protagonist of a tragedy, it would not be unfair to say that
Freud himself remained in the grip of that tragedy. There is no sign in
the published works of Freud that he knew the Oedipus legend in any
form but Sophocles' *Oedipus the King;* he does not even mention

11. For the Lévi-Strauss article in question, see Bibliography 1.
12. For the Propp article, see Bibliography 3.
13. For Nilsson and Bachofen, see Bibliography 1.

Sophocles' *Oedipus at Colonus,* though it is difficult to believe that he
had never read this tragedy.[14]

In Freud's thought, the question of the end of the story was replaced
by the problem of the overcoming of the Oedipus complex, to which
Freud returned again and again. But what was the end of the story? The
end of *Oedipus the King* leaves it unclear what will become of Oedipus,
since the end of the tragedy and the end of the story are not the same.
At the end of the tragedy, Oedipus is still alive, and Creon will consult
the Delphic oracle as to what is to be done with Oedipus (1438-39,
1442-43). Once again, in the matter of the end of the story, one senses
that the power of *Oedipus the King* has determined the conception of
the legend. Freud was not alone in his neglect of the ending. In *The
Types of the Folktale,* Stith Thompson concludes the list of motifs
under 931 (Oedipus) with "Parricide prophecy unwittingly fulfilled"
and "Mother-son incest," and thus leaves the story without an ending.[15]
Nevertheless, every storyteller has to answer the questions: How were
the hero's crimes discovered? What happened after the discovery? The
answers are important not only to storytellers and their audiences but
also to students of folktales. Thompson's silence was in fact forced
upon him by typology, since the end of the Oedipus story belongs to
another type, 933 (the legend of Pope Gregory), as the comparative
study of the ancient evidence for Oedipus and the modern analogues
will show.

The problem of the end of the story is, however—again because of
Oedipus the King—often posed in terms not primarily of narrative but
of the hero's subjective state after the discovery of his crimes. The view
of Benjamin, adumbrated above, belongs to what would have to be called
the minor interpretive tradition, though it includes such an illustrious
forebear as Hölderlin, who spoke of the Sophoclean Oedipus as attain-
ing "a consciousness that destroys consciousness."[16] The major tradition is eloquently expressed by André Gide in the closing pages of his
Theseus, where Oedipus tells Theseus: "Only since my eyes of flesh
were torn with my own hand from the world of appearances have I

14. In a letter to Zweig of May 2, 1935, Freud alludes to Antigone's role in
Oedipus at Colonus when he refers to himself as "supported by my faithful Anna-
Antigone": E. L. Freud, ed., *The Letters of Sigmund Freud and Arnold Zweig,*
trans. Elaine and William Robson-Scott (New York, 1970), p. 106.
15. Aarne and Thompson, *Types of the Folktale,* (see Bibliography 1).
16. Friedrich Hölderlin, *Sämtliche Werke und Briefe,* ed. G. Mieth, vol. 3 (Berlin
and Weimar, 1970), p. 453 (section 3 of his notes to his translation of *Antigone*);
cf. p. 391: "das närrischwilde Nachsuchen nach einem Bewusstsein" (section 2 of
his notes to his translation of *Oedipus the King*).

begun, it seems to me, to see truly. Yes; at the moment when the outer world was hidden forever from the eyes of my body, a kind of new eyesight opened out within myself upon the infinite perspectives of an inner world, which the world of appearances (the only one which had existed for me until that time) had led me to disdain. And this imperceptible world (inaccesible, I mean, to our senses) is, I now know, the only true one."[17] Oedipus and Theseus have met at Colonus. Sophocles' *Oedipus at Colonus*, which dramatizes Oedipus's final hour, provides Gide with the scene. In Gide's *Theseus*, then, the tragedy has ultimately been subjectivized, and the defect that Murray found has been completely repaired. Gide's presentation of the old Oedipus is, however, only an elegant fictional expression of a common tendency amongst scholars to interpret *Oedipus at Colonus* in terms of the inner Oedipus, of qualities that he has attained through suffering, endurance, and deeper wisdom. But as soon as the ancient legend is studied with reference to folklore analogues, the problem of the end of Oedipus's life in relation to his earlier crimes is necessarily recast in terms of the story pattern, and the goal becomes one of explaining this relationship, not as a development of the hero's inner self, but as a unified action forming a definable kind of biography or pattern of life.

2. THE ANCIENT OEDIPUS LEGEND

The famous tragedy concerning Oedipus is, in folkloristic terms, only one version of several that must have existed. Although we lack any comparably full source for these other variants, their existence can be ascertained from fragments of and passages in other poets, from Euripides' *Phoenician Women*, and from the mythographical tradition.[18] The evidence for the ancient legend will be divided into sections corresponding roughly to the division of the ensuing discussion of the same motifs in the analogues. The evidence is treated synchronically, not merely for convenience's sake, but because I believe that it is incorrect to present the evidence diachronically.[19] The legend did not "develop"

17. Gide, *Two Legends: Oedipus and Theseus*, trans. John Russell (New York, 1950), p. 107. (In Gide's *Oedipe* (1932), the self-blinding of Oedipus has a different significance: paradoxically, it is a path to freedom.) Cf. Propp, "Edipo," p. 133: "l'oscurità è segno ed espressione della sua rinunzia al mondo."

18. By the mythographical tradition, I mean especially the principal compilers of the Greeks myths and legends, Apollodorus and Hyginus, and also other post-classical writers who mention the Greek myths for one reason or another, for example, Diodorus Siculus and Pausanias. See the article, "Mythographers," in *The Oxford Classical Dictionary*, 2d ed.

19. For complete surveys, see Daly, "Oedipus," and Höfer, "Oidipus." De Kock,

into the form in which we find it in *Oedipus the King*. Although that tragedy postdates Homer's *Odyssey* by several hundred years, the self-blinding of the Sophoclean Oedipus may represent a variant of the legend earlier than Homer's in *Odyssey* 11.271–80, where Oedipus lives on apparently unscathed after the discovery of his crimes. The epic poems tended to stylize legend to suit their own canons of style and propriety.[20]

a. Curse and Oracle

In the fifth century B.C. there were alternate accounts of the pre-monition of Oedipus's crimes. According to one account, Oedipus's father, Laius, went to Elis in the Peloponnesus and there raped a boy, Chrysippus.[21] The boy's father, Pelops, cursed Laius: may you never have a son; if you do, may you be destroyed by him.[22] But later, Laius begot a son, Oedipus. The sources vary considerably in details: Laius's reasons for being absent from Thebes; his relationship with Chrysippus before the rape; and the fate of Chrysippus. According to one source, the boy committed suicide out of shame.[23] It was commonplace in antiquity that, by the rape of Chrysippus, Laius became the inventor of pederasty. In anger at Laius's misdeed, Hera sent the Sphinx to prey on Thebes.[24] According to another tradition, it was fated that Oedipus should commit his crimes, and his fate was foretold by oracles both to him and to Laius. Pindar's Second Olympian Ode (476 B.C.) is the earli-est evidence for the oracular revelation of Oedipus's destiny:

> Many are the streams that come to men,
> Now with the heart's delight, and now with sorrow.
> So Fate . . .
> With heaven-born joy brings grief,
> Itself to turn about with time;
> Ever since his doomed son encountered Laios

"The Sophoklean Oidipus and Its Antecedents," is historical in conception, as is the magisterial *Oidipus* of Robert. (For all of these, see Bibliography 1.)

20. For example, Phoenix is not blinded but rather is cursed by his father in *Iliad* 9.437–84. In Euripides' lost *Phoenix*, he was blinded (see Aristophanes, *Acharnians* 421; Apollod. 3.13.8; Menander, *Samia* 498–500).

21. Apollod. 3.5.5; Athen. 13.602f; Hyg. *Fab.* 85; hypoth. Aesch. *Sept.;* hypoth. Eur. *Phoen.;* Ps.-Plut. *parall. min.* 305Aff.; schol. Eur. *Phoen.* 1760 = Peisander *FGrH* 16F10.

22. For the curse of Pelops on Laius: hypoth. Aesch. *Sept.*; hypoth. Soph. *OT* (in the oracle); hypoth. Eur. *Phoen.* from MS Vat. 909; schol. Eur. *Phoen.* 60, 69.

23. schol. Eur. *Phoen.* 1760 = Peisander *FGrH* 16F10.

24. schol. Eur. *Phoen.* 1760 = Peisander *FGrH* 16F10; Apollod. 3.5.8 (her motive not given here, however); Dio Chrys. *Or.* 11.8.

And killed him, fulfilling the oracle
Spoken in Pytho long before.
The sharp-eyed Fury saw
And destroyed the warrior-race
In slaughter one of another.[25]

The adjective here translated "doomed" can also mean "fated," "appointed by fate."

For the most part, Aeschylus, Sophocles, and Euripides—and, through their influence, the later mythographical tradition—follow the account that makes fate, as revealed through oracles, the cause of Oedipus's crimes. Amongst the tragedians, Euripides is the only exception, emphasizing Pelops's curse upon Laius. He makes Oedipus say in *Phoenician Women* 1608-11:

So mine own father did I slay, and came—
Ah wretch!—unto mine hapless mother's couch.
Sons I begat, my brethren, and destroyed,
Passing to them the curse of Laius.[26]

Earlier in the play, we hear only of the oracle (15-20; 1595-99).

The mythographical tradition, when it wished to acknowledge both the curse and the oracle, tended to meld them. For example, the Byzantine hypothesis[27] to Aeschylus's *Seven Against Thebes* gives the following story:

Laius, the son of Labdacus, was king of Thebes. He married Iocasta,
the daughter of Menoeceus. Out of fear of Pelops' curses, he did
not dare to have intercourse with her and beget children. For they
say that Laius fell in love with Chrysippus, the son of Pelops,
and carried him off and had intercourse with him. Laius gave the first
example of sodomy amongst mankind, just as Zeus had done amongst
the gods through the rape of Ganymede. When Pelops discovered the
rape, he cursed Laius with destruction through his own offspring.
After Laius, childless for the reason just given, had passed his prime,
he went to the oracle of Apollo to ask if he ought to beget children.
This oracle was given him: "Do not, contrary to the gods, seed the
furrow of children" [= Eur. *Phoen.* 18]. With this oracular response
he went home and took care not to sleep with his wife. But one

25. Translated by C.M. Bowra, *The Odes of Pindar* (Harmondsworth, 1969), pp. 81-82.
26. Translated by A.S. Way, *Euripides*, vol. 4 (Loeb Classical Library, 1912), pp. 475-77.
27. See "hypoth." under "Abbreviations." For discussion of this particular hypothesis, see Robert, *Oidipus*, 1: 401-2.

day, overcome by wine, he had intercourse with his wife and she conceived Oedipus. Fearing the oracular response that had said, "For if you beget a son, the one who is born will murder you," [= Eur. *Phoen.* 19] just as Pelops had cursed him. . . . [My translation]

Oracle and curse are similarly melded in the oracle, in dactylic hexameters, the normal meter of oracles, which is quoted in the hypothesis to Sophocles' *Oedipus the King* and to Euripides' *Phoenician Women.* The text differs slightly in the two places, but the meaning is the same. In the hypothesis to *Oedipus the King* the oracle runs:

Laius, son of Labdacus, you crave blessed issue of children.
I shall give you a son. But it is fated
For you to leave the light at your own son's hands. For thus has consented
Zeus, son of Kronos, in obedience to the hateful curses of Pelops,
Whose son you raped. All this has he imprecated upon you.
[My translation]

Both curse and oracle are usually limited to parricide. In only one source, Nicolaus of Damascus, is it prophesied to Laius that his son will kill him and marry his own mother.[28] In two sources, Malalas and Cedrenus, only mother incest is prophesied.[29]

After he had grown up in Corinth, Oedipus too went to Delphi to consult the oracle, and it was prophesied to him that he would kill his father and marry his mother.[30]

b. Mutilation; Exposure

Laius exposed his child soon after its birth. According to the usual version, the infant was set out on Mount Cithaeron[31] or in some unspecified place on dry land; but another version tells that he was set adrift in a chest and came to shore at Sicyon or at Corinth, where Periboea, the king's wife, was doing her laundry.[32] In Aristophanes' *Frogs* 1190, it is a pot in which the child is abandoned, but whether on sea or land is not clear.

28. Nic. Dam. *FGrH* 90F8.
29. Malalas and Cedrenus are cited below, n. 93.
30. Apollod. 3.5.7; hypoth. Aesch. *Sept.*; schol. Eur. *Phoen.* 44, 1044; Soph. *OT* 787-93, 994-96.
31. Apollod. 3.5.7; Eur. *Phoen.* 25; Nic. Dam. *FGrH* 90F8; Paus. 9.2.4; Sen. *Phoen.* 31-33; Soph. *OT.*
32. Scene on a cup from Tanagra: *CVA:* France, Fasc. 23: Louvre, Fasc. 15: pp. 9-10; pl. 10, 1-4; Robert, *Oidipus* (Bibliography 1), vol. 1, p. 326, Abb. 49.

Before Laius exposed the child, he pierced its ankles with brooches,[33] or, in the most common version, with iron spikes.[34] The Byzantine chroniclers say that the child's feet were nailed into wooden shackles.[35] The child was given the name Oedipus, "Swollen-Foot," because of the wound. In two places, it is said that the swaddling clothing caused the swelling of the feet.[36] The hanging of the exposed child by its feet from a tree is not attested in any ancient source.[37]

c. Rescue; Youth; Return to Boeotia

Accounts of the immediate fate of the exposed child vary.

1. The agents of Laius, "compassionate executioners," took pity on the child and gave it to a shepherd or directly to the wife of Polybus, who passed it off as her own.[38]
2. The child was found by Polybus himself while hunting, or by herdsman of Polybus who delivered it to him.[39]
3. The child was found and raised by a rustic, Meliboeus, or by a herdsman, or by horse herders from Sicyon.[40]

The foster father is always Polybus and usually Corinth is his city. His wife is usually called Merope.

When Oedipus grew up, he excelled his age-mates in strength, and was the most important citizen of Corinth.[41] In an argument or from a drunken friend or from the envious taunts of his fellows, he learned

33. Apollod. 3.5.7; cf. Eur. *Phoen.* 805.

34. Diod. 4.64.1; Eur. *Phoen.* 26; Paus. 10.5.3; schol. Eur. *Phoen.* 26; Sen. *Phoen.* 254; Soph. *OT.*

35. Malalas O59; Cedrenus 25B. For Malalas and Cedrenus see n. 93, below. For the wooden shackles, also Joh. Antioch. *FHG* 4 fr. 8 (p. 545).

36. Nic. Dam. *FGrH* 90F8; schol. Eur. *Phoen.* 26; cf. Soph. *OT* 1035.

37. This form of the exposure motif might have seemed a medieval literary invention (see the articles by Edmunds in Bibliography 2); but it appears in a south Slavic folktale published by Friedrich S. Krauss, "Die Ödipussage in südslawischer Volksüberlieferung," *Imago* 21 (1935): 359. The question thus arises whether the medieval literary attestations are borrowings from a folk tradition or whether the occurrence of this form of the motif in a folktale represents borrowing from literature. In the absence of further examples in folklore, the question cannot be answered. (A translation of the article by Krauss appears in Edmunds and Dundes (Bibliography 3), pp. 10–22)

38. Apollod. 3.5.7; hypoth. Eur. *Phoen.*; cf. Diod. 4.64.2.

39. The child found by Polybus: Myth. Vat. 2.230; schol. Stat. *Theb.* 1.64. By Polybus's men: Apollod. 3.5.7.

40. Eur. *Phoen.* 28–31; hypoth. Eur. *Phoen.*; Soph. *OT* 1026; schol. Hom. *Od.* 11.271 = Androtion *FGrH* 3B 324F62; schol. Eur. *Phoen.* 1760 = Peisander *FGrH* 16F10.

41. Apollod. 3.5.7; Soph. *OT* 775–76; Zen. 2.68.

that Polybus was not his natural father.[42] He questioned his parents on the matter, but they told him nothing.[43] He started off for Delphi to consult the oracle and, on the way, killed Laius;[44] alternately, he went to Delphi, received the oracle, and, returning from Delphi, killed Laius.[45] Or he went directly to Thebes in search of his parents.[46] At any rate, he killed Laius, who was himself on the way to Delphi to inquire about the child he had exposed long ago. According to one source, Laius went contrary to the advice of Teiresias, who counseled him to sacrifice to Hera.[47]

d. Murder of Laius; Sphinx; Marriage

Laius and Oedipus meet at a crossroads, or a triple crossroads.[48] Laius has five attendants.[49] His herald or driver orders Oedipus out of the way. Oedipus, on foot, advances nonetheless. Laius tries to run him off the road, striking him and running the chariot wheels over his feet.[50] Oedipus attacks and kills Laius and his attendants,[51] although one escapes.[52]

After the death of Laius, Creon became king. Most sources are silent about this interregnum, except for the matter of the Sphinx. In Sophocles' *Oedipus the King,* Creon tells Oedipus that no thorough search was made for the murderers of Laius because "the subtle Sphinx caused

42. Apollod. 3.5.7; Eur. *Phoen.* 33; Hyg. *Fab.* 67; hypoth. Eur. *Phoen.*; schol. Eur. *Phoen.* 33; Soph. *OT* 779; Zen. 2.68.

43. Apollod. 3.5.7; Soph. *OT* 782-87.

44. Apollod. 3.5.4; Diod. 4.64.2; Eur. *Phoen.* 35-38; Hyg. *Fab.* 67; Myth. Vat. 2.230.

45. Apollod. 3.5.7; hypoth. Eur. *Phoen.*; Soph. *OT* 785-97; Zen. 2.68.

46. schol. Hom. *Od.* 11.271 = Androtion *FGrH* 3B 324F62.

47. schol. Eur. *Phoen.* 1760 = Peisander *FGrH* 16F10.

48. Eur. *Phoen.* 38; papyrus fr. in Alfred Koerte, "Literarische Texte mit Ausschluss der christlichen," *Archiv für Papyrosforschung und verwandte Gebiete* 11 1935), no. 807 (p. 259); schol. Eur. *Phoen.* 1760 = Peisander *FGrH* 16F10; Sen. *Oed.* 276-83; Soph. *OT* 800-804; Stat. *Theb.* 11.64; Paus. 10.5.3.

49. Apollod. 3.5.7; Soph. *OT* 752-53; schol. Eur. *Phoen.* 39 = Pherecydes *FGrH* 3F94; Soph. *OT* 752-53.

50. Apollod. 3.5.7 (L.'s herald killed one of O.'s horses); Eur. *Phoen.* 41-42 (L.'s horses bloodied O.'s ankles with their hooves); Hyg. *Fab.* 67 (the wheel of L.'s chariot rolled over O.'s foot); schol. Eur. *Phoen.* 1760 = Peisander *FGrH* 16F10 (either L. or his driver hit O. with a whip—the syntax of the Greek is ambiguous); Soph. *OT* 806-7, 810-13; 804-5, 807-9 (L. hits O. with goad); Zen. 2.68 (L.'s driver strikes O.).

51. Apollod. 3.5.7; Eur. *Phoen.* 44 (attendants not mentioned); Nic. Dam. *FGrH* 90F8; schol. Eur. *Phoen.* 1760 = Peisander *FGrH* 16F10; Soph. *OT* 806-7, 810-13; Zen. 2.68.

52. Soph. *OT* 756, cf. 813.

us to let go of obscure problems and drew us on to consider what was closer to home" (130-31).

The "subtle Sphinx" is, of course, the monster who posed a riddle to passersby on the condition that they answer or die. Her dwelling place was Mount Phicion (named after her) or an unnamed mountain or the acropolis of Thebes or a steep cliff beside a road near Thebes—in other words, always a high place.[53] When the passerby failed to answer, she would devour him.[54] Alternately, the Sphinx posed her riddle to all the Thebans. They would meet every day to attempt a solution. When they failed, she would carry off a victim.[55]

The wording and form of the riddle vary from source to source, but it is always fundamentally the same riddle. Its fullest form is found in Athenaeus: "There walks on land a creature of two feet, of four feet, and of three; it has òne voice, but sole among animals that grow on land or in the sea, it can change its nature; nay, when it walks propped on most feet, then is the speed of its limbs less that it has ever been before."[56] The answer to the riddle is man.

Whether because of the loss of his son, Haemon, or because of the general menace, Creon offered the kingdom and the hand of Iocasta, Laius's widow, to whoever could solve the riddle.[57] Oedipus, with his native intelligence, solved it.[58] The Sphinx then killed herself.[59] The solving of the riddle seems to be an overdetermination of the monster-

53. Apollod. 3.5.8 (the acropolis of Thebes); Eur. *Phoen.* 806 (a mountain); Myth. Vat. 2.230 (a mountain); Paus. 9.26.2 (a mountain); schol. Hes. *Theog.* 326 (Mount Phicium, named after her); schol. Ov. *Ib.* 378 (a steep cliff); schol. Stat. *Theb.* 1.66 (a steep cliff).

54. Diod. 4.64 (devoured victims); Hyg. *Fab.* 67 (devoured victims); hypoth. Aesch. *Sept.* (devoured victims); Myth. Vat. 2.230 (decapitated victims); Ov. *Ib.* 377-78 (killed victims); Palaephat. 4 (devoured victims); schol. Ov. *Ib.* 378 (devoured victims); schol. Stat. *Theb.* 1.66 (carried victims up to her cliff).

55. Apollod. 3.5.8; hypoth. Eur. *Phoen.*; schol. Eur. *Phoen.* 45 = Asclepiades *FGrH* 12F7b.

56. *AP* 14.64; Apollod. 3.5.8; Athen. 10.456b (citing Asclepiades, *Stories from Greek Tragedy* = *FGrH* 12F7b); Diod. 4.64.3-4; hypoth. Aesch. *Sept.*; hypoth. Eur. *Phoen.*; Myth. Vat. 2.230; schol. Eur. *Phoen.* 50; schol. Hom. *Od.* 11.271; Tz. on Lyc. 7 (p. 282).

57. Apollod. 3.5.8; Eur. *Phoen.* 45-51; Diod. 4.64.3; Hyg. *Fab.* 67; hypoth. Aesch. *Sept.*; hypoth. Eur. *Phoen.*; Zen. 2.68.

58. Eur. *Phoen.* 1505-7, 1728-31; Pind. *Pyth.* 4. 263; Soph. *OT* 393-98, cf. 38. The scene in which Oedipus ponders the Sphinx's riddle is the favorite with fifth-century vase painters: see *Enciclopedia dell' Arte Antica*, s.v. "Edipo," 3: 218 ("E. davanti alla Sfinge" under "Monumenti considerati").

59. It has been thought that certain vase paintings show Oedipus killing the Sphinx with a weapon. For references, see L. Edmunds, *The Sphinx in the Oedipus Legend* (Bibliography 1), p. 35, n. 37. The forthcoming book on the Sphinx by

slaying motif. In folklore, either riddle solving or monster slaying by itself is sufficient to win a bride.[60]

In the Byzantine tradition, the Sphinx is a robber woman. Oedipus, coming with an army from Corinth, destroys her; or he pretends to join her band and kills her when she is off guard. This latter deceit is a version of the Sphinx's death that can be traced back to Palaephatus (fourth century B.C.).[61] The poetess Corinna said that Oedipus also killed the Teumesian fox.[62]

After solving the riddle of the Sphinx and freeing Thebes of this menace, Oedipus married his mother, whose name is usually Iocasta or Epicaste.[63] They married in ignorance of their kinship. The only piece of evidence that could suggest they knowingly entered an incestuous relationship is Aeschylus's *Seven against Thebes* 756, but the frenzy (*paranoia*) referred to here is not that of Oedipus and Iocasta but that of Laius and Iocasta, who produced a son despite warnings. Another tradition has it that there were no offspring of the incestuous union, but rather Oedipus's children came from a second marriage. In Homer's *Odyssey* 11.271-80 Odysseus tells how he saw the mother of Oedipus in the underworld, and his words imply that the gods revealed the crime very soon after the marriage. Thus, there would have been no children. This tradition assigns the four children to a second wife, who is called Euryganeia or Eurygane.[64]

e. Discovery; Blinding; Exaltation; Deaths of Oedipus and Iocasta

The recognition of Oedipus's identity comes about in various ways.

1. In the passage from the *Odyssey* quoted above, the gods make it known, but it is not said how they do so.

J.-M. Moret will show that none of these vase paintings has any value as evidence for such a variant.

60. For further discussion, see Edmunds, *The Sphinx*.

61. Palaephat. 4. Cf. section 3 below.

62. Fr. 19(672)Page.

63. In the epic tradition she is Epicaste: Hom. *Od.* 11.271; Nic. Dam. *FGrH* 90F8; schol. Eur. *Phoen.* 12; cf. Apollod. 3.5.7. In tragedy, Iocasta: Soph. *OT* 632, 950, 1053, 1235; Eur. *Phoen.* 12, 289, 444, 691, 803, 987, 1068, 1318, 1665; hypoth. Aesch. *Sept.*; Diod. 4.64.1, 3; Hyg. *Fab.* 67, 68; Myth. Vat. 2.230; Zen. 2.68; Athen. 160b, 222 a-b. (In the latter place Athen. cites Antiphanes: "Let me but mention Oedipus, and they know all the rest: his father was Laius, his mother Iocasta. . . . " Antiphanes, a fourth-century comic poet, was speaking of the advantages of the tragedian.)

64. Apollod. 3.5.8; Paus. 9.5.11; cf. schol. Eur. *Phoen.* 53 = Pherecydes *FGrH* 3F95; schol. Eur. *Phoen.* 1760 = Peisander *FGrH* 16F10.

2. Iocasta discovers Oedipus's identity by the scars on his feet.[65]
3. Iocasta questions Oedipus about his origins. He tells her that he was raised by Meliboeus. She sends for Meliboeus, who tells her that he found Oedipus in the woods. She calculates the time that has passed and discovers the identity of her husband.[66]
4. The death of Polybus in Corinth sets off a chain of events that leads to the discovery. In Sophocles, Iocasta's account of the murder of Laius awaits clarification by the sole survivor of the affray at the crossroads, who is now a herdsman. In the meantime, a messenger comes from Corinth with news of the death of Polybus. This messenger reveals that he himself had received the infant Oedipus on Mount Cithaeron from another herdsman. When the Theban herdsman arrives, he is forced to acknowledge that he had received the infant from the wife of Laius.[67] The only other source that makes the discovery begin with the death of Polybus is Hyginus, *Fabulae* 67, which, like Sophocles' *Oedipus the King,* tells of a plague: ". . . barrenness of crops and want fell upon Thebes on account of the crimes of Oedipus. Asked why Thebes was so oppressed, Teiresias gave this reply: if there remained any descendant of those sprung from the dragon's teeth, and if he died for his fatherland, he would free it from the plague. Then Menoeceus threw himself from the walls. While these events took place at Thebes, Polybus died in Corinth. Hearing this, Oedipus was aggrieved, believing that his father had died. Periboea [the name of Polybus's wife in this variant] revealed to him that he was supposititious. Likewise, the old man Menoetes, who had exposed him, recognized from the scars on his feet and ankles that he was the son of Laius."

Teiresias's role in Hyginus's version of the discovery can be compared with his role in Sophocles' *Oedipus the King* 200-462, where Teiresias denounces Oedipus as the polluter of the city. In both places, Teiresias is ineffectual. The denouement comes, not through his intervention, but through the process of discovery in which the death of Polybus is the turning point.[68] Why then does Teiresias appear at all? The answer,

65. Myth. Vat. 2.230.
66. Cedrenus 25C; Joh. Antioch. *FHG* 4 fr. 8 (p. 545); Malalas O61. For complete references, see n. 93, below.
67. This is, of course, the version of Soph. *OT.*
68. In Eur. *Phoen.* the self-sacrifice of Menoeceus takes place at the time of the Seven's attack on Thebes. It is possible, of course, that Hyginus has simply transferred this incident to the time of the plague. On the other hand, Hyginus seems to have been in possession of authentic nontragic traditions; see Section 3, below.

in general terms, must be that Teiresias had such importance in Theban legend that he was bound to appear somewhere in the legend of Oedipus. Carl Robert suggested that originally it would have been Teiresias, not the Delphic oracle, who prophesied to the parents the destiny of their son,[69] a suggestion that is corroborated by the folklore analogues.[70] In Sophocles and Hyginus, then, the role of Teiresias has been transferred from the beginning of the story to a penultimate position, to the discovery. In the tragedy, *Oedipus the King,* Teiresias does not prophecy the crimes of Oedipus at the beginning of the story but denounces them on what is to be the last day of Oedipus's kingship; it is noteworthy, however, that Teiresias' place in the structure of the tragedy corresponds to his putative place in an earlier, pre-Delphic version of the legend, i.e., at the beginning, and that he still has a prophecy to dispense: that Oedipus will be driven from Thebes as a blind beggar (417, 454–56). The prophetic role of Teiresias in the legend of Oedipus is attested in the Peisander scholium[71] and in the fragments of what was apparently a minor Thebaid, which by a broad consensus is attributed to Stesichorus.[72] The text of this poem becomes readable at line 201, where the queen (unnamed) is speaking. She prays that Apollo may not bring to pass the prophecies of Teiresias, who has said that her sons will die and that her city will be captured. (Oedipus's curse on his sons does not appear in this version.) In Stesichorus, then, Teiresias is still a prophet before the fact, although the association with Apollo, which will become complete in *Oedipus the King* 284–85, has already begun.

Iocasta, according to one of two main traditions, hanged herself immediately after the discovery of Oedipus' identity.[73] According to the other, it was not until later, at the time of the campaign of the Seven against Thebes, that she killed herself with a sword over the bodies of her sons.[74] A third tradition, attested once, has it that she was killed by Oedipus.[75]

In one ancient and one medieval source, Oedipus dies through self-blinding at the same time as the death of Iocasta, immediately after the discovery.[76] Usually, after blinding himself with brooches from his

69. Robert, *Oidipus,* vol. 1, pp. 69–70.

70. See Section 4a, below.

71. See n. 47, above, and accompanying text.

72. For the text, see P.J. Parsons, "The Lille "Stesichorus,'" *Zeitschrift für Papyrologie und Epigraphik* 26 (1977): 7–36.

73. Apollod. 3.5.9; Hom. *Od.* 11.277–78; Joh. Antioch. *FHG* 4 fr. 8 (p. 545); Sen. *Oed.* (she killed herself with a sword); Soph. *OT* 1263–64, *Ant.* 53–54 (O. died at the same time, as the result of the self-blinding); Zen. 2.68.

74. Eur. *Phoen.* 1455–59; hypoth. Eur. *Phoen.*: Stat. *Theb.* 11.634–41.

75. schol. Eur. *Phoen.* 26.

76. Soph. *Ant.* 53–54; Hyg. *Fab.* 67.

mother's robe, he lives on.[77] There are three other traditions for the blinding of Oedipus:

1. Blindness came upon him as the result of his own curse on the murderer of Laius.[78]
2. Oedipus was blinded by Polybus because of the oracle concerning parricide.
3. The servants of Laius blinded Oedipus.[79]

Three Etruscan urns with reliefs show the blinding of a rather youthful Oedipus.[80] Two soldiers hold him, and a third plunges a dagger into his left eye as Creon looks on. Another soldier restrains a young woman —Antigone or Iocasta. Two small boys appear, the sons of Oedipus. The scene must illustrate the lost *Oedipus* of Euripides.[81]

There are two main traditions concerning the death of Oedipus, one that he died in Thebes,[82] the other that he was driven out of Thebes and died elsewhere.[83] According to the first, Oedipus fell in battle (so much is implied by the verb used by Homer, *Iliad* 23.678); there were funeral games in his honor; Argeia, the daughter of Adrastus and wife of Polynices, came to the funeral. According to the second, Oedipus is expelled from Thebes by Creon, who follows the bidding of Teiresias. Oedipus had heard an oracle (in Sophocles' *Oedipus at Colonus,* he refers to it as the same oracle that also foretold incest and parricide long ago) that he would end his days in Athens in a precinct of the Eumenides.[84]

f. Oedipus's Curse on his Sons

In his anger at his sons, Oedipus laid upon them the curse of strife for the throne of Thebes. In Euripides' *Phoenician Women,* he speaks of

77. E.g., Aesch. *Sept.* 783–84; Soph. *OT* 1268–70, cf. 830–33; Eur. *Phoen.* 59–62, 327, 870, 1613–14.

78. schol. Eur. *Phoen.* 61.

79. Oedipus blinded by Polybus: schol. Eur. *Phoen.* 26. O. blinded by servants of L.: schol. Eur. *Phoen.* 61 = Eur. *Oed.* fr. 541N 2d ed.

80. Robert, *Oidipus,* vol. 1, p. 307, Abb. 48. For full references, see Ingrid Krauskopf, *Der thebanische Sagenkreis und andere griechische Sagen in der etruskischen Kunst,* Heidelberger Akademie der Wissenschaften: Kommission für Antike Mythologie, Schriften zur antiken Mythologie 2 (Mainz am Rhein, 1974), Öd 39–41, with discussion, pp. 52–53.

81. Fragments in Nauck, 2d ed.

82. Hom. *Il.* 23.679; schol. Hom. *Od.* 11.275; schol. T. Hom. *Il.* 23.679 = Hes. fr. 192 Merkelbach and West; Soph. *Ant.* 53–54; in the Byzantine encyclopedists, O. dies at the time of his self-blinding: Malalas O62; Cedrenus 26A; Joh. Antioch. *FHG* 4 fr. 8 (p. 545).

83. See L. Edmunds, "The Cults and the Legend of Oedipus" (Bibliography 1).

84. For Oedipus's association with the Eumenides, see ibid.

his curse as a continuation of the curse on Laius. The reason for Oedipus's anger is variously given.

1. His sons sequestered him in some dark place in Thebes. Sources for this version of the legend often emphasize the darkness of his prison.[85]
2. His sons drove him out of Thebes.[86]
3. His sons sent him the hip joint instead of the shoulder of a sacrificial victim, and he felt himself slighted. This version is attributed to the now lost *Thebaid.* [87]

Athenaeus, in a discussion of cups, attributes another version to the *Thebaid:*

And it was on account of cups that Oedipus cursed his sons, according to the author of the Cyclic poem *Thebaid,* because they had set before him a cup which he had forbidden; the author says: "But the divine hero, yellow-haired Polyneices, first set the beautiful silver table of godly Cadmus before Oedipus, and then he filled a fair golden cup with sweet wine. But when Oedipus recognized the precious possessions of his own father set before him, mighty woe fell upon his spirit, and swiftly he called down harsh curses upon both his sons—and it escaped not the avenging fury of the gods—that they should never divide his father's goods in loving kindness, but that wars and fights should ever be upon them both."[88]

3. THE HISTORICAL RELATION OF THE ANALOGUES TO THE ANCIENT OEDIPUS LEGEND

The earliest datable folktales in this collection are medieval, and they fall quite distinctly into two groups corresponding to 931 (Oedipus) and 933 (Gregory).[89] The subject of the first of these groups is Judas; of the second, the legendary Pope Gregory. As will be seen, in the context of the collection as a whole, the distinction between the two types blurs, but for the purpose of studying the historical relation of the col-

85. Diod. 4.65.1; Eur. *Phoen.* 64, 1539–45 and schol. Eur. *Phoen.* 1539; hypoth. Aesch. *Sept.*; Myth. Vat. 2.230; Stat. *Theb.* 1.47–52, 8.241, 11.580–81; cf. Soph. *OT* 1424–31.

86. Soph. *OC* 1348–96; Zen. 5.43.

87. *Thebaid* fr. 3.

88. Translated by C. B. Gulick, *Athenaeus: The Deipnosophists,* vol. 5 (Loeb Classical Library 1933), pp. 31–33.

89. For the sake of stylistic convenience, I have permitted myself the inaccuracy of referring to the Gregory and Judas stories as folktales or tales. Properly speaking they are legends. See Rosenfeld (Bibliography 2).

lection to the ancient Oedipus legend, it is reasonable to begin with the earliest datable examples and to discuss the Judas and the Gregory folktales separately, since they present separate historical problems.

The Judas folktale, which more closely matches the story of Oedipus, is the easier to deal with. It was extremely popular in the Middle Ages. It is preserved in more than forty-two Latin manuscripts.[90] There are two main forms. Of these, one, represented by LT1, is so closely related to the ancient legend that a learned origin may be suspected. Mutilation of the shins of the exposed child is the element that especially suggests knowledge of Sophocles or Euripides or of a tradition deriving from them. Elsewhere in the medieval and modern examples, mutilation, when it occurs, is either of the upper body or unspecified. The other form of the Judas folktale, represented by LT2 from the *Legenda Aurea*, is distinguished by the anachronistic figure of Pilate, which suggests unlearned provenience, and by the exposure of the child on water and its rescue by a queen (cf. FI13). A similar exposure and rescue of Oedipus are found in Hyginus (date unknown), *Fabulae* 66, which also, like LT2, contains the superiority of the foundling and the jealousy of his age-mates. Exposure of Oedipus on water and his rescue by a queen are also depicted on a Boeotian cup of the first century B.C., and exposure on water is mentioned in the scholium (undatable) on Euripides, *Phoenician Women* 27. In short, the exposure of Judas on water can be connected with a variant of the Oedipus legend for which there is ancient evidence, but the evidence does not strongly indicate a written tradition for this form of the Judas folktale.

The medieval Greek Judas tale (GK1) shares elements of both LT1 and LT2, of which the most notable is the parricide in the orchard or the garden, where the son is a trespasser. This trespasser's parricide, as it can be called, is (with the omission of the Sphinx) the main innovation in the Judas tale as compared with the ancient Oedipus legend, but how it came about cannot be shown. The garden of Naboth (1 *Kings* 21) has often been suggested as the model for the innovation, but such an explanation assumes direct borrowing from a separate tradition. In twenty-seven of the modern folktales, the motif is inverted: the son has been hired to guard his father's property and kills his father, of whose identity he is ignorant, in the line of duty. This form of the motif can be called the guardian's parricide. In these folktales, the hero is often forgiven in the end (RM2(GM), FI1,3-7,10,12(?), KR3, IR5) or exalted

90. See Baum in Bibliography 2 and also Paul Lehmann, "Judas Ischariot in der lateinischen Legenden-Überlieferung des Mittelalters," *Studi Medievali*, NS 3 (1930): 289-346; reprinted in *Erforschung des Mittelalters*, vol. 2 (Stuttgart 1959), pp. 229-85.

to the status of pope or saint (LI3, PL2, UK1, OR1, RS2). Here is evidence for the contention that types 931 and 933 are fundamentally the same folktale. With the inversion of one motif (guardian's for trespasser's parricide) and a different ending, Judas becomes Gregory, the legendary pope.[91]

But in the medieval folktales, type 931, represented by Judas, and type 933, represented by Gregory, are quite distinct, and it is parricide that especially sets the Judas group apart from the Gregory group. In the European Gregory folktales, parricide is absent. If, however, one places this Gregory folktale in another context, the absence of parricide appears to be only a variant in a story pattern that admits parricide. In some non-European tales that may be cognate with the Gregory tale, parricide does occur. In the Arabic "Nimrud" (AR1), the protagonist defeats and kills his father, Kana'an, in battle. Nimrud is the leader of an army. In AR2(GM), a parricide that takes place under these circumstances leads directly to the hero's marriage with his mother. The date of the Zulu "Usikulumi" (ZL1) cannot be established,[92] but if it can be discussed in the context of the medieval tales, it provides another example of parricide in a military engagement, though the narrator does not tell us in so many words that Usikulumi killed his own father. Amongst the modern tales, FI14 and RS1 seem to be the descendants of the tradition represented by "Nimrud" and "Usikulumi" (cf. AL1, TK1).

This form of parricide, i.e., a military parricide, provides a point of contact with the ancient Oedipus legend. The Byzantine encyclopedists, Malalas, Cedrenus, and John of Antioch, give a version of the Oedipus legend in which, after he killed the Sphinx, Oedipus was named king by popular acclaim, and Laius raised an army against him.[93] Laius was killed in the ensuing battle, though it is not said that Oedipus himself did the deed. What is the relation of the Byzantines to the ancient legend? In at least one respect, namely the manner of Oedipus's killing the Sphinx, the encyclopedists' version can be traced back to Palaephatus, a rationalizing mythographer of the fourth century B.C. (cf.

91. Cf. Pellizer (Bibliography 1), p. 66: " . . . è sufficiente invertire il segno di un solo elemento per mettere in moto una serie di sviluppi che portano dalla possibilità di una conclusione tragica a quella opposta di un lieto fine."

92. Propp in "Edipo alla Luce del Folclore" (Bibliography 3) assumes that "Usikulumi" is the oldest Oedipus folktale and bases much of his argument on this assumption.

93. A. I. Bekker, *Georgius Cedrenus*, 2 vols., in *CSHB* (1838). In this text, see 25C on Oedipus. The fragments of John of Antioch are in Carl Müller, *Fragmenta Historicorum Graecorum* (Paris, 1851), 4:532-622. There are no translations of Cedrenus and John of Antioch. For Malalas: Ludwig Dindorf, *Ioannis Malalae Chronographia*, in *CSHB* (1831) O61, with Latin translation by Dindorf.

Pausanias 9.26.2).[94] It is possible, then, that their account of the parricide also goes back to an ancient version of the legend in which Oedipus returned to Thebes at the head of an army. In the brief summary of Oedipus's life at *Odyssey* 11.271–80, Homer uses the term *exenarizō* of the parricide. This verb, which elsewhere refers to encounters on the battlefield,[95] might indicate that Homer knew of a military parricide. In the received form of the ancient legend, the parricide at the crossroads obviously connects the legend with Delphi, but that connection can have been made only after the oracle came into prominence, in the eighth century B.C., while the legend of Oedipus is surely much older.[96]

But in the commonest form of the Gregory folktale, parricide is omitted and incest is reduplicated, occurring at the beginning of the tale and motivating the exposure of the hero, who is the offspring of brother and sister or of father and daughter. As in the Byzantine version of the Oedipus legend, the hero returns to his homeland at the head of an army, but his father has already died or disappeared from the scene. He successfully defeats his mother's enemies, and then marries her. The earliest example of this folktale is "Jean" (AR?1(FR)), the product of a Christian community in Egypt, and written in either Coptic or Arabic, probably the latter (see the headnotes to the folktale), in the fourth to seventh centuries A.D. The medieval European version (LT3) is almost identical to "Jean."

In the form of the Gregory folktale in which parricide is omitted, the hero is finally exalted, and this conclusion corresponds to the end of Oedipus in Sophocles' *Oedipus at Colonus*. In this tragedy, Oedipus foretells the power he will have after death, and his burial suggests hero cult. The honor due the dead Oedipus was not Sophocles' invention, but had already taken the form of funeral games in the epic version of the legend.[97] The Gregory folktale, then, looks back to a story pattern

94. Nicolaus Festa, *Palaephati Peri Apiston,* . . . (in *Mythographi Graeci*, vol. 2, fasc. 2) (Leipzig, 1902) sec. 4. See section 3.d, below.

95. The verb usually means to strip or despoil a slain foe in a fight. Thus consider the ancient tradition that Oedipus took spoils from Laius: the main source is the much discussed Peisander scholium, on which see de Kock, "The Peisander Scholion" (Bibliography 1). Consider also Antimachus fr. 6 in E. Diehl, *Fragmenta Lyrica Graeca*, 3d. ed. (Leipzig, 1949), 1: 110–11.

96. See H. W. Parke and D. E. W. Wormell, *The Delphic Oracle*, 2d ed. (Oxford, 1956). Cf. J.-M. Moret, "L' 'Apollinisation' de l'imagerie légendaire à Athènes dans le second moitié du ve siècle," *Rev. Arch.* (1982): 109–36, especially 121 and 126.

97. Homer, *Il.* 23.677–80; Hesiod, frs. 192–93, in the edition of R. Merkelbach and M. L. West.

attested in the ancient Oedipus legend, a pattern linking earlier crime and later exaltation.

In sum, there is evidence to connect the medieval tales of both Judas and Gregory with the ancient legend, but for the most part the historical problem lacks any clear and detailed solution. If we are in fact dealing with a tradition, or two independent traditions, coming down from Greek antiquity, we simply lack sufficient examples to fill in the gaps and to explain when and how the principal mutations of the ancient legend occurred. This predicament is not peculiar to the Oedipus story but holds for all the stories for which there are both ancient literary and modern oral examples. Each such story presents its own problems and the question of the tradition must be judged on its own merits, which differ from one story to another. In my opinion, the probability of a continuous oral tradition, from antiquity to the present century, of the stories of Meleager, of Polyphemus, and of the sailor who went inland has been convincingly argued.[98] The Aesopic fables are another case and one that has been accorded an intuitive acceptance. Everyone knows of the ancient literary redaction of these fables that goes under the name of Aesop; at the same time, everyone is aware that many of these fables have turned up in modern oral forms amongst peoples who are not likely to have taken them from books.[99] There is, I think, an intuitive sense that a literary and a popular, oral tradition have coexisted for many centuries.

I believe that the Oedipus story too has come down to us in a double tradition. Not all the stories but many in my collection represent an ancient popular, oral tradition that in antiquity coexisted with the illustrious literary tradition, of which Sophocles' *Oedipus the King* is the chef d'oeuvre. To return to the example of the exposure of the child on water, this form of the exposure motif never entered the ancient literary tradition; it does not appear in any extant poem or

98. The story of Meleager: J. T. Kakridis, *Homeric Researches* (Lund, 1949); "Probleme der griechischen Heldensage," *Poetica* 5 (1972): 152-63. The story of Polyphemus: Justin Glenn, "The Polyphemus Folktale and Homer's *Kyklôpeia*," *Transactions of the American Philological Association* 102 (1971): 133-81. The story of the sailor who went inland: W. F. Hansen, "The Story of the Sailor Who Went Inland," in *Folklore Today: A Festschrift for Richard M. Dorson*, ed. Linda Dégh, Henry Glassie, and Felix Oinas (Bloomington; Ind.: 1976), pp. 221-30; "Odysseus' Last Journey," *Quaderni Urbinati di Cultura Classica* 24 (1977): 27-48. For general discussion, see J. T. Kakridis, "Problem der grieschen Heldensage," *Poetica* 5 (1972): 152-63. For references to folklore in Greek literature, see Johannes Bolte, *Zeugnisse zur Geschichte der Märchen*, FFC 39 (Helsinki, 1921), pp. 1-14.

99. For discussion, see G. A. Megas, "Some Oral Greek Parallels to Aesop's Fables," in *Humaniora*, ed. W. D. Hand and G. O. Arlt, (Locust Valley, N.Y.), 1960, pp. 195-207.

tragedy concerning Oedipus. If it did appear in some work now lost, it would have turned up in Apollodorus or elsewhere in the Greek mythographical tradition, but it does not.[100] Therefore the appearance of this form of the exposure motif in the popular and not the learned form of the medieval Judas folktale is not surprising. I believe, then, that many of the folktales in my collection descend from an ancient popular, oral tradition.

Although one must be tentative concerning the historical relationship between these folktales and classical antiquity, one can be bolder concerning a more broadly conceived model or stemma. If the two ancient Greek traditions, the learned or literary and the popular, are regarded not as the only possible ancestors of the medieval and modern Oedipus folktales but only as the representatives of one ancient tradition, *amongst others,* for the Oedipus story, then these folktales present themselves as *cognates* of the Greek traditions. This more broadly conceived stemma would explain why the Judas and the Gregory stories are dissimilar enough to have been assigned different type numbers in *The Types of the Folktale* but similar enough to appear, under analysis, as variants of one another. This complex relationship would be the result of relatively distant positions on a shared stemma.

4. THE ANALOGUES

a. Prophecy or Forewarning or Other Reason for the Exposure of the Child

For Vladimir Propp, prophecy is the key to the historical genesis of the ancient Oedipus legend.[101] The Oedipus legend as we have it arises from the historical clash of two conflicting social orders, one matri-

---

100. The scholium on Euripides, *Phoenician Women* 27 could be interpreted as referring to an oral tradition. Hyginus *Fabulae* 66, which has the exposure of Oedipus on water, is more difficult. Hyginus's sources were Greek, but in the case of the exposure of Oedipus, he may have been in touch with an extraliterary tradition. Hyginus had a mind, so to speak, of his own. For example, the Vatican palimpsest of a fragment of Hyginus (transcription in Mauricius Schmidt, *Hygini Fabulae* [Jena, 1872], p. xlix) gives Sikyon as the city of Polybus and Periboea, the foster parents of Oedipus (cf. *Fabulae* 66), whereas Corinth was firmly established as their city in the literary and thus the mythographical tradition. Hyginus's reference to Sikyon attaches him to what was at best a minor literary tradition or perhaps a popular tradition. This tradition is reflected in only a few other places: schol. Eur. *Phoen.* 26, 1760 = Peisander *FGrH* 16F10; schol. Hom. *Od.* 11.271 = Androtion *FGrH* 3B 324F62. See also on Sikyon, L. Edmunds, "The Cults and the Legend of Oedipus," p. 227, n. 23 (Bibliography 1).

101. Propp, "Edipo," pp. 89-95 and passim.

lineal—in which succession to the throne is by the son-in-law, who kills his father-in-law, the old king—and the other patriarchal. According to Propp, the narrative originally concerned regicide by the son-in-law. The motif of parricide enters the narrative when, in changed historical circumstances, the conflictual succession by the son-in-law is ascribed to what ought to be the nonconflictual succession by the son.

The form of the prophecy in the ancient legend is the key to this development. On the hypothesis that the prophecy is based on the outcome—that is why prophecies always come true in folklore—the prophecy in the Oedipus legend ought, according to Propp, to have spoken of regicide and of marrying the king's widow. But it speaks only of parricide and mother-incest. This inconsistency or incompleteness of the prophecy shows that what needed to be motivated was the father's hostility toward his son, a hostility that would make no sense in a patriarchal context, in which a son and heir is to be desired. To repeat, the conflict between father and son represents the historical transposition into new social and political circumstances of an earlier conflict between father-in-law and son-in-law.

Propp's account of the origin of the Oedipus legend stands or falls on the truth of the historical development he assumes. At present, there is considerable skepticism concerning matriarchy or matriliny—Propp does not make the necessary distinction between the two[102]—as a universal stage in the evolution of human society. Such a stage is not at all clearly attested in Greece,[103] and Propp would have to argue that the Oedipus legend as we know it was borrowed by the Greeks for reasons of their own from some other people.

But Propp's handling of the prophecy can also be challenged on mythological and folkloristic grounds. In the first place, the oracle was not the only forewarning received by Laius in ancient legend. There was the variant in which Laius was cursed by Pelops, whose son, Chrysippus, Laius had raped, and not abstract fate but this curse, sanctioned by Zeus, was the ultimate cause of the parricide. As I have already suggested, the importance of Apollo's prophecy in the Oedipus legend must postdate the establishment of Delphi as the oracular center of Greece, but the Oedipus legend itself antedates this development.

Study of the medieval and modern Oedipus folktale shows, furthermore, that the prophecy or other forewarning is not related to the nar-

102. Sarah B. Pomeroy, *Goddesses, Whores, Wives, and Slaves: Women in Classical Antiquity* (New York, 1975), p. 22.
103. C. G. Thomas, "Matriarchy in Early Greece: The Bronze and Dark Ages," *Arethusa* 6 (1973): 190: "The culture of the first Hellenes was patriarchal in nature."

rative as a whole—though it may be generally true that the content of prophecies is based on and is secondary to the plots of folktales. Prophecy functions principally to motivate the exposure. Therefore, the content of the prophecy concerning the newborn son is paralleled in some Finnish tales by a prophecy concerning a newborn lamb,[104] and only the fulfillment of the latter prophecy causes the parents to expose their child. In other words, the motif has been reinforced in order to provide sufficient cause for the exposure, and motivation of the exposure is thus shown to be the function of the prophecy motif.

Since the function of the motif is more important than whatever belief or doctrine it may point to in the particular society in which the tale is told, the source of the prophecy varies considerably and is not restricted to the most authoritative source in that society. It may be semidivine persons, the Apostles (FI1), Peter and Jesus (FI7), the Nile Maidens (AR(GM)), a fairy (AL1), or the Ursitori (RM2(GM)); it may be those who, for one reason or another, have clairvoyance—astrologers (AR1), wizards (FI3, 6, 8), sorcerers (FI4, LP1(NG), (AR?4(HE))), wisemen (FI5), a witch (FI13), scholars (IR1-3, IR6), a magician (RS1), or a priest (LI3); but just as well ordinary persons, a young artisan (HU3), a stranger (FI2, 10), a traveler (FI16). These prophetic figures are the ones who represent the role that Teiresias would have played (cf. section 2.e, above) before Delphi became the source of the prophecy and thus, ultimately, of the still widely held view that the story of Oedipus is a "tale of fate."

Prophecy may be omitted altogether, as in UL1, PO1, or ML1(FR), or it may be replaced by some other cause, usually illegitimacy (RM1 (GM), HU1(GM), HU2, SP3) or, in the Gregory folktales, the fact that the child is the offspring of father and daughter or of brother and sister (IT1(GM), IT2, IT3, AR?1(FR), LT3, BL2, SC2). When the hero is the offspring of an incestuous union, parricide does not occur in any of the examples we have, and the cause of the exposure thus seems to be an emphatic repetition of the incest motif. Instead of committing two crimes, parricide and incest, the hero is twice associated with incest, once as product and once as perpetrator thereof. Likewise, the criminality of the hero may be intensified at the end of the tale, for example, by paedophagy (AR?2-3(HE)), the murder of priests (FI3, 7, 10, etc.) or the rape of nuns (KR1, OR1).

Since the main purpose of the prophecy or other forewarning is to motivate the exposure of the child, it is incorrect to treat the prophecy or forewarning as embodying the fundamental belief on which the whole story is based. Such, however, is the power of the scene in which the

104. FI1, 9-10, 16, LP1(NG).

blind and ruined Oedipus appears on stage and says that it was Apollo, the god of prophecy, who brought his ills to pass (Sophocles, *Oedipus the King* 1329ff.) that it is difficult to escape the feeling that the Oedipus legend embodies the idea of fate. Sophocles even influenced Freud to speak of the Oedipus complex as fate: Oedipus's "destiny moves us only because it might have been ours—because the oracle laid the same curse upon us before our birth as upon him. It is the fate of all of us, perhaps, to direct our first sexual impulse towards our mother and our first hatred and our first murderous wish against our father."[105] And yet, from the folkloristic point of view, the conclusion must be that both Sophocles' *Oedipus the King* and Freud's Oedipus complex are versions of the legend that, for reasons of their own, choose to make fate—though Sophocles and Freud of course mean different things by fate—the ultimate source of all that happens.[106] The evidence for the ancient Oedipus legend attests the variant of Pelops's curse on Laius, and the medieval and modern analogues with their many variants of this motif confirm what is plausibly inferred from the ancient variant of the curse: namely, that prophecy is not the indispensable form of the motif. Since prophecy is thus only a variant, the doctrine of fate embodied in this variant can hardly be taken as the basis or significance either of the ancient legend or of the medieval and modern analogues.

When storytellers point to fate as the moral of the tale (e.g., KV1 (GR)), they are unknowingly and innocently appropriating a variant as the whole truth, and indeed for them it is the whole truth. The scholar, who has the broader tradition in his purview, has one sort of advantage over folk wisdom. For the scholar, the meaning of the tale does not belong to individual story-tellers and perhaps not even to communities and societies but only to the tradition as a whole *in its variability*. The individual storyteller for his part must seize upon a single variant of the tale and present it, at least on the occasion of the telling, as the truth. It is natural that in many places in the Western world, fate has been regarded both by storytellers and by scholars as the essential meaning of the Oedipus folktale, but this "truth" is relativized most strikingly by the examples of the Oedipus folktale from societies in Oceania where the concept of fate is unknown.[107]

105. Sigmund Freud, *The Interpretation of Dreams*, trans. James Strachey (New York: Discus Books, 1967), p. 296.

106. Though some would deny that in Sophocles all of Oedipus's actions are determined by fate: see Bernard Knox, "The Freedom of Oedipus," *The New Republic*, Aug. 30, 1982, pp. 28-34, based on his introduction to the translation of *Oedipus the King* by Robert Fagles in *Sophocles: The Three Theban Plays* (N.Y.: Viking Press, 1982).

107. See Lessa's discussions (Bibliography 3).

b. Exposure; Mutilation; Feral Nursing; Compassionate Executioner

In this section of the tale, exposure is the most important motif, and the others are subsidiary to it. The exposure of the child signifies that he is a future hero (usually a leader) or villain of great stature. This function of the exposure motif is shown in its earliest attestation, in the autobiographical inscription attributed to Sargon, a Babylonian king of the third millennium, but composed at a much later date.[108] Sargon tells how his mother bore him in secret, apparently illegitimately, and set him adrift on the Euphrates in a basket of rushes with its lid sealed with bitumen. "My father I knew not," he says. The story is, of course, fictitious and reflects what a later age wished to believe about the great founder of the dynasty of Agade. Sargon's story was later attached to Cyrus;[109] and Dārāb, a hero and destined king in the Persian epic, *Shāh-nāma*, whose story is similar to the medieval Gregory's, followed Sargon down the Euphrates. But the story is too well known to require further illustration.

Although it has sometimes been argued that the exposure motif in folklore derives from rituals of initiation,[110] the valence of the motif in narrative is plain enough from a comparative study of folklore. The exposed child will be saved for some great destiny, usually kingship. In the ancient Oedipus legend and in the medieval and modern folktales, however, the motif has an additional function. Since the child has been separated from its parents, it can later commit parricide and incest unknowingly. Although this is not the usual function of the motif, and incest and parricide are sometimes committed deliberately and knowingly in folklore,[111] the use of the exposure motif to provide a background of

108. For Sargon, see the inscription translated by E. A. Speiser in *Ancient Near Eastern Texts Relating to the Old Testament*, ed. J. P. Pritchard, 3d ed. (Princeton, N.J., 1969), p. 110. The inscription belongs to a genre called *"narû* literature." O. R. Gurney, "The Sultantepe Tablets (Continued): IV. The Cuthaen Legend of Naram-Sim," *Anatolian Studies* 5 (1955): 93, states: "A *narû* was an engraved stele, on which a king would record the events of his reign; . . . the so-called *narû*-literature consists of a small group of apocryphal *narû*-inscriptions, composed probably in the early second millenium B.C. but in the name of famous kings of a bygone age." A. K. Grayson and W. G. Lambert, "Akkadian Prophecies," *Journal of Cuneiform Studies* 18 (1964): 8, propose the term "poetic autobiography."

109. Robert Drews, "Sargon, Cyrus, and Mesopotamian Folk History," *Journal of Near Eastern Studies* 33 (1974): 387–93.

110. Especially by Delcourt (See Bibliography 1).

111. In the Dunnu myth, parricide and incest seem amost automatic. For the text, see Albright and Lambert and Walcot (Bibliography 1). This myth is also discussed by Littleton (Bibliography 1). For intentional parricide and incest in folklore, see the story of Kauha in M. A. Biesele, "Folklore and Ritual of the !Kung

ignorance for later crime appears very early. With the Oedipus legend, one can compare in this respect a Hittite text dated to the sixteenth or fifteenth century B.C. The queen of Kanis (= Neša, the Hittite capital = modern Költepe, fifteen kilometers northeast of Kayseri) bore thirty sons in the course of one year. In dismay, she filled containers with filth, set her sons therein, and put them in the river (the Halys). The river brought them to the sea (the Black Sea) and to the land of Zalpa (in the neighborhood of modern Bafra). The gods(?) took the children from the sea and raised them. As the years passed, the queen again gave birth, this time to thirty daughters. She raised them. The sons returned, after an interlude at Tamarmara, to Neša. Through some delusion perpetrated by the gods, the mother failed to recognize her sons, and she gave her daughters to them in marriage. The youngest son was the only one to see that he and his brothers were marrying their sisters. Guilty, they return to Zalpa, where they had grown up. The rest of the story concerns the conflict between Zalpa and another city.[112] The exposure of the sons provides, then, the background for their later incestuous marriages. In the Oedipus legend, however, the motif has a double function: as in the Hittite text, it is the necessary condition for incest (and parricide); it also has the generic function of preparing the child for a great destiny, kingship.[113] Since this is the generic function of the motif, the variance between exposure on water and exposure on land is insignificant for interpretation. But this variance bears on the geographical-historical problem, as I have already suggested in discussing the medieval analogues. In my collection, only nine tales have exposure on land, and in two of these the motif has obviously been remade (HU2, KV1(GR)). In all the others in which the motif appears, exposure is on water.[114] In

Hunter-Gatherers," Ph.D. diss., Harvard Univ., 1975, 1: 266–70. The story is also included in Edmunds and Dundes (Bibliography 3), pp. 39–42.

112. I have followed the translation and summary in Heinrich Otten, *Eine althethische Erzählung um die Stadt Zalpha,* Studien zu den Boğazköy Texten 17 (Wiesbaden, 1973).

113. I have borrowed the term *generic* from David Bynum, *The Daemon in the Wood* (Cambridge, Mass., 1978), who distinguishes between the "generic" and "nominal" forms of motifs. The nominal is the particular treatment of a motif, determined by the exigencies of the storyteller's own place, time, and idiosyncrasies, but still preserving the same narrative function that the motif has in other folktales.

114. Those medieval and modern tales that have exposure on land present interesting configurations. Two are "Nimrud" (AR1) and "Usikulumi" (ZU1), both of which have multiple exposures, and which share other similarities already noted. Two others are FC1 and TK1, which are similar in many respects, despite the geographical, linguistic, and ethnic space that separates them. Another pair consists, however, of AR?3(HE) and 4, which are clearly related to the Judas group, whereas "Nimrud" belongs to the Gregory group. Exposure on water must, then, have been

the canonical form of the ancient legend, Oedipus is to be set out on a mountain, Cithaeron, but the compassionate executioner hands him over to a shepherd from Corinth. There is, however, some ancient evidence, already cited, for exposure on water.

The role of the compassionate executioner is simply to spare the life of the protagonist, which is inevitably spared anyway. This subsidiary motif occurs in only three of the analogues in this collection (TK1, FC1, OR1). The compassionate executioner is, as it were, supernumerary, and represents an elaboration of the exposure motif. Similarly, the protagonist may be nursed by a wild or domestic animal, again as a token of his destiny.[115] This subsidiary motif is absent in the ancient Oedipus legend as we know it, but occurs in seven of the analogues. Its occurrence in FC1, which closely resembles the ancient legend in other respects, suggests that Oedipus may also have been thus nursed.

Paradoxically, the mutilation also reinforces the exposure motif as guarantee of the protagonist's future. Like exposure, mutilation is an attempt at infanticide that is not intended to succeed. As Propp saw, the symbolic nature of the mutilation as a mark of death is shown by the contradiction of this motif with the solicitude shown by the parents in preparing the vessel in which their child is exposed. One can also point to various attempts by storytellers to motivate the mutilation, e.g., a fit of anger on the father's part, as in some of the Finnish folktales. The storyteller has no sense of the original function of the motif and tries to give it a psychological cause. Already in the ancient Oedipus legend, the motif has become a difficulty. It is restricted to the single function of explaining the name Oedipus, "Swollen Foot," and thus the feet are the locus of the mutilation. But in my collection, significantly, only LT1 has this locus; in the other twenty-four tales in which the motif occurs, the upper body is the locus, since the protagonist is not named "Swollen Foot" and there is no reason for the strange wounding of the infant's feet.

Another difference between the ancient legend and the modern analogues is that in the former the scars resulting from the mutilation have not yet become the means by which the hero's identity is ascertained. In *Oedipus the King*, the scars only corroborate a conclusion that has already been reached otherwise. In the *Odyssey* Homer says that "presently the gods brought all to light" (11.274). One can only

---

extremely common in the story. The only other tale that has exposure on land is LT1, which, as I have said, may be of learned origin.

115. Cf. Binder, s.v. "Ziege" in the Index, and McCartney (Bibliography 1). See also Cosquin (Bibliography 3).

guess at the exact means by which Oedipus's crimes and identity were discovered, but Homer does not seem to be referring to scars. In the mythographical tradition, it is not, in fact, until the time of the medieval Second Vatican Mythographer that the scars serve the purpose of identifying the hero.[116] But in the modern analogues, the scars always serve this purpose, and thus mutilation leads ultimately to the discovery. In short, the motif of mutilation, like the motif of exposure, has a double function. Mutilation reinforces the exposure of the destined hero or villain—both attempts at infanticide are symbolic and necessarily fail—and leads later to the recognition scene. The scars are, of course, unnecessary, and the recognition can come about in conversation or through documents or tokens that have been placed with the exposed child.

Besides prophecy, with which are coordinated the subsidiary motifs just discussed, there is another reason for the exposure of the child, and that is illegitimacy, either endogamous or exogamous. Propp saw the incestuous marriage of the hero's parents as further proof of his thesis concerning the historical genesis of the Oedipus legend, and he did not discuss cases of exogamous illegitimacy, which is a traditional reason for exposure (as, for example, in the legends of the Greek heroes Perseus and Telephus) and is already attested in the inscription of Sargon. Endogamous illegitimacy, a double illegitimacy, as it were, is simply a multiform of exogamous illegitimacy. In the analogues here discussed, what require explanation is the fact that in the folktales in which either form occurs, exogamous (RM1(GM), HU1(GM), HU2, SP3) or endogamous (IT1(GM), IT2-3, AR?1(FR), LT3, BL1, SC2), parricide is always omitted. The omission of parricide is easy for a storyteller (compare FI17 with the other Finnish tales), but how did the rule of compensation come about, by which the criminality the protagonist loses in one place, parricide, he recovers, at least by association, in another, i.e., the incest of his parents?

c. Rescue; Rearing; Precocity; Conflict with Foster-Brother(s) or Other Children; Departure from Foster Home

The child must be rescued and reared, and then must leave its foster home. This section of the tale might seem to be merely transitional, but it is not left unmarked by the tale's fundamental concern with the future greatness, for better or worse, of the protagonist. This concern, which is sometimes even stated in the prophecy and is developed in the exposure

116. George Bode, *Scriptores Rerum Mythicarum Latini Tres Romae Nuper Reperti*, 2 vols. (Celle, 1834) is the most recent edition.

and related motifs, appears, in the section beginning with the rescue, in the motifs of precocity and conflict with other children. The mode of rescue and the identity of the foster-parents are of less importance.[117]

The precocity of the destined child is either physical, taking the form of rapid growth (only UL1 and PO1, but cf. FI13), or of mental quickness displayed by the child as a student (e.g., LT3, RM1(GM), SC1). Physical precocity is obviously magical, a sign of the protagonist's special powers. In Greek mythology, one can compare the rapid growth of, for example, the infant Zeus (Hesiod *Theogony* 492-93, cf. Aratus *Phaenomena* 34ff.).[118] Likewise, mental precocity is a sign of the magical wisdom of the future leader. Propp cites the story of Habis, told in Justin's *Epitome* (third century A.D.) of the lost *Historiae Philippicae* by the Augustan historian Trogus. The story is clearly analogous to the Oedipus legend, although it does not contain incest or parricide. Habis survived several exposures and finally succeeded his father as king of the Tartessii, a people in Spain. He then gave laws to his people and taught them plowing and sowing (*Epit.* 44.4). In other words, Habis is an inspired founder of civilized life. Propp's instinct was sound. A middle term linking Habis and Oedipus can be found in Perdicas, who gave up his incestuous love of his mother in order to become a farmer and love mother earth (Fulgentius *Myth.* 3.2). Perdicas was also the inventor of the saw.

The motif of precocity in the analogues may contribute to the elucidation of a rather puzzling point in the ancient Oedipus legend, and that is the intelligence of Oedipus, a well-known theme of Sophocles' *Oedipus the King*. This trait makes perfect sense in the context of the tragedy, but, given the story pattern of the Oedipus legend, the appearance of the trait in the legend, as distinct from individual dramatic elaborations of the legend, is difficult to explain. Why should this hero have become known for outstanding intelligence? Oedipus demonstrated this intelligence, of course, by solving the riddle of the Sphinx, and one can speculate that the protagonist's precious intelligence, displayed in some of the analogues, became attached in the Greek legend to the motif of monster slaying. The confrontation of hero and winged maiden was a favorite theme of fifth-century vase painters—it was practically the only episode of his life they illustrated—and his wisdom became proverbial.[119]

117. My interpretation of this section of the tale differs widely from Propp's historical explanation of the foster parents. See Propp, "Edipo," pp. 105-18.

118. For further references, see the notes of M. L. West on these lines of the *Theogony* in his edition of that poem (*Hesiod: Theogony* [Oxford, 1966]), and also Jacques Laager, *Gebürt und Kindheit des Gottes in der griechischen Mythologie* (Wintherthur, 1957), Index, s.v. "Wachstum, rasches."

119. It has been argued that certain vase paintings attest a version of the myth

Like other motifs already discussed, precocity may have a double function. It may bear a relation not only to the child's destiny as leader but also, more immediately, to the child's relation with his coevals. His precocity may provoke their jealousy, and this in turn may lead to their taunting him with bastardy, which leads finally to his departure from his foster home. These motifs may be thus causally linked, but this is not always the case, since each of the motifs is more fundamentally coordinated with the hero's ultimate destiny, or, in narrative terms, with the fundamental story pattern, in which causal connections are not the most important thing. The storyteller may say simply, "When he grew up he said goodbye . . . and went out to earn his living" (UK1), and the absence of any cause, psychological or other, in no way detracts from the coherence of the story.[120]

The conflict belongs to the fundamental story pattern because it too demonstrates the protagonist's superiority. If he is a villain, the conflict demonstrates his villainy, as in "Nimrud" and the Judas folktales, in which the young Judas murders his brother or foster brother (LT2, GK1, GR2, GR3, FI15, KR2, IR2). The most highly developed form of the conflict motif is found in the Cyrus legend, in which the young hero plays a game with other children in which he takes the role of king and has a disobedient playmate beaten (Herodotus 1.114). But a trace of the conflict motif appears in Sophocles' *Oedipus the King* 779, where Oedipus says that a drunken companion taunted him with not being the son of Polybus. The mythographical tradition makes this taunt a matter of his companions' envy (Apollodorus 3.5.7, Hyginus *Fabulae* 67). Although we hear nothing of precocity as such, Oedipus was, he says in *Oedipus the King* 775-76, the most important man in Corinth, and Apollodorus reports that Oedipus excelled in strength (again 3.5.7). Here is perhaps a faint trace of the precocity of the child who will be king.

In sum, the analogues bring into relief two motifs that have faded in the ancient sources for the Oedipus legend—the superiority of the foundling and his conflict with his age-mates. Furthermore, the folktales show how these motifs are to be understood in relation to the story pattern. They are further signs of the protagonist's future greatness.

---

in which Oedipus killed the Sphinx with a sword or a club. See Ulrich Hausmann, "Oidipus und die Sphinx," *Jahrbuch der staatlichen Kunstsammlungen in Baden-Württemberg* 9 (1972): 7-36. J.-M. Moret, however, in chapter 5 ("Le Combat d'Oedipe") of his forthcoming book on the Sphinx in Greek art, has argued persuasively that the vase paintings do not allow the conclusion that the slaying of the Sphinx existed in Greek myth independently of the riddle solving.

120. As Propp, "Edipo," p. 118, rightly observes, "i nessi causali nello svillupo dell' intreccio non svolgono una funzione decisiva."

d. Act of Valor; Parricide; Incest

The act of valor takes one main form in the analogues. The hero returns to his native city at the head of an army and rescues his mother from her enemies (LT3, AR?1(FR), IT2). This heroic deed may once in the ancient legend have encompassed the parricide and still does so twice in modern folklore (RS1, FI14). The only other valorous deeds are the slaying of a wild animal in "The Sultan's Son" (TK1) and the solving of a riddle in LA1. In the Turkish folktale, the queen has offered her hand and the kingdom to anyone who can kill a savage wolf. This is a test that the hero must undergo in order to prove himself. The Turkish wolf may be a descendant of the Teumesian fox that Oedipus killed. In any case, the Turkish tale indicates that the function of this motif in the ancient legend is to qualify the hero for his marriage, and this function, which is already implicit in *Phoenician Women* 45-51, is explicit in the mythographical tradition (Diodorus Siculus 4.6.2, Apollodorus 3.5.8, Hyginus *Fabulae* 67). The Sphinx is thus related causally to what follows in the legend, although her appearance in the legend is completely adventitious. She was a local Boeotian monster (Hesiod *Theogony* 326) who was available for slaying by Oedipus.

"A Tale About How Riddles Came into Existence" (LA1) is anomalous both because of the monster slaying and because of the riddle, the only occurrence amongst the analogues of the famous riddle of the Sphinx. At first sight, this tale might seem to be derived, at least indirectly, from the ancient Greek legend and thus to be an offshoot of literary history and not a genuine piece of folklore. The exposure on water, however, as was argued above in the conclusion of section 3, belongs to a popular, oral tradition of the Oedipus story. Furthermore, the apparently literary form of the parricide in LA1—the hero's father is riding in a carriage, as in Sophocles' *Oedipus the King*—has far-flung parallels in the collection of analogues (AL1 and FC1). The wizard-monster of LA1 that poses the famous riddle is male, not female like the Sphinx, and in this respect, too, the folktale has parted company with any learned origin it may have had. Finally, the total ineptitude of the moral ("Thus, from that time on, riddles came to be") suggests that any deliberate borrowing from the ancient myth has long since lost its original point, whatever it was.

But the absence, with the lone exceptions of TK1 and LA1, of the monster-slaying motif in the analogues would imply that the Sphinx was only a variant in the ancient Oedipus legend. This suggestion might be greeted with amused incredulity, since we know that the Sphinx is essential to the legend. Robert regarded the slaying of the Sphinx as the nucleus of the legend, and even those who disagreed with Robert's thesis of a cult origin of the Oedipus legend preserved, for reasons of their own, the notion that slaying the monster and winning the bride were the basic elements in the legend.[121] Of the episodes in Oedipus's life, his confrontation with the Sphinx was by far the favorite of vase painters, and this fact by itself would suggest that for the Greeks, too, this episode was the most important one. Furthermore, the intelligence demonstrated by Oedipus in solving the Sphinx's riddle seems to be central to his character.[122]

But there is a text, *Odyssey* 11.271-80, that summarizes the life of Oedipus without any mention of the Sphinx:

I saw the mother of Oedipus, lovely Epicaste,
Who did an enormous deed in the ignorance of her mind
And married her son. He slew his own father
And married her. The gods soon made these things known to men.
But he suffered pains in his much-beloved Thebes,
And ruled the Cadmeians through the destructive plans of the gods;
And she went to the place of the mighty gatekeeper Hades.
She hung up a high noose from the lofty roofbeam,
Possessed by her grief. For him she left many pains
Behind her, the kind a mother's Furies bring to pass.[123]

The absence of the Sphinx here can be explained neither by the brevity of the passage nor by the fact that it is focused on Epikaste. The author explicitly links the marriage to the parricide. ("He slew his own father / And married her.") The passage is noteworthy in other respects, too: the immediate discovery of the incestuous marriage, with the result, as Pausanias observed, that Oedipus's children would have been by a second wife;[124] the absence of the self-blinding;[125] Oedipus' living on as king of Thebes. In short, the passage constitutes a rather complete variant of the legend, and, from this point of view, the absence of the Sphinx is less surprising.[126]

121. For the doxography, see Edmunds, *The Sphinx in the Oedipus Legend* (Bibliography 1), pp. 2-4.
122. See the first section of this introduction, above.
123. *Homer: The Odyssey*, trans. Albert Cook (New York, 1967), p. 152.
124. Paus. 9.5.11. Note that Pausanias says that the author of the *Oedipodeia* "also" (i.e., in addition to what he infers from the passage in the *Odyssey*) makes Euryganeia the mother of Oedipus's children.
125. See Robert, *Oidipus*, 1:112.
126. Jean-Marc Moret, objecting to my interpretation of this passage in the *Odyssey* as a variant of the Oedipus legend in which the Sphinx is missing, has pointed out that in *Iliad* 6.179-83 Bellerophon's slaying of the Chimaera is described without mention of Pegasus. I would agree with what seems to be M. L. West's suggestion in his note on *Theogony* 325 that, in the *Iliad*, the last three

The common opinion, on the other hand, has held that this passage represents the content of the lost *Oedipodeia,* and it is natural that in the attempt to reconstruct the epic, no stone should be left unturned and that no likely stone should be left unused. Indeed, Bethe believed that the *Oedipodeia* was the source of the passage in the *Odyssey.*[127] For present purposes, however, the common opinion is worth discussing only as a means of distinguishing two different methods of studying the Oedipus legend. Robert, Bethe, and others wrote the history of the legend as the history of literature. The subtitle of Robert's book is *Geschichte eines poetischen Stoffs im griechischen Altertum.* As historians, their method was diachronic; and there is even an implicit teleology in their thinking: the history of the legend *culminates* in fifth-century tragedy, especially in Sophocles' *Oedipus the King.* In any case, the diachronic approach almost imposes upon them a certain way of reading passages like *Odyssey* 11.271-80: with respect to tragedy, this passage is early, and as such, it can be *combined* with everything else that is early, since earliness in and of itself is a common denominator.

The method adopted in section 2 above was synchronic, and the purpose of the survey of the ancient evidence for the Oedipus legend was not to reconstruct lost Theban epics but to identify variants, as background to a comparative analysis of the analogues. The two principles of synchrony and variation allow a passage like *Odyssey* 11.271-80 to stand on its own as what it is—to repeat, an authentic variant of the legend, and the analogues corroborate absence of the monster-slaying motif as a variant. As for the problem of the relation of the passage to the *Oedipodeia,* it is known from the single fragment that the Sphinx was preying on the youth of Thebes.[128] Therefore, the *Oedipodeia* is not the source of the passage in the *Odyssey.*

I have already suggested why it was appropriate for Oedipus to become a riddle solver—it was a display of the mental superiority that the hero of this type often displays as a child. But how did the Sphinx become a riddler in the first place? The most likely explanation is that the riddle that princesses of folklore set for their suitors has been transferred

---

words of 6.183 indicate the source of Bellerophon's power to overcome the monster—"trusting to the portents of the gods." It is not clear to me what this phrase means, but it indicates some different sort of aid from that supplied by Pegasus in the other sources for the story.

127. Bethe, pp. 3ff. Legras simply assumes that the passage in the *Odyssey* is a source for the *Oedipodeia.* De Kock, "The Sophoklean Oidipus and Its Antecedents" (note the teleological perspective), p. 15, mentions "liberation of Thebes" in a list of motifs found in this passage, unconsciously conflating it with the standard version that includes the Sphinx. For Bethe, Legras, and de Kock, see Bibliography 1.

128. Fr. 2, from schol. Eur. *Phoen.* 1760.

from the princess to the monster.[129] In a modern Greek folktale, the riddle of the Sphinx is, in fact, proposed by a queen to her suitor.[130] It is also worth noting that the Oedipus tale has a special affinity for riddles the subject of which is the offspring of an incestuous union.[131] The riddle may take the form of a lullaby (AL1) or an epitaph (IT3) or an inscription on a tablet accompanying the exposed child (AR?1(FR)). Or the whole tale may be an explanation of an incest riddle (SP1-3). These incest riddles are formally the same as the Sphinx's riddle in that one and the same thing is given several different and apparently mutually exclusive descriptions.

But monster slaying as a test of the hero is absent from the modern analogues, with the exceptions already noted (TK1, LA1). It is only necessary that the hero kill his father, and this parricide always precedes the incestuous marriage, with the exception of HU3, and of UL1 and PO1. The first of these seems like a conflation of the Oedipus with the St. Julian folktale. The second and third present a more difficult problem. On the one hand, they look like cognates of the others and belong probably to the Gregory group. On the other, their peculiarities, rapid growth, etc., as well as the inverted sequence of parricide and incest, cannot be found in other tales, and they remain apparently unique examples of this form of the Gregory group.

In either sequence, parricide and incest are the centerpiece of the narrative. In the case of the villain, they raise his villainy to such a degree that he can become a suitable enemy of God (Nimrud) or the destroyer of Christ (Judas). In the case of the hero, they are the mode by which he attains kingship. Although in one version of the ancient legend, Oedipus lived on as king of Thebes after the discovery of his crimes, and although in *Oedipus the King* his kingship is nearly divine, the modern analogues find it difficult to maintain the ambiguity of greatness and criminality in the hero, and this ambiguity is secured only in his later exaltation. One can speculate that it is for this reason that the Gregory folktales tended to omit the parricide and to replace it— if this was in fact the process of evolution—with the hero's passive fault of being the offspring of incest; these folktales wanted to reduce the criminality of the hero, which was felt as ill-suited to the temporal greatness that he achieves. Nevertheless, it is certain that parricide and incest do not simply represent the inevitability of fate, even in those

129. See A. Lesky, "Sphinx," in *Real-Encyclopaedie der classischen Altertums-wissenschaft*, ed. A. Pauly, G. Wissowa, et al. (1893-), second ser., 6th half vol. (1929), cols. 1717-18.

130. In Bernhard Schmidt, "Die Räthselwette," *Griechische Märchen, Sagen, und Volkslieder* (Leipzig, 1877), pp. 143-44.

131. Cf. Brewster (Bibliography 3).

analogues in which the storyteller explicitly draws such a conclusion. The folktale has no such abstract concern. All of the principal motifs contribute to the story pattern of the exposed child who will finally achieve greatness for better or worse. Parricide and incest are the paradoxical way in which this greatness is achieved, finally for the villain and penultimately for the hero, who must undergo penance before his final exaltation. It is vouchsafed to him to commit the ultimate crimes of which humans are capable—that is why cannibalism is sometimes attracted into the story. Only to the gods, as practically all mythologies show, are incest and parricide permitted. In committing these crimes, the protagonist becomes superhuman. The villain's superhuman nature is shown in his role of adversary to the divine. The hero's is shown in his ultimate attainment of a quasi-divinity of his own.

The parricide motif must also be discussed apropos the relation of types 933 and 931. Thompson concludes his description of 933 with the statement, "The parents come to the pope to be confessed." Of the Gregory folktales in my collection,[132] only two end in this way (IT1 (GM), IT3). More often, the hero's father simply departs or otherwise disappears from the story and is never heard of again (LT3, HU1(GM), IT1(GM), UK2). Death is another way of removing the father (KV1 (GR), IT2, SC2) and thus the motif of parricide. The early death of the father in FI17 is especially interesting. Taken in the context of the FI group, it shows how simply the parricide is deleted from a Judas folktale and thus how close the Judas and Gregory folktales potentially are. Contrariwise, in RS1, obviously of the Gregory type, the parricide has been, so to speak, retained. Again, the boundary between 933 and 931 is blurred. In short, the Judas folktale may, through the early death of the hero's father, delete the motif of parricide; and the Gregory folktale, through preservation of the father, may include this motif.

e. Discovery; Further Crimes; Penance; Exaltation

The discovery motif has already been discussed apropos of mutilation. In *Oedipus the King,* the plague gives the impetus to the quest for Laius's murderer, but this plague appears only in TK1 in the analogues. One is inclined to agree with Carl Robert that the plague was Sophocles' invention.[133] There is no one to correspond to the figure of Teiresias (except perhaps for the spaewife in AL1 and the priest in LI2). In the analogues, the discovery is subject to considerable variation. It may

132. A minimal list: AR?1(FR), LT1, 3, IT2-3, BL1. I say minimal because I have not attempted to include the many cases in which 933 is combined with other types.

133. Robert, *Oidipus,* 1: 292 (Bibliography 1).

come about through scars or tokens, or a third party may reveal the truth (AL1, UL1, LI1, FC1). In two tales (AR?3-4(HE)) paedophagy leads to the discovery of incest and parricide, and the protagonist is thus encumbered with another extreme crime. Here the discovery motif too is given a double function.

The crimes of the protagonist are the mode in which his superhuman nature is revealed, and therefore it is not surprising that they should be reduplicated in new forms in the stage of the narrative that follows discovery. This stage is a brief reprise of what has already happened. Again the protagonist leaves home, he commits new crimes, and again he is exalted or, if he is a villain, he usually takes his own life. The first exaltation is sometimes obscured in the tales, although in the Gregory group and in several other folktales, the hero becomes, through marriage, a king. In the second exaltation, the hero becomes a priest (IT2, IR5) or a bishop (IR6, OR1) or pope (LT3, cf. AR?1(FR), IT1(GM), IT3, LI3, PL2) or a saint (SC2, UK1-2) or a sage (AR?2(HE)). Just as, in the first exaltation, the hero marries his mother, so, in the second, they are sometimes reunited (LT3, AR?1(FR), HU2, IT1(GM), IT3, LI3, IR6, PL2), and sometimes die together. In FI3 and FI7, they continue to live together but now as mother and son. In UL1 the marriage continues. In short, there is a marked tendency in the analogues to reduplicate the incest in some form of union of mother and son.

In the folktales that have a Christian setting, the second exaltation is the result of penance, and thus the folktale could be a lesson, like the medieval Greek folktale (GK1), which comes from a synaxarium, or BL1, presented as a sermon by John Chrysostom, of which the homiletic point is: "How much more the apostles rejoice in heaven over one sinner who repents than over a righteous man." There is a group of folktales about St. Andrew that explain the origin of his Canon of Repentance. The etiological tendency is so strong in the case of St. Andrew that he is even made the son of Mary of Egypt (UK2), whose help is invoked in the Canon, and to whom St. Andrew was especially devoted.

The period of penance in the folktales corresponds with the period of wandering in the ancient Oedipus legend that culminates in the hero's death and burial at Colonus, where he becomes a sort of cult hero and his corpse will have the power to protect the land from its enemies. The folktales, as Propp saw, confirm the unity of the two parts of the ancient legend represented by the two tragedies, *Oedipus the King* and *Oedipus at Colonus*.[134]

There is a further correspondence between the form of penance in the analogues and the form of Oedipus's final heroization in *Oedipus*

---

134. Propp, "Edipo," pp. 129-34.

at Colonus. Oedipus miraculously enters the earth at the time of his death, and as a cult hero he becomes a chthonic power. In the analogues, the hero's exaltation is connected, not with earth, but with heaven. And yet his penance sometimes causes him to dig a well in a cliff (FI3-5, FI7) or to be buried in a well or cave (KR3, UK1-2, OR1, RS1-2, IT1(GM)) or chained to a rock. His chthonic nature is so pronounced that his knees take root (IT1(GM)) or his hair grows into the cover of the well (KR3). Similarly, the hero may be required to water a dead stump or a charred piece of wood until it puts forth new growth (FI6, HU1(GM), UK1).[135] In short, the analogues present the penance as a chthonic phase in the hero's exaltation.

When the hero is imprisoned in a well, a tower, etc., he is also chained, and the key is thrown into the sea and swallowed by a fish. At a certain point, the fish is caught, and in its belly is discovered the long-lost key. If the key stands for the hero, as Propp suggests, then even in this element of the later stage of the folktale, we have a reprise of the earlier stage.[136] The hero is once again cast into the sea. It is worth noting that in one folktale (HE1) the hero is swallowed by a fish and thus makes his way to his foster father, who discovers him in the fish at a banquet. This example, which was unknown to Propp, lends some credence to his suggestion concerning the key to the penitent's chains.

5. CONCLUSIONS AND CRITIQUE OF TWENTIETH-CENTURY INTERPRETATIONS OF THE ANCIENT OEDIPUS LEGEND

Study of the analogues shows that we are dealing with the tale of the child who, despite all obstacles, achieves greatness as villain or as hero. This interpretation is secured especially by the part of the narrative that follows the discovery of the crimes. This part is a reprise of the earlier part. The essential motifs are repeated as the hero moves toward his conflict with the divine or to a quasi-divinity of his own. In either case, the hero is repeating the earlier climax that took the form of parricide and incest. As I have already argued (section 4.a, above), the hero's achievements, whether good or bad, have nothing essentially to do with fate, although it is of course open to storytellers to perceive fate as the moral of the tale, and the ancient Oedipus legend itself was accommodated to the Delphic oracle. The tale's air of fatality derives, not from its content, but from what might be called fatality of narrative,

135. These motifs constitute for Thompson an independent type or types: 756B and 756C.

136. Propp, "Edipo," p. 132.

which consists in the characteristic double function and overdetermination of the tale's motifs. In order, as it were, to make its point, the tale acquired an ever denser narrative structure, which entailed the reprise discussed in the preceding section (4.e). In other words, this narrative fatality is the signifier, not the signified.

This observation concerning narrative also has a bearing on the problem of the hero's subjectivity (cf. section 1). In the folktales, with their brevity and lack of adornment, it is quite obvious that psychological motivation is kept to a minimum and is indeed unnecessary (cf. section 4.c on the hero's departure from his foster home). The action does not flow from the protagonist's inner self; nor does it culminate in any sort of self-consciousness. Judas, dying at the very threshold of the new era of grace, dies unaware of his place in the scheme of salvation, perhaps the last man to die according to the law of the Old Testament.[137] Such self-consciousness as is to be found is attached, like the sense of fatality, to the narrative itself. The part of the tale I have called the reprise represents a self-consciousness on the part of the narrative tradition, a capacity of the tradition itself for self-reflection.

In the comparative perspective provided by the analogues, the self-consciousness, or, more generally, the subjectivity of Oedipus would have to be regarded as the peculiar property of tragedy. The question would then become the degree and kind of subjectivity manifested by Oedipus in tragedy, a question for literary criticism. To the debates of this field, folklore can add only one suggestion, namely that the action of *Oedipus the King* and *Oedipus at Colonus* does not flow from the subjectivity of Oedipus but constitutes it, such as it may be. Toward the end of his essay, Propp raises the question of the powerful attraction of the Oedipus story outside of the ancient setting to which his analysis mainly refers. Propp finds the answer in a single feature of the ancient story: the suffering of Oedipus, the personal nature of which is, according to Propp, unusual for a Greek hero. Oedipus is an outcast. He has lost all contact with human society. His blindness expresses renunciation of the world. He loses his sons. But he has a daughter, Antigone, who accompanies him in his wanderings, and, says Propp, "it is precisely through the affection of his daughter that he can later find a partial return to the world. The scene of leave-taking [Propp refers to the final scene of *Oedipus at Colonus*] is the most disturbing in all tragedy, it is the moment of the birth of man, it is the moment of the birth of man in European history."[138] Propp's words are deliberately

137. See Ohly (Bibliography 2), pp. 31–32.
138. Propp, "Edipo," p. 133 (my translation): "Ed è appunto attraverso l' affetto della figlia che egli più tardi in parte trova una via di ritorno verso il mondo.

paradoxical because what follows immediately after the leave-taking is the death of Oedipus.

For Propp, then, it is only at the very end of his life that Oedipus attains something that signifies the origin of man in European history. What is this thing? The answer must come from Propp's remark concerning the personal nature of Oedipus's suffering, which was endured for the most part in isolation. Through this suffering, Oedipus attains an individuality of which it can be said that it makes him the first European. Propp's discussion of the end of *Oedipus at Colonus* may have been inspired by Hegel's statement on that tragedy in his *Aesthetics*. For Hegel, Greek tragedy was not a matter of the depths of the individual but rather of the destructive conflict of opposing forces, one of which the tragic hero embodied and lived out. But *Oedipus at Colonus*, in virtue of its subjectivity, was almost modern.[139] Hegel traces the progressive isolation of Oedipus; his purification of himself from all inner conflict; and his death as the savior of Athens. "This transfiguration in death is his and our evident reconciliation in his own individuality and personality."[140] Why "and our"? Hegel has already called attention to the modernity of *Oedipus at Colonus*, to the "inner reconciliation" that takes place in that tragedy. The specifically modern inwardness of the reconciliation with which the tragedy ends is what engages us. Both Hegel and Propp, then, find the characteristically modern subjectivity of Oedipus in the scene of his death, and for them this subjectivity is not a given in the tragedies but is attained for an instant only at the very end. In the perspective of the analogues, this qualification of the subjectivity of Oedipus comes as no surprise.

But the most important result of the comparison of the modern analogues with the ancient Oedipus legend is the demonstration of the unity of the stages of the ancient legend represented by *Oedipus the King* and *Oedipus at Colonus*. The comparison also leads to various other insights into the ancient legend. First, the exposure of the infant on water must have been a more common variant in antiquity than our meager evidence would suggest, and Oedipus would thus have stood closer, in this respect, to other well-known exposed children. Second, the compassionate executioner, who would be unnecessary in the case of exposure on water, was not essential to the ancient legend but rather was a dramatic emphasis of the intent—perhaps one should speak of the

---

La scena del congedo e forse la più sconvolgente di tutta la tragedia, è il momento della nascita dell' uomo, è il momento della nascita dell' uomo nella storia europea."

139. G. W. F. Hegel, *Ästhetik*, vol. 3, *Die Poesie*, ed. R. Bubner (Stuttgart, 1971), p. 336.

140. Hegel, *Ästhetik*, p. 337 (my translation).

intent of the legend itself, not of the parents' intent—that the child be preserved. Third, the motifs surrounding the exposure may have included feral nursing. Fourth, the precocity of the foundling and his conflict with his age-mates had much more importance than they do in our sources for the ancient legend, and these motifs are coordinated with the future greatness of the child. Sixth, the Sphinx would seem to be a rough reduplication of the parricide, a means of motivating the marriage with the mother. The mental precocity of the foundling in the modern folktales seems to have been expressed in the ancient legend in the intelligence that Oedipus displayed in solving the riddle of the Sphinx. Seventh, originally or in another version of the legend now lost, the parricide may have taken place in a military engagement.

But the comparison of the analogues and the ancient legend, confirming as it does the unity of the earlier and later stages of the ancient legend, reveals a fundamental similarity in the ancient and the modern protagonists. In the case of the hero, he combines the worst and the best that human life is capable of in his society; in the case of the villain, his being capable of the best is shown inversely, as it were, in that he— and by implication he alone—is capable of direct conflict with the best. The hero is, in a medieval expression, a *pars totalis*. Unlike many heroes of folklore who found, protect, give order to, or otherwise make possible human society, Oedipus or the hero of the analogues here discussed is the individual part of society who in the vicissitudes of his life manages to incorporate in himself all the moral and other possibilities of his society. His life is a description of the dimensions of his society, a description that, in virtue of his crimes, includes all that lies outside those dimensions. The worst is everywhere and always the same. Thus the hero commits parricide and incest (and sometimes also cannibalism). These are the worst crimes of which humans are capable. But the best differs. In the Greek setting, kingship (or tyranny) and hero cult were the best attainments (though from an early period Greek culture provided alternatives in, for example, Pythagoreanism, Orphism, the mystery religions, and, later, philosophy). The evidence for kingship in the earlier history of Greece is scanty, but mythological, as distinguished from historical, kingship in Greece waxed strong in the figure of Zeus, the divine king of the Greek pantheon. The resemblance between the story patterns of Zeus and Oedipus points to kingship as that element in the ancient legend in which the greatness of the hero is fulfilled, at least in a preliminary way, to be finally consecrated in hero cult. For obvious reasons, royalty ceases to be the hero's achievement in most of the modern folktales, but those in which it persists willy-nilly are the exceptions that prove the principle. What is more typical of the modern hero is that he becomes a leader of the church or a saint. For this reason, the part of the folktale that I have called the reprise must emphasize the penance of the hero, who must, in the Christian setting, undergo a spiritual change. In the ancient legend, at least in *Oedipus at Colonus,* Oedipus is impenitent. He is angry; curses his sons to death; resents all that he has been made to suffer.

It remains to compare the present interpretation of the Oedipus legend and of the modern analogues with the main twentieth-century interpretations of the Oedipus legend, those of Freud, Propp, and Lévi-Strauss. Propp's is the only one of these that used folklore, and yet for Propp, as for Freud and Lévi-Strauss, the ancient Oedipus legend was only a case in point. The legend illustrated something else that was of greater interest. Propp used modern folklore diagnostically in order to uncover what he took to be the historical genesis of the ancient legend. This approach caused him to give historical explanations even where a more obvious folkloristic explanation was ready to hand. For example, he spends pages on the incestuous union of the hero's parents, arguing that this represents a particular stage of history, and never considers the obvious possibility that this incestuous union is simply a multiform of illegitimacy as a reason for the exposure of the child. Nor does Propp point out what I have called the law of compensation, by which the incestuous union of the hero's parents is always coordinated with omission of parricide. When the Russian Propp speaks of the shepherds in the ancient legend as reflecting the original foster parents in some early stage of society, before the origin of the state and class differentiation, or when he speaks of the foundling's age-mates as reflecting some primitive "collective," the Western reader inevitably suspects deliberate conformity with officially prescribed views on the origin of society. When Propp speaks of the plot of the Oedipus legend as originating "in a post-hunting, herding society," in a postmatriarchal stage, one can even hear an echo of Frederick Engel's *The Origin of the Family, Private Property, and the State.* [141]

Folklorist though he was, Propp's interest in interpreting the ancient legend was the change in the history of human society that he thought he could discern in the legend. The two other great interpreters of the Oedipus legend, Freud and Lévi-Strauss, no matter what the differences between them, are like Propp in using the legend to make a point about something else beside the legend. For Freud, the legend, which had its

141. Propp, "Edipo," p. 108, Cf. Engels, *The Origin,* p. 119, in the translation by Alec West (New York, 1972): "Once it had passed into the private possession of families and there begun to augment, this wealth [i.e., cattle] dealt a severe blow to the society founded on pairing marriage and the matriarchal gens." But in fairness to Propp, it must be pointed out that he was not afraid to risk official disfavor: see Bynum, *Demon,* p. 252.

origins, not in history, but in incest dreams of the sort that he heard from his patients, represented the primary desires of the child, which must be overcome if the child is to attain adulthood. In short, the legend exemplified, and provided confirmation for, the Oedipus complex.[142]

In discussing Freud and the Oedipus legend, one must distinguish between two problems: the truth of the Oedipus complex *for us* and the truth of the Oedipus complex as an interpretation of the ancient legend. I shall discuss only the latter problem, and shall limit myself to those points that are suggested by the interpretation of the ancient legend to which study of the modern analogues has led. The most salient point is the severe reduction in the number of motifs that the complex can account for. Freud has nothing to say about the stage of the legend, which has been shown to be integral to the legend, represented by *Oedipus at Colonus,* a tragedy that he must have known but never mentions in his published works. Furthermore, such motifs as exposure and precocity can have no meaning in relation to the complex. Only parricide and incest are meaningful, and these, in the complex, are, of course, not deeds but desires, and they are the child's, not those of the adult who has overcome the Oedipus complex. Parricide and incest are specifically royal in the ancient legend, as folklore confirms, but are democratized in the complex and become the desires of everyman.

Freud has taken the possibility of the story pattern represented by the Judas folktale and modified it so that not only is the Oedipus of the Oedipus complex not a hero, he is not even a Judas, a worthy villain. The comparison of the Oedipus complex with folklore and with the ancient legend as interpreted in relation to folklore demonstrates starkly what has sometimes been said of Freud on other grounds, namely, that the Oedipus complex was an attempt to denigrate human nature, an attack on the idealistic humanism of the Western tradition. "Like Oedipus," Freud says, "we live in ignorance of these wishes, repugnant to morality, which have been forced upon us by Nature, and after their revelation we may all of us seek to close our eyes to the scenes of our childhood."[143]

Freud held that the Oedipus legend "sprang from some primaeval dream material," which itself sprang from the Oedipus complex. But where did the Oedipus complex come from? In order to answer this

142. The first complete statement of the Oedipus complex appeared in *The Interpretation of Dreams* (1900), in *The Standard Edition of the Complete Psychological Works of Sigmund Freud,* ed. James Strachey (London, 1966-), 4: 261-64. The canonical account of the Oedipus complex appears in *Introductory Lectures on Psycho-Analysis* (1916-17), in *The Standard Edition,* 16: 329-38.

143. Freud, *The Interpretation of Dreams,* trans. James Strachey (New York, 1965), p. 297.

question, Freud created in *Totem and Taboo* the legend of the primal horde. Freud took over from Darwin the notion of a primal horde ruled by a patriarch who expelled his envious sons. They then banded together (unlike the quarrelsome foster brothers of folklore) and killed their father and ate him. Overcome by guilt, they refrained from the women. Here is the origin of the incest taboo. (In terms of narrative, the crime of incest has been omitted and has been replaced by cannibalism. There is an analogous process in the Gregory folktales, where parricide is omitted and incest reduplicated.) The sons then exalt the father in the form of the totem animal. Here is the origin of totemism.

The Freudian legend of the primal horde shares with the Freudian interpretation of the Oedipus legend the failure to unite in the hero the crimes and the exaltation. In the primal horde, the sons commit the crimes, and the father is exalted because of their guilt. Although the sons do achieve parricide, and consume their father to boot, their deed remains incomplete with respect to the women, just as the desires of the Oedipus complex are repressed. Such was "the great event with which culture began and which ever since has not let mankind come to rest."[144]

Whereas in Freud's interpretation of the ancient legend, parricide and incest are the central message of the legend—they express the primary desires of the complex—in Lévi-Strauss these motifs are not a message but only elements of a code.[145] The legend, to the extent that it is about anything at all, to the extent that it has a content, is about something else. Parricide, incest, the other motifs, and also such elements as the names of the characters—all these form a code deployed in a system in which one side of a binary opposition (denial of autochthony; affirmation thereof) is related analogously to the other (overrating of kinship relations; underrating thereof). Incest, for example, is an element in the code that comes under the heading of overrating of kinship relations. The legend is not so much about autochthony as it is a logical model that, according to Lévi-Strauss, palliates the problem of autochthony by transposing it into other terms. Lévi-Strauss regarded autochthony as a central problem in Greek culture. Classicists have received his interpretation of the Oedipus legend with near contempt,[146] and yet, whatever the truth of his broader claim concerning autochthony, he was surely right about the Oedipus legend. This analogy is discernible in the principle texts, including, as an astute reading has shown, Aeschylus'

144. Freud, *Totem and Taboo*, trans. A. A. Brill (New York, 1946), p. 187.
145. Lévi-Strauss, "The Structural Study of Myth," *Journal of American Folklore* 68 (1955): 428–44, reprinted with very slight changes in Lévi-Strauss's *Structural Anthropology* (New York, 1967), pp. 202–28.
146. See Vernant (Bibliography 1), p. 19.

Seven against Thebes. [147] To return, however, to the comparison of Lévi-Strauss and Freud, what distinguishes the former from the latter is the emphasis on the form as opposed to the content of the ancient legend, but they are just alike in taking that legend as a case in point.

Lévi-Strauss offered his interpretation as an example of method and also as a theory of myth. The theory is more or less implicit in the essay on the Oedipus legend but has been made clear in his other writings. Myths are models of their societies. This theory is, in fact, corroborated by the interpretation of the ancient Oedipus legend and of the modern analogues that I have offered, but a large area of disagreement remains. The Oedipus legend and the analogues do not function as models of societies through a code and a system of binary oppositions. Rather, they employ motifs that have certain generic meanings (e.g., exposure) and, at the same time, content that is specific to particular places and periods, e.g., hero cult or sainthood. To use Lévi-Strauss's own terms, he has overemphasized the synchronic (also called paradigmatic) elements of the legend and has not allowed the diachronic (also called syntagmatic) elements to speak for themselves, as they can do to a large extent. For example, the reprise, by repeating and at the same time varying the earlier motifs, in effect provides an interpretation of those motifs.

By putting Freud, Propp, and Lévi-Strauss in the perspective afforded by folklore and the interpretation of the ancient Oedipus legend that folklore suggests, one has done them no injustice. If their interpretations of the legend appear, in this perspective, to be more closely related to their own thought than to the demonstrable concerns of the narrative, they yet belong to a distinguished tradition. Hegel, when he makes the transition in his *Philosophy of History* from the Egyptians to the Greeks, takes Oedipus as the representative of Greek consciousness. [148] Nietzsche also, in section 9 of *The Birth of Tragedy,* takes Oedipus as the exemplar of a certain mental power: "Oedipus the murderer of his father, the husband of his mother, Oedipus the solver of the Sphinx riddle. What is the meaning of the mysterious triad of these fated deeds [*die geheimnisvolle Dreiheit dieser Schicksalstaten*]?" (my translation). For Nietzsche, Oedipus is the man of Dionysiac wisdom who reaches toward "the maternal womb of being" (sec. 16). Heidegger, in chapter 4 of *An Introduction to Metaphysics,* took Oedipus as exemplifying the conflict of being and appearance.

147. F. Zeitlin, "Language, Structure, and the Son of Oedipus in Aeschylus' *Seven against Thebes,*" in *Contemporary Literary Hermeneutics and the Interpretation of Classical Texts* (Ottawa, 1981), pp. 556–59.

148. *Vorlesungen über die Philosophie der Weltgeschichte,* vol. 2, ed. G. Lasson (Leipzig, 1923), pp. 510–11.

These various applications of the Oedipus legend do not mean that it is infinitely malleable. On the contrary, the motifs and the story pattern provide a certain range of possibilities, and modern thinkers will exploit one or another of these. It happens that Hegel and Nietzsche in seizing upon Oedipus the riddle solver have isolated a motif that was probably the last to enter the ancient narrative and was certainly the first to be omitted, but it is a motif, after all, that is connected with the future greatness of the hero. Freud sees the negative side of the riddle solving, the greater ignorance that engulfed Oedipus's cleverness. Modern thought will thus oscillate between limits laid down in the tradition, and the same is true of twentieth-century artistic reinterpretations of the ancient legend. Paradoxically, the Oedipus of Stravinsky in his opera-oratorio *Oedipus Rex* is closest to Freud's—a fundamentally guilty and culpable man, though Stravinsky's point of view was Christian. Hof-mannsthal (*Oidipus und die Sphinx*), Gide (*Oedipe* and the last pages of *Thesée*), Cocteau (*La machine infernale*) and Pasolini (the film *Edipo Re*) all found something admirable in the hero, and he achieves a kind of triumph in all these works.

While these works of thought and art were being created in various cities of Europe, it was still possible (note the dates in the headnotes to folktales that come from archives) to collect the Oedipus folktale in the countryside. This folktale was, and may still be,[149] a living inheritance from the Middle Ages and perhaps even from antiquity. This folktale preserves in rather pristine form the ambiguity of the protagonist that has been difficult to grasp in modern art and thought.

149. It was collected as recently as 1971: see Karpati (Bibliography 3).

Ancient Sources
for the Oedipus Legend

The passages printed in this section—and Homer, *Odyssey* 11.271-80 (quoted above)—are the main narrative accounts of the story of Oedipus in ancient sources. The first of them, from Euripides' *Phoenician Women,* is a primary source, and as such stands apart from the others, all of which belong to the post-fifth-century mythological tradition. This Euripidean account of the life of Oedipus obviously differs from the canonical Sophoclean version in several ways, and thus poses three questions. (1) To what extent is Euripides drawing upon earlier poetic traditions different from Sophocles'? (2) To what extent is Euripides drawing upon popular traditions, i.e., folklore? (3) To what extent does Euripides invent? The first of these questions is nearly impossible to answer because of the loss of the Theban epics and of all Oedipus tragedies before Sophocles'. The second question can be answered only in general terms. Scholia sometimes point out that Euripides has used a "popular" element of a myth (for example, the scholium on the first line of the *Alcestis*), and it may be that such elements are lurking in the passage quoted here. But how to be sure that the element was not already in the poetic tradition? As for the third question, such a detail as the bloodying of Oedipus's feet by Laius's carriage, especially since it involves a pun on the title of the tragedy, might seem to be a Euripidean invention. But the loss of the earlier texts obscures the answer to this question as much as the others.

After the passage from the *Phoenician Women,* the rest are from the mythographical tradition. They provide a further sense of the variation within the poetic tradition from which they mainly descend. Mainly, but not entirely. It has been argued above that the exposure of the infant Oedipus on a body of water, in Hyginus, must be a popular tradition. Therefore, the same questions must be raised concerning the mythographers as were asked about Euripides. The relation of the mythographers to the earlier poetic tradition has been set out by Robert in tabular form in chapter 8 of his study of the Oedipus legend (see Bibliography 1), and he provides copious discussion. But the existence of a folk tradition and its possible contamination of the literary and mythographical traditions is never considered, since Robert is writing literary history. For example, he begins his discussion of Hyginus thus: "Hyginus begins with the *Oedipus* of Euripides [of which a few fragments survive], but immediately contaminates this with the prologue to the *Phoenician Women* and Sophocles' *Oedipus the King.*" In other words, each element in the mythographer must be traced to a tragedy, lost or extant.

Although the general problem of the relation of these sources to earlier literature is shadowed over by the loss of most of that literature, these sources at least provide a sure sense of variation within the literary tradition. It is especially useful to compare them with the now canonical Sophoclean version of the Oedipus story, which can be summarized as follows on the basis of the two Oedipus tragedies: Once upon a time Laius received an oracle from Delphi that he was fated to die at the hands of a son who should be born of him and his wife, Iocasta. When a son was born, Laius fastened his feet together and had him set out on Mount Cithaeron. But the servant, a shepherd, to whom Laius entrusted this task took pity on the baby and gave him to a fellow shepherd from Corinth, who gave the baby to Polybus, king of Corinth. Oedipus got his name, meaning "Swollen Foot," from the condition in which he had been found. Oedipus grew up in Corinth as the son of Polybus and his queen, Merope. One day, a drunken companion at a banquet said that Oedipus was not the son of Polybus. Oedipus questioned Polybus and Merope, but they told him nothing. He then went to Delphi, where he was told that he was destined to murder his father and marry his mother. He resolved never to return to Corinth. At a place where three roads meet, he encountered a man in a carriage who struck him with a stick when Oedipus would not give way. Oedipus then killed the man and all his attendants but one, who escaped. Continuing on his way, Oedipus encountered the Sphinx, whose riddle he solved and whom he thus vanquished. (The relative chronology of the murder of Laius and the encounter with the Sphinx is not certain in *Oedipus the King.*) The city of Thebes gave Oedipus the widowed queen as a reward, and he had four children by her, two sons, Polyneices and Eteocles, and two daughters, Ismene and Antigone. After Oedipus had reigned prosperously for many years, a plague fell on the city. Oedipus sent to Delphi and received the response that the murderer of Laius must be driven from the city. In the course of his investigation of the murder, he discovered his own identity. Jocasta hanged herself, and he blinded himself. Thereafter, Oedipus went into exile and wandered as a beggar for many years, attended only by Antigone, until he reached Colonus, a town near Athens. There he remembered a detail in the earlier oracle concerning the fated parricide and incest: he would end his life in a place sacred to the Eumenides, a boon to those who received him and a bane to those who drove him forth, the Thebans. In the meantime, Eteocles and Polyneices had attempted to arrange an alternating kingship, but Eteocles had reneged on the agreement, and war had broken out. Both sides attempted, without success, to enlist Oedipus's aid. He cursed both his sons to death, prepared for his own death, and then miraculously disappeared into the earth.

EURIPIDES

Source: Phoenician Women, lines 1–87, from E. P. Coleridge, trans., *The Plays of Euripides,* vol. 2 (London, 1907), pp. 219–21.

O sun-god, who cleavest thy way along the starry sky, mounted on golden-studded car, rolling on thy path of flame behind fleet coursers, how curst the beam thou didst shed on Thebes, the day that Cadmus left Phoenicia's realm beside the sea and reached this land! He it was that in days long gone wedded Harmonia, the daughter of Cypris, and begat Polydore from whom they say sprang Labdacus, and Laius from him. I am known as the daughter of Menoeceus, and Creon is my brother by the same mother. Men call me Jocasta, for so my father named me, and I am married to Laius. Now when he was still childless after being wedded to me a long time, he went and questioned Phoebus, craving moreover that our love might be crowned with sons born to his house. But the god said, "King of Thebes for horses famed! seek not to beget children against the will of heaven; for if thou beget a son, that child shall slay thee, and all thy house shall wade through blood." But he, yielding to his lust in a drunken fit, begat a son of me, and when his babe was born, conscious of his sin and of the god's warning, he gave the child to shepherds to expose in Hera's meadow on mount Cithaeron, after piercing his ankles with iron spikes; whence it was that Hellas named him Oedipus. But the keepers of the horses of Polybus finding him took him home and laid him in the arms of their mistress. So she suckled the child that I had born and persuaded her husband she was its mother. Soon as my son was grown to man's estate, the tawny beard upon his cheek, either because he had guessed the fraud or learnt it from another, he set out for the shrine of Phoebus, eager to know for certain who his parents were; and likewise Laius, my husband, was on his way thither, anxious to find out if the child he had exposed was dead. And they twain met where the branching roads to Phocis unite; and the charioteer of Laius called to him "Out of the way, stranger, room for my lord!" But he, with never a word, strode on in his pride, and the horses with their hoofs drew blood from the tendons of his feet. Then—but why need I tell aught beyond the sad issue?—son slew father, and taking his chariot gave it to Polybus his foster-father. Now when the Sphinx was grievously harrying our city after my husband's death, my brother Creon proclaimed that he would wed me to any who should guess the riddle of that crafty maiden. By some strange chance, my own son, Oedipus, guessed the Sphinx's riddle, and so he became king of this land and received its sceptre as his prize, and married his mother, all unwitting, luckless wretch! nor did I his mother know that I was wedded to my son; and I bore him two sons, Eteocles and the hero Polynices, and two daughters as well, the one her father called Ismene, the other, which was the elder, I named Antigone. Now when Oedipus, that awful sufferer, learnt that I his wedded wife was his mother too, he inflicted a ghastly outrage upon his eyes, tearing the bleeding orbs with a golden brooch. But since my sons have grown to bearded men, they have confined their father closely, that his misfortune, needing as it did full many a shift to hide it, might be forgotten. He is still living in the palace, but his misfortunes have so unhinged him that he imprecates the most unholy curses on his sons, praying that they may have to draw the sword before they share this house between them. So they, fearful that heaven may accomplish his prayer if they dwell together, have made an agreement, arranging that Polynices, the younger, should first leave the land in voluntary exile, while Eteocles should stay and hold the sceptre for a year and then change places. But as soon as Eteocles was seated high in power, he refused to give up the throne, and drove Polynices into exile from the kingdom; so Polynices went to Argos and married into the family of Adrastus, and having collected a numerous force of Argives is leading them hither; and he is come up against our seven-gated walls, demanding the sceptre of his father and his share in the kingdom. Wherefore I, to end their strife, have prevailed on one son to meet the other under truce, before appealing to arms, and the messenger I sent tells me that he will come. O Zeus, whose home is heaven's radiant vault, save us, and grant that my sons may be reconciled! For thou, if thou art really wise, must not suffer the same poor mortal to be for ever wretched.

PALAEPHATUS

Source: Palaephatus 4(7) in Nicolaus Festa, ed., Palaephati *Peri Apistōn,* in Mythographi Graeci, vol. 3, fasc. 2 (Leipzig, 1902), pp. 10–11. My translation.

Concerning the Cadmean Sphinx it is said that she was a beast with the body of a dog, the head and features of a girl, the wings of a bird, and a human voice. Sitting upon Mount Phicium, she sang a riddle to each of the citizens. She used to destroy whomever she found unable to answer. When Oedipus answered the riddle, she threw herself [from the mountain] and destroyed herself. Such a form cannot come to be; that those unable to answer the riddle were eaten by her is puerile; that the Cadmeans did not shoot down the beast but allowed their citizens to be eaten like enemies is foolish. The truth is as follows. Cadmus came to Thebes with an Amazon wife whose name was Sphinx, and having killed Draco, he took over his property and kingdom, and later also the sister of Draco, whose name was Harmonia. When Sphinx perceived that he was taking a second wife, she persuaded many of the citizens to revolt along with her, and seizing most of the property and taking also the swift-footed dog that Cadmus had brought with him—with all this she went up into the so-called Mount Phicium, and from this place she made war on Cadmus. Setting ambushes during the summer season, she used to destroy those whom she carried off. The Cadmeans called an ambush an "enigma." Accordingly the citizens were muttering: "The fierce Sphinx lying concealed in ambush carries us off and it is impossible to fight her in the open. For she does not run but flies—both the woman and the dog." Cadmus made a proclamation that he would give much money to the one who killed the Sphinx. Then came Oedipus, a Corinthian skilled in warfare, with a swift-footed horse, and, forming the Cadmeans into armed bands and going out at night and lying in wait for her, he discovered the enigma and killed the Sphinx. After this happened, the rest was invented.

APOLLODORUS

Source: The Library 3.5.7–9, from J. G. Frazer, trans., *Apollodorus: The Library* (Loeb Classical Library, 1921), pp. 343–51. Frazer supplies copious notes, which are not reprinted here.

After Amphion's death Laius succeeded to the Kingdom. And he married a daughter of Menoeceus; some say that she was Jocasta, and some that she was Epicasta. The oracle had warned him not to beget a son, for the son that should be begotten would kill his father; nevertheless, flushed with wine, he had intercourse with his wife. And when the babe was born he pierced the child's ankles with brooches and gave it to a herdsman to expose. But the herdsman exposed it on Cithaeron; and the neatherds of Polybus, king of Corinth, found the infant and brought it to his wife Periboea. She adopted him and passed him off as her own, and after she had healed his ankles she called him Oedipus, giving him that name on account of his swollen feet. When the boy grew up and excelled his fellows in strength, they spitefully twitted him with being supposititious. He inquired of Periboea, but could learn nothing; so he went to Delphi and inquired about his true parents. The god told him not to go to his native land, because he would murder his father and lie with his mother. On hearing that, and believing himself to be the son of his nominal parents, he left Corinth, and riding in a chariot through Phocis he fell in with Laius driving in a chariot in a certain narrow road. And when Polyphontes, the herald of Laius, ordered him to make way and killed one of his horses because he disobeyed and delayed, Oedipus in a rage killed both Polyphontes and Laius, and arrived in Thebes. Laius was buried by Damasistratus, king of Plataea, and Creon, son of Menoeceus, succeeded to the kingdom. In his reign a heavy calamity befell Thebes. For Hera sent the Sphinx, whose mother was Echidna and her father Typhon; and she had the face of a woman, the breast and feet and tail of a lion, and the wings of a bird. And having learned a riddle from the Muses, she sat on Mount Phicium, and propounded it to the Thebans. And the riddle was this:—What is that which has one voice and yet becomes four-footed and two-footed and three-footed? Now the Thebans were in possession of an oracle which declared that they should be rid of the Sphinx whenever they had read her riddle; so they often met and discussed the answer, and when they could not find it the Sphinx used to snatch away one of them and gobble him up. When many had perished, and last of all Creon's son Haemon, Creon made a proclamation that to him who should read the riddle he would give both the kingdom and the wife of Laius. On hearing that, Oedipus found the solution, declaring that the riddle of the Sphinx referred to man, for as a babe he is four-footed, going on four limbs, as an adult he is two-footed, and as an old man, he gets besides a third support in a staff. So the Sphinx threw herself from the citadel, and Oedipus both succeeded to the kingdom and unwittingly married his mother, and begat sons by her, Polynices and Eteocles, and daughters, Ismene and Antigone. But some say the children were borne to him by Eurygania, daughter of Hyperphas. When the secret afterwards came to light, Jocasta hanged herself in a noose, and Oedipus was driven from Thebes, after he had put out his eyes and cursed his sons, who saw him cast out of the city without lifting a hand to help him. And having come with

Antigone to Colonus in Attica, where is the precinct of the Eumenides, he sat down there as a suppliant, was kindly received by Theseus, and died not long afterwards.

PEISANDER

Source: Schol. Eur. *Phoen.* 1760 = FGrH 16F10. This scholium seems to date from Hellenistic times. "Peisander" is probably a pseudonym. The author is unknown. See *FGrH*, pt. 1a (Commentary), pp. 493–94. For a discussion of the scholium, with references to other secondary literature, see de Kock, "The Peisandros Scholion" (Bibliography 1). My translation.

Peisander reports that the Sphinx was sent to Thebes, from the farthest parts of Aethiopia through the anger of Hera, because the Thebans had not punished Laius for the impiety of his unlawful love for Chrysippus, whom he had carried off from Pisa. Just as in the pictures of her, the Sphinx had the tail of a dragon. She snatched up and ate both large and small, including Haemon the son of Creon and Hippios the son of Eurynomos, the one who fought the Centaurs. Eurynomos and Eioneus were the sons of Magnes the Aeolian and Phylodice. Hippios, guest though he was, was snatched up by the Sphinx; Eioneus was killed by Oenomaos, in the same way as the rest of the suitors. Laius was the first to have this lawless love. Chrysippus killed himself with a sword out of shame. Then Teiresias, knowing as a seer that Laius was abominated by the gods, tried to turn him from the road to Apollo, and [to persuade him] to sacrifice rather to Hera the god of marriage (*gamostolos*). Laius paid no attention. Departing, he was killed at the crossroads, both he and his driver, after he had struck Oedipus with his whip. Oedipus buried them immediately after he had killed them, taking, along with the reins, the belt and the sword of Laius, which he wore. Upon his return [to Sicyon], he gave the chariot to Polybus. Next he married his mother, having solved the riddle. Having thereafter performed some sacrifices on Mount Cithaeron, he was starting down the mountain with Jocasta in the carriage, and, when they reached the vicinity of the crossroads, Oedipus remembered the place and pointed it out to Jocasta and recounted what had happened and showed her the belt. She was very disturbed but kept quiet, for she did not know that he was her son. And thereafter came an old horse herder from Sicyon, who told him everything—how he had found him and taken him up and given him to Merope, and he also showed him the swaddling clothes and the pins [with which his ankles had been pierced] and asked him for a reward for having saved his life. So everything became clear. They say after the death of Jocasta and his blinding, he married the maiden Eurygane, from whom his four children were born. So says Peisander.

DIODORUS SICULUS

Source: Diodorus Siculus 4.64.1–65.1, from C. H. Oldfather, trans., *Diodorus of Sicily,* vol. 3 (Loeb Classical Library, 1939), pp. 19–23.

We shall now give the account of The Seven against Thebes, taking up the original causes of the war. Laius, the king of Thebes, married Jocaste, the daughter of Creon, and since he was childless for some time he inquired of the god regarding his begetting children. The Pythian priestess made reply that it would not be to his interest that children should be born to him, since the son who should be begotten of him would be the murderer of his father and would bring great misfortunes upon all of the house; but Laius forgot the oracle and begat a son, and he exposed the babe after he had pierced its ankles through with a piece of iron, this being the reason why it was later given the name Oedipus. But the household slaves who took the infant were unwilling to expose it, and gave it as a present to the wife of Polybus, since she could bear no children. Later, after the boy had attained to manhood, Laius decided to inquire of the god regarding the babe which had been exposed, and Oedipus likewise, having learned from someone of the substitution which had been made in his case, set about to inquire of the Pythian priestess who were his true parents. In Phocis these two met face to face, and when Laius in a disdainful manner ordered Oedipus to make way for him, the latter in anger slew Laius, not knowing that he was his father.

At this very time, the myths go on to say, a sphinx, a beast of double form, had come to Thebes and was propounding a riddle to anyone who might be able to solve it, and many were being slain by her because of their inability to do so. And although a generous reward was offered to the man who should solve it, that he should marry Jocaste and be king of Thebes, yet no man was able to comprehend what was propounded except Oedipus, who alone solved the riddle. What had been propounded by the sphinx was this: What is it that is at the same time a biped, a triped, and a quadruped? And while all the rest were perplexed, Oedipus declared that the animal proposed in the riddle was "man," since as an infant he is a quadruped, when grown a biped, and in old age a triped, using, because of his infirmity, a staff. At this answer the sphinx, in accordance with the oracle which the myth recounts, threw herself down a precipice, and Oedipus then married the woman who, unknown to himself, was his mother, and begat two sons, Eteocles and Polyneices, and two daughters, Antigone and Ismene.

When the sons had attained to manhood, they go on to say, and the impious deeds of the family became known, Oedipus, because of the disgrace, was compelled by his sons to remain always in retirement, and the young men, taking over the throne, agreed together that they should reign in alternate years. Eteocles, being the elder, was the first to reign, and upon the termination of the period he did not wish to give over the kingship. But Polyneices demanded of him the throne as they had agreed, and when his brother would not comply with his demand he fled to Argos to king Adrastus.

NICOLAUS OF DAMASCUS

Source: Nicolaus of Damascus, *Excerpta de insidiis*, p. 7, 1 = *FGrH* 90F8. On Nicolaus, see the article in the *Oxford Classical Dictionary*, 2d ed. For commentary on the passage here translated, see *FGrH*, Pt. 2C, p. 237. My translation.

King Laius and his wife Epicaste did not have children. For this reason, he went to Delphi to consult the oracle. The god prophesied to him that he would have a child who would kill him and take his mother to wife. After this prophecy, a son was born to Laius, whom, as soon as he was born, Laius set out on Mount Cithaeron that he might perish. Herdsmen of Polybus took up this child (Polybus is said to be the son of Hermes), and they took their discovery to their master. He took the child and raised him as if he were his own son, naming him Oedipus, for his feet were swollen because of the swaddling clothes. After time passed and he grew up, he came to Orchomenus in Boeotia in quest of horses, and somehow Laius, who was going as a sacred ambassador to Delphi with his wife, Epicaste, met him. The herald who accompanied them went forward and bade Oedipus get out of the king's way. Oedipus struck him with his sword out of pride and killed Laius when he came to help, but he did not touch the wife. After he had done these things, he fled to the mountain and disappeared into the woods. Epicaste, her servants arriving a little later, sought the murderer of Laius. When she could not find him, burying Laius and the herald there on Laphystium, where they had died, she returned to Thebes. Oedipus returned from Orchomenus to Corinth to the house to Polybus, and he brought Polybus the mules of Laius, for he was driving these as well as horses, and . . . [here a word or two in the text is corrupt] and considered him his father as before.

PAUSANIAS

Source: Pausanias 9.5.1–13, from W. H. S. Jones, trans., *Pausanias: Description of Greece,* vol. 4 (Loeb Classical Library, 1935), pp. 195–97.

When Laius was king and married to Iocasta, an oracle came from Delphi that, if Iocasta bore a child, Laius would meet his death at his son's hands. Whereupon Oedipus was exposed, who was fated when he grew up to kill his father; he also married his mother. But I do not think that he had children by her; my witness is Homer, who says in the *Odyssey:*—

And I saw the mother of Oedipodes, fair Epicaste,
Who wrought a dreadful deed unwittingly,
Marrying her son, who slew his father and
Wedded her. But forthwith the gods made it known among men.

How could they have "made it known forthwith," if Epicaste had borne four children to Oedipus? But the mother of these children was Euryganeia, daughter of Hyperphas. Among the proofs of this are the words of the author of the poem called the *Oedipodia;* moreover, Onasias painted a picture at Plataea of Euryganeia bowed with grief because of the fight between her children. Polyneices retired from Thebes while Oedipus was still alive and reigning, in fear lest the curses of the father should be brought to pass upon the sons. He went to Argos and married a daughter of Adrastus, but returned to Thebes, being fetched by Eteocles after the death of Oedipus. On his return he quarrelled with Eteocles, and so went into exile a second time. He begged Adrastus to give him a force to effect his return, but lost his army and fought a duel with Eteocles as the result of a challenge. Both fell in the duel, and the kingdom devolved on Laodamas, son of Eteocles; Creon, the son of Menoeceus, was in power as regent and guardian of Laodamas.

HYGINUS

Source: Hyginus, *Fabulae* 66–67, from Mary Grant, trans., *The Myths of Hyginus* (Lawrence, Kans., 1960), pp. 65–66. The translator provides notes. See also the notes of H. J. Rose, *Hygini Fabulae* (Leyden, 1934).

66. Laius

The oracle of Apollo warned Laius, son of Labdacus, that he should beware of death at his son's hands, and so when his wife Jocasta bore a son, he ordered him to be exposed. Periboea, wife of King Polybus, found the child as she was washing garments at the shore, and rescued him. With Polybus' consent, since they were childless, they brought him up as their son, and because he had pierced feet they named him Oedipus.

67. Oedipus

After Oedipus, son of Laius and Jocasta, had come to manhood, he was courageous beyond the rest, and through envy his companions taunted him with not being Polybus' son, since Polybus was so mild, and he so assertive. Oedipus felt that the taunt was true. And so he set out for Delphi to inquire [about his parents. In the meantime,] it was revealed to Laius by prodigies that death at his son's hands was near. When he was going to Delphi, Oedipus met him, and when servants bade him give way to the King, he refused. The King urged on his horses, and a wheel grazed Oedipus' foot. Enraged, he dragged his father from the chariot, not knowing who he was, and killed him. After Laius' death Creon, son of Menoeceus, ruled; in the meantime the Sphinx, off-spring of Typhon, was sent into Boeotia, and was laying waste the fields of the Thebans. She proposed a contest to Creon, that if anyone inter-preted the riddle which she gave, she would depart, but that she would destroy whoever failed, and under no other circumstances would she leave the country. When the King heard this, he made a proclamation throughout Greece. He promised that he would give the kingdom and his sister Jocasta in marriage to the person solving the riddle of the Sphinx. Many came out of greed for the kingdom, and were devoured by the Sphinx, but Oedipus, son of Laius, came and interpreted the rid-dle. The Sphinx leaped to her death. Oedipus received his father's king-dom, and Jocasta his mother as wife, unwittingly, and begat on her Eteocles, Polynices, Antigona, and Ismene. Meanwhile barrenness of crops and want fell on Thebes because of the crimes of Oedipus, and Tiresias, questioned as to why Thebes was so harassed, replied that if anyone from the dragon's blood survived and died for his country, he would free Thebes from the plague. Then Menoeceus [father of Jocasta] threw himself from the walls. While these things were taking place in Thebes, at Corinth Polybus died, and Oedipus took the news hard, thinking his father had died. But Periboea revealed his adoption, and Menoetes, too, the old man who had exposed him, recognized him as the son of Laius by the scars on his feet and ankles. When Oedipus heard this and realized he had committed such atrocious crimes, he tore the brooches from his mother's garment and blinded himself, gave the kingdom to his sons for alternate years, and fled from Thebes, his daughter Antigona leading him.

Texts of
The Analogues

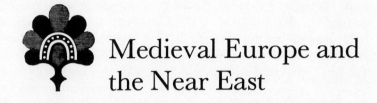

Medieval Europe and the Near East

LT1 JUDAS ISCARIOT

Source: E. K. Rand, "Mediaeval Lives of Judas Iscariot," in *Anniversary Papers by Colleagues and Pupils of George Lyman Kittredge* (Boston, 1913), pp. 313–14. Reprinted in P. F. Baum, "The Mediaeval Legend of Judas Iscariot," *PMLA*, NS 24 (1916): 490–91. This twelfth century life of Judas comes from the oldest of the forty-two Latin texts of the Judas legend known to Baum. My translation.

There is nothing hidden that will not be brought to light and nothing concealed that will not be known. Who sets forth from evil and persists in evil will receive the gift, not of a crown, but of the penalty for his desert. I have composed the life of Judas the betrayer, who was evil in his origin, worse in his life, and worst of all in his end. Now his father, so far as he had repute amongst men, was of abundant means and esteemed honorable in the eyes of all his neighbors. One night he saw in a vision that he had a son who threatened him with death (for his wife was now pregnant)—the son from whom this deceitful trick was to come. When, however, the child was born, the father, reflecting upon and feeling terror at such an omen, pierced its shins and exposed it in underbrush rather far from the city of Jerusalem. Certain shepherds, hearing its wailing and weeping, took it from the place, and bringing it to Scariot, caused it to be nursed by a certain woman. Nourished and grown to manhood, he attached himself to King Herod and mingling with his servants served the king and the soldiers with complete honesty. And yet, as is the custom of servants, he gave out lavishly whatever he had and kept as much as possible for himself. It happened, however, that once Herod held a ceremonial banquet with the nobles in Jerusalem and, amongst dishes of many sorts, the king sought fresh fruit. Hastening to satisfy the king's desire and going into his father's orchard (he did not know it was his father), by force he plucked the fruit and stripped the trees bare. The man whose property this was, in high dudgeon and full of bitterness, pitted himself against the upstart, but Judas, prevailing, struck and killed him. The whole city was stirred up against Judas and, falling upon him, determined to put him to death. But Judas, fleeing to Herod's protection, escaped the danger of death. Herod, himself frightened, proceeded in such a way that Judas might win forgiveness from the friends of the murdered man, lest, because of a single crime, he pass on to some greater risk. Taking counsel, therefore, Herod joined Judas to the wife of the murdered man, he himself and everyone else ignorant that she was his mother. One day it happened that Judas appeared nude before his mother and wife, and when she saw the scars of the wounds on his shins, she suspected that it was her own son, whom she had once abandoned, cast out in the underbrush. Thus, she asked him who his father was, who his mother was, who his parents were, and whence, from what province, he sprang, by whom he had been reared. He said that he did not know but had heard only this from his nurse, that he had been thrown out in that place in the underbrush, found by shepherds, brought to Scariot, and raised there. And that when he had reached manhood, he had joined the servants of Herod and had pleased many with his services. Hearing this, she collapsed and, crying out that she was wretched, said, "Unfortunate the vision of my husband, which has been fulfilled by the son and moreover the madness of the sin and malice redounds to me. May the day of my birth perish and may the darkness of the shadows cover him over." Judas, however, perceiving that he had committed such a villainy, felt remorse and, penitent at such a crime, left his mother. But at that time Jesus was dwelling in those places, who by his preaching and aid healed the bodies of many and recalled their minds from many sins. Those who came to him weighed down with many sins he took to himself and like a shepherd he rescued from attack sheep snatched from the jaws of wolves. Perceiving his virtue and piety, Judas went to him and asked that Jesus take pity on him. Jesus agreed to his desire, and also allowed Judas to stay with him amongst his disciples. Jesus even entrusted what he had to Judas, that he might provide the necessities of life to him and the others. He held the purse strings and stole what he could. And what the design of Judas was appeared in the end, because he sold his master for a price and betrayed him to the Jews. At last he hanged himself and ended his life with a wretched death. But you, Lord, have mercy on us. He who perseveres in good until the end shall be saved.

LT2 JUDAS

Source: Jacobus de Voragine or Jacopo da Varaggio, *Legenda Aurea* (thirteenth century). Text: Theodor Graesse, *Jacobi a Voragine Legenda Aurea, . . .* 3rd ed. (Breslau, 1890) ch. 45 ("De sancto Mathia apostolo"), pp. 183–86. Translation: William Caxton, *The Golden Legend* or *Lives of the Saints,* vol. 3 (London, 1900; reprint ed. New York, 1973), pp. 55–58.

Caxton's translation, nearly as famous as the original, was his last publication. He brought printing to England in 1476 and worked constantly, as translator and printer, until his death in 1492. In the introduction to his *Golden Legend,* Caxton says that he had before him three versions, one Latin, one French, and one English. The nature of some of his mistakes suggests that the Latin was not the primary source for the translation, but Caxton's tale of Judas reproduces faithfully the substance of the original.

The Latin sentences with which Jacobus introduces and concludes the tale of Judas in the life of St. Matthew have been added in brackets.

S. Matthias the apostle was in the place of Judas the traitor, and therefore first we shall rehearse here the birth and beginning of Judas. It is read in a history, though it be named apocrypha [*legitur enim quadam hystoria licet apocrypha*], that there was a man in Jerusalem named Reuben, and by another named Simeon, of the kindred of David, or, after S. Jerome, of the tribe of Issachar, which had a wife named Ciborea, and on the night that Judas was conceived his mother had a marvelous dream whereof she was so sore afeard. For her seemed that she had conceived a child that should destroy their people, and because of the loss of all their people her husband blamed her much, and said to her: Thou sayest a thing over evil, or the devils will deceive thee. She said: Certainly if so be that I shall have a son, I trow it shall be so, as I have had a revelation and none illusion. When the child was born the father and mother were in great doubt, and thought what was best to do, for they durst not slay the child for the horror that they should have therein, neither they wist not how they might nourish one that should destroy their lineage. Then they put him to a little fiscelle or basket well pitched, and set it in the sea, and abandoned him to drive whither it would. And anon the floods and waves of the sea brought and made him arrive in an island named Scarioth, and of this name was he called Judas Scariotes. Now it happed that the queen of this country went for to play on the rivage of the sea, and beheld this little nacelle and the child therein, which was fair, and then she sighed and said: O Lord God, how should I be eased if I had such a child, then at the least should not my realm be without heir. Then commanded she that the child should be taken up, and be nourished, and she fained herself to be great with child and after published that she had borne a fair son. When her husband heard say hereof he had great joy, and all the people of the country made great feast. The king and queen did do nourish and keep this child like the son of a king. Anon after, it happed that the queen conceived a son, and when it was born and grown Judas beat oft that child, for he weened that he had been his brother, and oft he was chastised therefore, but alway he made him to weep so long that the queen which knew well that Judas was not her son, and at the last she said the truth, and told how that Judas was found in the sea. And ere this yet was known Judas slew the child that he had supposed to be his brother, and was son to the king, and in eschewing the sentence of death he fled anon and came into Jerusalem, and entered into the court of Pilate which then was provost. And he so pleased him that he was great with him, and had in great cherety and nothing was done without him.

Now it happed on a day that Pilate went for to disport him by a garden belonging to the father of Judas, and was so desirous to eat of the fruit of the apples that he might not forbear them. And the father of Judas knew not Judas his son, for he supposed that he had been drowned in the sea long tofore, ne the son knew not the father. When Pilate had told to Judas of his desire, he sprang into the garden of his father and gathered of the fruit for to bear to his master, but the father of Judas defended him, and there began between them much strife and debate, first by words and after with fighting, so much that Judas smote his father with a stone on the head that he slew him, and after brought the apples unto Pilate, and told to him how that he had slain him that owned the garden. Then sent Pilate to seize all the good that the father of Judas had, and after gave his wife to Judas in marriage, and thus Judas wedded his own mother.

Now it happed on a day that the lady wept and sighed much strongly and said: Alas! how unhappy that I am! I have lost my son and my husband. My son was laid on the sea, and I suppose that he be drowned, and my husband is dead suddenly, and yet it is more grievous to me that Pilate hath remarried me against my will. Then demanded Judas of this child, and she told him how he was set in the sea, and Judas told to her how he had been found in the sea, in such wise that she wist that she was his mother, and that he had slain his father and wedded his mother. Wherefore then he went to Jesu Christ, which did so many miracles, and prayed him of mercy and forgiveness of his sins. Thus far it is read in the history which is not authentic [*Hucusque in praedicta hystoria aprocrypha legitur*].

Our Lord made Judas one of his apostles and retained him in his company, and was so privy with him that he was made his procurator, and bare the purse for all the other, and stole of that which was given to Christ. Then it happed that he was sorry and angry for the ointment that Mary Magdalene poured on the head and feet of our Lord Jesu Christ and said that it was worth three hundred pence, and said that so much he had lost, and therefore sold he Jesu Christ for thirty pence of that money usual, of which every penny was worth ten pence, and so he recovered three hundred pence. Or after that some say that he ought to have of all the gifts that was given to Jesu Christ the tenth penny, and so he recovered thirty pence of that he sold him, and nevertheless at the last he brought them again to the temple, and after hung himself in despair, and his body opened and cleft asunder and his bowels fell out. And so it appertained well that it should so be, for the mouth which God had kissed ought not to be befouled in touching, and also he ought not to die on the earth because all earthly creatures ought to hate him, but in the air where devils and wicked spirits be, because he had deserved to be in their company.

GK1 JUDAS

Source: G. Megas, "Ho Ioudas eis tas Paradoseis tou Laou," *Epetēris tou Laographikou Archeiou* 3 (1941–42), pp. 29–32 (a French summary of the article appears on pp. 219–23). This excerpt is from Ms. 260 in the Monastery of St. Dionysius on Mount Athos and Ms. 15 in the Archbishopric of Cyprus, collated and edited by Megas. It is from a synaxarium, or compilation of saints' lives, arranged according to the months of the year, to be used in the church for the celebration of the saints' anniversaries. Translated by Margaret M. Thorne.

. . . Let us consider how even the very origins of Judas were stained by every evil, as the prophet David testifies in the paslm: "Set thou a wicked man over him and let a devil stand at his right hand . . . let his children be fatherless and his wife a widow . . . let the iniquity of his fathers be remembered and let not the sin of his mother be blotted out . . . and he delighted not in blessing and it was far from him . . . and he clad himself in cursing as with his garment" and so the psalm proceeds.

O my friends, let us hear his story.

One of the wise men saith that the sinner Judas was of the land of Iskara in the nation of Judaea, and that his father was named Robel. This Robel had a wife, and once in the night she dreamed a dreadful dream and was amazed, and in great fear she began to cry aloud. Her husband said to her, "What has happened to thee, wife, that thou art in such anguish?" And she said, "I dreamed a dreadful dream, that if I conceive and bear a male, that child will be the ruin of the Jews." And her husband reproved her for believing in dreams.

But the woman had indeed conceived that very night, and in her time she bore a male child. And she wished to destroy it, that it might not destroy the race of the Jews, so in secret from her husband she made a box, and in it she put the child and cast it into the sea.

But across from Iskara there was a small island whereon herdsmen dwelt, and thither the box was borne upon the waves. The herdsmen took it and found the boy within. They nursed him on the milk of their beasts and called him Judas, believing him to be a Judaean, and when the child was weaned they carried him across the strait to Iskara, asking who would undertake to raise him.

The child was very beautiful, and his own father, Robel, adopted him, not knowing he was his son, and his mother loved him, remembering the child she had cast into the sea. Then she conceived and bore another son, and two were raised together. But Judas was wicked and would beat his brother, so that his mother chided him and said, "Beat him not, for he is thy brother, and all that your father and I possess is for you both." But he, the bad seed, was consumed with envy and the love of gold, and he desired to kill his brother. So one day, when the boys were away together, Judas rose and slew his brother, striking him on the temple with a stone so that he died, and he himself fled away to Jerusalem. And his father and mother mourned the loss of their sons.

But Judas came to Jerusalem, greedy of gain, and became known to Herod, the king of the Jews. When the king beheld this strong and handsome man he made him his steward and put him in charge of buying and supplying for his needs.

After a long time there was a rising in the country of Iskara and Robel took his wife and his goods and went to Jerusalem. He was a rich man, and he bought a great house near to that of Herod, and it had gardens, and in the gardens there were trees. But Judas, because of the long lapse of time, did not know his father and mother again, nor did they know him.

One day the king leaned out of the window and gazed on Robel's garden. Judas stood beside him and he said, "Lord, dost desire that I go down and gather blooms from those trees?" And he said, "Go thou." So Judas went into the garden and took as many blossoms and fruits as he desired, but as he turned to go, he met his father, Robel. Robel said to him, "Young man, how durst thou enter my garden in my absence? Was it perchance to steal the fruit?" But Judas, cruel and violent as always, stood up against Robel, and, looking about him to see that there was no one there, he killed his father with a stone, as he had killed his brother, unbeknownst to all. Then he bore the fruit and the flowers to the king and told him also of the death of Robel.

Herod was grieved. He kept the deed dark, and they buried Robel.

Then the king said to Judas, "I would that thou take this widow to wife and become heir to her inheritance." And Herod sent word to the woman, saying, "It is my royal will that thou take another husband, else thy wealth reverts to me." Hearing this, the woman obeyed and agreed to take a husband, lest her riches vanish utterly. She took her son as her husband, to wit, Judas, not knowing that he was her son, and she had sons by him, and they lived together a good number of years.

One day the woman bethought herself and remembered all that she had suffered on account of her children and the cruel death of her husband, and she beat her breast and mourned aloud that she had taken another husband against her will. And lo, Judas—who, as we have said, was her husband, came and asked her, "What is this mourning of thine, and this breast-beating?" And at his pressing, the woman began to recount all her trials, and how she had cast a son into the sea (now, the herdsmen had told Judas that they had drawn him up from the sea), and she told, too, of his brother's death and of the death of Robel.

When Judas heard all these things, he said to her, "I am thy son whom thou didst cast into the sea, and I have killed my own brother and my father, Robel."

When the woman heard that he was her son, she longed to die a cruel death, and she groaned and cried, "Alas for me, wretched that I am! Where shall I hide myself? Where may I escape the wrath of the Lord? No longer may I live among you."

But when Judas learned what evil his greed had caused and heard that Christ, the healer of soul and body, was in Jerusalem, he went to him to confess, and Christ in his mercy made him a disciple. And because the disease he suffered from was greed, he gave him the purse to carry, with the money therein, to wit, the alms given for the support of the apostles, but Judas used to steal the money and send it to his wife and children. So ye see, from ancient evil and former sinfulness no new virtue can come. Behold then, how the word of the prophet David was fulfilled? "Let his children be fatherless and his wife a widow, and let the iniquity of his father and his mother be remembered." Was he not mindful to be merciful? Did he not repent, and become an apostle, and work miracles? Yet still his greed made him betray the Saviour. Truly, new virtue can hardly spring from ancient evil.

HE1 JOSHUA SON OF NUN

Source: Rabbi Abraham of Vilna, *Rav Po'olim* (Warsaw, 1894), p. 23a.
On the date of the tale, see P. F. Baum, "The Mediaeval Legend of
Judas Iscariot," *PMLA,* NS 24 (1916): 601. Baum concludes: "We have
no direct authority for dating the legend of Joshua bin Noun earlier
than the sixteenth century; but it is certainly older." For the portent of
the mother's milk, see Cosquin (Bibliography 3). Translated by Isaac
Mann.

An accepted scholar by the name of Rabbi Nathan Nata wrote that
he found in a Midrashic work a reason for Joshua the son of Nun being
called by that name.[1] And the spies [who had been sent into the
Promised Land by Moses] called him *resh katiya*[2] because the father of
Joshua lived in Jerusalem and his wife was barren and this pious man
[the husband] prayed opposite his wife and God hearkened to his
prayers. When this woman became pregnant, the pious man fasted and
wept day and night without pause. His wife looked upon this with displeasure and she said to him, "You should rejoice, for God has hearkened unto your prayer." And he did not answer her. Since she spoke to
him daily of this matter, she finally compelled him [to tell her the rea-
son], and he told her everything in his heart: that he was told from
above that the son that would be born to him would cut off his head.
And she believed him, for she knew that all his words were words of
truth. And the time came when she gave birth, and, behold, it was a son,
and his mother brought a chest and coated it with clay and pitch and
she placed therein the child and cast the child into the river. God prepared a large fish to swallow the chest. On a certain day the king gave a
feast for all his princes and servants. The fish that had swallowed the
chest was caught and brought before the king. He cut it open and, behold, there was a crying child. The king ordered that a woman be
brought to suckle the child. The child grew up in the house of the king,
and the king appointed him his executioner. It was after these events
that the pious man, the father [of Joshua] sinned before the king of
Egypt. The king commanded his executioner to behead him and to take
his wife, children, and belongings, as was the law at that time. When he
approached his mother to come upon her, then the whole bed was full

---

1. Author's note: This story of Joshua son of Nun is also found in a book of
stories that Rabbi Nissim wrote.

2. Author's note: The name *resh katiya* is cited in the Talmud, Sotha, p. 35a:
"*resh katiya* will speak." On that Rashi comments that what it means is literally: he
whose head is cut off (i.e., he will have no sons to inherit a portion of the land) will
speak for us. The Aruch (Aruch R̄Sh) explains the reason for his being called *resh
katiya:* that Moses called him Joshua, i.e., the beginning of his name was cut off,
because the Yod (the first letter of his name) is often dropped.

of milk from her breasts. Thereupon a great trembling arose within him, and he was about to take his spear and kill her, thinking that she was a sorceress. Then his mother remembered the words of his father, the pious man (may he rest in peace), and she answered him: "This is not sorcery but the milk that nourished you, for I am your mother." And she told him the whole story. Immediately he left the bed, for he also remembered the tale that he had been found in a fish, but he didn't know that it was his father [whom he had killed]; and then he repented. Therefore they call him the son of Nun, because he was found in a fish, which in Aramaic is "nun"; and the spies called him *resh katiya*[3] on account of his former deeds.

AR1 NIMRUD*

Source: Qissat 'Antara ibn Shaddad Al-'Absi (Cairo, 1961) 1:9-15. This work is commonly known as "Sirat 'Antar," or "The Romance of 'Antar." The hero, 'Antar, was an Arab poet and warrior of the sixth century A.D. The date of origin of the poem is unknown. The earliest reference to it comes from around A.D. 800. In its present form and length (10,000 verses), it represents a vast conflation of materials. See Bernard Heller, s.v. "Sirat 'ANTAR," in *The Encyclopaedia of Islam*, new ed. (1960), 1:518-21. On Nimrud, see the same author, s.v. "NAMRŪD" in *The Encyclopaedia of Islām* (1936), 3:843-44. Translated by Peter Heath.

Under Kush, who was a descendent of Ham, son of Noah:

The land [of Iraq] flourished, and no desolate place remained in it. And he continued to dwell in it until he had a son named Kana'an. He already had another son older than Kana'an, named Alhas, who was the designated successor of his father and to whom the kingship was already assigned.

Kana'an was a violent man who was fond of hunting, shooting, and roaming the plains and mountains. One day, he was in the country-side of Kutaria hunting lions, whose hearts used to crack from terror because of his shout. While hunting, he suddenly saw a woman herding cattle and driving them before her. After the death of his father, his brother had ascended to the throne of the kingdom. When he saw the herdswoman, he was attracted to her and tried to seduce her. But she resisted him. When he repeatedly asked and pressed her, she said "Get away from me, you! I have a husband whom I expect here at any moment, and I am afraid of what he would do to you if he saw us doing what you suggest, for he would kill you straightaway."

---

3. Author's note: Now *resh katiya* assumes the meaning, "he who cut off the head (of his father)."

But he said to her, "Is there anyone on the face of the earth who may resist or contest with me? I am the son of Kush, the son of Ham, the son of Noah. We have conquered this whole land, both plains and mountains, and we have complete control of it."

The herdswoman laughed at his words and was not afraid of him, nor was her heart alarmed on his account. She said, "Listen you! Do not mention kings when you are just a hunter." While Kana'an was involved with her in this way, and was increasing his threats and promises, her husband suddenly arrived. Seeing them in this state, he became very angry. He approached Kana'an and attacked him with the knife he had in his hand. Kana'an met his attack and the two grappled and struggled, clutching and pulling and pushing at each other. Then the man threw Kana'an down on a rock, so that he fell on his back on the ground. The husband of the herdswoman sat on his chest and wanted to slit his throat with his knife, but Kana'an continuously tried to soften him with words, yielding to him in this question and humbling himself before him, until the man got up from his chest. Then Kana'an jumped up from the ground, attacked the man, and overcame him. He picked him up in his hands, and raised him until the black of his armpits showed, then he whipped the earth with him until he smashed his bones apart and his length became indistinguishable from his width, so that he killed him.

He approached the herdswoman whose name was Sulkha', and said to her, "Do you see how strong I am?" Then he stretched out his hand to her and wanted to make use of her. She said, "How can you do this when you claim you are a son of great kings, while I am a poor destitute herdswoman?" But he paid no attention to her words and made love to her right there. Afterwards, he took her with him and brought her to his house, where she was the favorite and most beloved of his women.

[Kana'an, hunting in the wilderness, encounters his cousin, Jauhar, who has just been defeated in a battle. Jauhar promises him his daughter in return for his aid. Together they defeat the enemy, but Jauhar reneges. Then Kana'an goes to his brother, the king, and asks for troops with which to punish Jauhar. His brother refuses, and Kana'an murders him and becomes king in his place. He then carries out his vengeance on Jauhar. Thereafter he defeats Ballch, the son of Jauhar.]

After this matter was finished, one night Kana'an had a terrifying dream, and he woke up very frightened. He immediately called for the astrologers and dream interpreters. When they came before him, he said, "Know, Oh People, that I dreamt that I wrestled with a man, and he with me. And he crushed my bones and neck and he said to me, 'I am ill-omened for my people, and my residence is darkness, and I will emerge from darkness to the light of the world through your offspring.'"

Then the astrologers said to Kana'an, "All right. Let us have today and tonight to examine this matter." And they quieted his fear and terror. After the appointed amount of time had elapsed, they returned to him and said, "Oh King, we inform you that a child will be born to you in whose hands lies your destruction and the cessation of your rule. And he is now in the womb of his mother." Then they withdrew and returned to their duties.

We had mentioned that Sulkha' was one of Kana'an's concubines. Lately, she had become pregnant through him. This was an affair that God Almighty had ordained and decreed through His will and power, and nothing occurs unless He wills it. He had decreed that from this headstrong tyrant and recalcitrant devil, Nimrud, may God curse and humiliate him and make his destination and dwelling place the Fire, should appear.

And when her pregnancy became clear to Sulkha', the herdswoman, she heard from her womb a great noise and a prodigious clamor. Then Kana'an heard it at various times, and he said to her, "Oh Sulkha', this which is in your womb is not human." And Kana'an wanted to trample on her womb to kill the child and do away with him once and for all. Suddenly, a voice called out to him. He heard the voice but did not see its owner, and it was saying, "Leave off from what you have decided, for you will not be able to do it." So Kana'an gave up this idea.

When the days of her pregnancy were complete, Sulkha', the herdswoman, gave birth to a son with a stern, flat-nosed, and scowling face. And when he emerged, suddenly a thin snake went out from under its rock and entered into the nose of that baby. Sulkha' became greatly afraid because of this. When Kana'an came to her, she informed him of what had happened. He said to her, "Woe unto you, allow me to kill him for I think he is an ill-omened child." Then she said to him, "Oh my Lord, killing him does not please my heart, for under any circumstances, he is my son." So he said to her, "I will show you something that is easier than killing him." She said, "What is this?" He said, "It is that you rise up and take him to someplace in the countryside and cast him there to die."

She consented to that and immediately gave him to her maid, and they both went secretly out of the city. While they were in the countryside, suddenly a shepherd, or some say he was a cowherd, appeared. Sulkha' said to him, "Would you take this child, accept him from me, and raise him as your lifelong slave?" The cowherd took him from her, and he put the child among the herd until he was through for the day and would take him home. But when he put him among the animals, they shied away from him and scattered in all directions. And it was difficult for the cowherd to collect them, for whenever he collected them, they scattered again. This continued until the end of the day.

As for Sulkha', she was not happy or fully decided about parting with her son, so she returned to see what had happened to him. She found the cowherd in the above-mentioned situation, and his heart had come to dislike the child. He was saying, "Why should I have a child whose father is displeased with him, and whom I do not need?" So Sulkha' told him what had happened to her, and what she had heard from him while he was still in her womb. He said to her, "These cattle have shied away from him, and his father and mother are afraid of him. He is a boy who brings bad luck to anyone with whom he seeks shelter." Then Sulkha' said to him, "If this is the case, then kill him so that we may have rest from this misfortune."

The herder refused and said, "I will not do this. I will not have his blood on my hands, nor will I take responsibility for him." Then he said to her, "Carry your son and leave him somewhere" So Sulkha' carried him away, brought him to the bank of a river, and left him there. For she said to herself, "Perhaps someone who wants water will come and take him," although the river was far from any road. She put him down and left him, with the child neither crying or moving, nor being afraid.

Then a leopard who wanted water came to drink and found him. God Almighty inspired her to nurse him, so she nursed him, and then went away from him. She continued to do this until one day a woman came seeking water and saw the leopard while it was nursing the child. The woman was very surprised and returned to her village and informed the people of what she had seen concerning the leopard and the child. The villagers went out from the village and came to the place the woman had told them about. They found everything just as she had said. They took the child and carried him to the village. There, one of them took him and named him Nimrud, after the leopard who had nursed him.

Nimrud continued to grow up in that village until he was two years old. He was quarrelsome with the older boys and threw stones at them, until he reached the age of seven. Then his evil doings towards his contemporaries so increased that they complained to his father, who was raising him. But he was not able to restrain his mischief, so they went to the head of the village and told him. He brought Nimrud's father, who had raised him, before him and said to him, "Limit the evil your son is doing to the people, or expel him from the village!" But Nimrud's father could not do it. When the village head saw his failure, he expelled Nimrud from the village. Then Nimrud became a highwayman and a thief and attacked travelers.

He would pay and reward everyone who gathered around him until he gathered every godless thief and hypocrite around himself. Many people joined him. The news of him reached Kana'an, and he sent general after general against him, and army after army. But Nimrud defeated everyone of them and took their booty and horses. Evil people heard of him and came to him from all sides until they were countless. Then he took them to the city of Kutaria and fought Kana'an, without knowing that he was his father, and killed him. Then he took possession of his rule and treasures and slave girls and thrones, among whom was Sulkha', the herdswoman. He took her for his private use and made her his concubine.

[The story continues for another sixty pages beyond the portion here translated, and tells of the struggle between Abraham and Nimrud that ends with God punishing and finally killing Nimrud. The story is an elaboration of that told in *Genesis*. But it is never told whether Nimrud learns that he has killed his father and married his mother.]

AR?1(FR) JEAN*

Source: E. Amélineau, *Contes et romans de l'Égypte chrétienne*, vol. 1 (Paris, 1888), from no. 8, "Histoire du roi Arménios" (pp. 175-89). Amélineau states that he has translated most of his collection from Arabic, some of it from Coptic, but gives no indication concerning the separate pieces (pp. x, xiii). Since he gives a footnote on an Arabic word in the story of Armenios (p. 166) and since *guebbeh* (outer garment) is kept in the text, the original was probably Arabic. Amélineau dates the origin of the stories in his collection to the fourth to seventh centuries A.D. (pp. xliv-xlv). The "Histoire du roi Arménios" falls into two parts, of which the first, modeled on the book of *Isaiah*, concerns the victory of the pious king, and the second the fortunes of his son, Jean. It is the second part that is offered here. Translated by George Bason.

Jean, his son, remained unhappy for some time. The viziers and patricians bowed themselves before him and said to him, "Oh, our lord, where are your fathers, and the fathers of your fathers, where the first men? Know that God has decided that all men drink from the cup of death. Now, arise, oh, our master, and take pity on your subjects, do as your father did, since you have seen the assistance that God gave him, slaying his enemies while he slept in his bed. You must know that it is only on account of his purity, charity, and obedience that this happened, and also because he was a fair and unerring observer of all the commandments." In a word, they wanted to console him, but this was in vain. They left him alone for several days, then they began the same efforts as before, but nonetheless, they did not get their way. Seeing that he paid no attention to their advice, they prepared a splendid banquet for him, stretched out carpets in a beautiful garden for him, and threw themselves at his feet and said to him, "We wish that you would give us the pleasure of coming to dine with us." At first, he refused, but their insistence made him yield. He arose with them, and they took him to the garden. There, they served him exquisite dishes, of which he ate only very little. Then, they offered him stoppered pitchers of beer, which gave off a very strong scent of musk and rose water. They begged him, implored him in the name of God, but he drank only a little. They, however, did not stop insisting until he had drunk as was fitting. As he was no longer accustomed to drinking wine, since he had stopped drinking some time ago, he lost his head, seeing the trees that surrounded him everywhere, and the little babbling streams. Soon he was so drunk, he forgot himself. They took him to his palace and left him in that state.

His sister received him at the door and began to embrace him: forthwith he threw her to the ground and had his business with her. As she became pregnant, she grew very sad. Some time later, her brother noticed that her belly was large and that her color was yellow. He said to her, "Oh dear sister, in what state do I see you?" She replied, "Oh brother, when you went with the viziers and returned drunk with wine, I betook myself to greet you, you threw me to the ground, and that which you now observe happened to me." As soon as he heard her story, he left in a hurry, ran here and there, and finally entered a monastery where he made himself a monk and assumed the monk's habit. As God knew his firm resolve and good intentions, he pardoned him for his sins. From that point, this was a fair and pure man.

The next day, when the viziers returned to the palace, they saw only his sister, who was crying bitterly. They continued to pay their visits to the palace for an entire month. Since he never returned, and since their waiting was in vain, they made his sister queen in his place. When she finished the nine months of pregnancy, she brought a male child into the world, for whom she had three tablets made, one of gold, the other of silver, and the third of ivory. On the last, she had these words engraved, "The father of this child is his uncle, and his mother is his aunt." She also ordered a cradle to be built, and that the child and the three tablets be put in it. She had written these words on a sheet of paper, "The tablet of gold will belong to the child when he grows up, that of silver will go to the one who takes charge of his upbringing." After having sealed the paper, she ordered the cradle to be thrown into the river.

There used to be, on the bank of the river, a monastery constructed in honor of the martyr James Intercisus. During that same day, the annual celebration was being held. It happened that on that day, the father superior went to the riverbank, encountered a fisherman and gave him a dinar for all that he would catch during the night. He left him, intending to send for the fish the next day. The fisherman continued his work until morning. All of a sudden, the cradle was caught in the net. The fisherman hauled it in and put it amongst the fish. A moment later, the father superior of the monastery arrived with his wagon, on which he would load the fish. The fisherman gave him the fish and the cradle saying, "We agreed that all that I would have caught should belong to you. For this reason, the cradle belongs to you." The father superior opened the cradle and found the tablets there. He took the gold tablet and kept it for the moment; he was full of astonishment concerning the tablet of ivory and kept that, too; finally, he took the tablet of silver and gave it to the fisherman, saying, "Take good care in bringing this child up and this tablet will belong to you." "Gladly!" replied the fisherman, who took the child and brought it to his wife, very gladly, since the tablet was worth one hundred dinars. He brought the child up well and taught him morals.

As soon as the child was grown up, he grew handsome and perfect, and started to strike the children of the fisherman. These said to him one day, "Is it to compensate us for having brought you up that your heart grows hard toward us?" He replied, "You speak to me as if you weren't my brothers, and as if my father weren't yours." They said to him, "We are not your brothers." He went to find the wife of the fisherman and said to her, "Are you not my mother?" "No," she replied, "it was a monk who brought you to us, and we brought you up." As soon as the fisherman returned, he said to him, "Take me to the monk, since that is my desire." The fisherman led the young boy to the monk. Seeing the fine figure of the monk, the young boy was very glad and said to him, "Oh monk, are you my father?" "No," replied the monk. "Who then is my father?" returned the young boy. "I have no idea," replied the monk, "but what I do know, is that I found you in a cradle where there were three tablets, one of gold; the other of silver, which I gave to the fisherman in return for the care that he has taken of you; the third was of ivory. Now, if I were to give you advice, it would be to don the monk's habit and become a monk." The boy replied, "No, I want to be a soldier." The monk then gave him the gold tablet. He took it to the market and sold it for a thousand dinars of gold. With these he bought a beautiful horse, all saddled, the arms of war, épée, lance and all the rest. He returned to the monk and said, "Who is my father? Tell me before I leave." The monk gave him the ivory tablet. As soon as the eyes of the young man fell on the inscription, he cried bitterly, took leave of the monk, and departed. God willed it that he should direct his footsteps to his birthplace.

He saw soldiers who surrounded the city, and asked, "What is this city, and why are the soldiers besieging it?" They replied, "It's a city that is governed by a woman, and here is a king and his soldiers who want to seize it." As soon as he heard this story, he directed his horse at a gallop to the gate of the city, which they opened for him. He entered, went to an inn, and spent the night. The next morning, the public crier began to cry, "Go to battle and may God have mercy on you, oh soldiers." When the young boy heard this proclamation, he went out and arrayed himself with the soldiers of the town. As the armies were arrayed for battle, ready to fight, a divine force urged him on, and he conquered the king and took him prisoner. At this sight, all the enemy soldiers fled and did not return. The young man led the king to the inn where he had stayed. The viziers went, in all haste, to tell the good news to the queen, and said to her, "The king who besieged the town was made prisoner by a young foreign soldier." She was astonished at this, and went to his inn, wanting to find him to reward him for what he had just done, but he accepted nothing. As she saw he was handsome, brave, young, and strong, she proposed to marry him, and make him king. The young boy said to her, "Gladly!" and accepted the proposition with as much joy as ingenuousness. The queen told him to mount his horse, and conducted him to her palace, where she arranged for him to spend the night. The next day, she had priests come to the church, and there they celebrated mass. She then ordered preparations for a great festival in honor of the victory won against the king who had besieged the city. With this done, she married the young boy, who never left her, night or day.

One day, when the queen was seated with her servants, she said, "Have you ever seen anyone more handsome than my young husband? He has, however, a disease," she continued, "which no one save myself knows about." What is this disease, Madam?" asked one servant. "Each time he goes to the watercloset," she said, "he comes out pale, with red eyes: there are, doubtless, evil spirits in him." The housekeeper of the palace said to her, "I will take charge of the matter." She waited for the prince to enter the watercloset, saw him take the ivory tablet, look at it, and then place it in a window. As soon as he left, the woman entered, took the tablet, and brought it to the queen. When she took the tablet in her hands, she cried aloud and fell in a dead faint.

Seeing her in this state, several servants went to tell the king that the queen had fainted. The king returned quickly to the palace, and as soon as his gaze lit on the queen, he said to her, "Don't cry; God will bring you salvation." "How can I not cry and lament since you are the son born of my flesh?" After these words from the queen, he went out to the field, without knowing where to go. He finally found himself on the shore of an ocean and saw a fisherman. "Take my clothing," he said to him, "and give me your *guebbeh*." The fisherman replied, "It is not appropriate for your grandeur, monseigneur." "It is I who wants them," said the king; forthwith he doffed his clothing and gave it to the fisherman. With this done, he said to him, "Will you do me a great service? Buy me a chain of iron." The fisherman went in all haste, bought it for him and brought it back to him. The king put the chain at his feet, threw the key into the sea, and said to the fisherman, "Will you do me a great favor? Take me over the sea to that isle which you see over there." The fisherman could not refuse him, especially when he heard him say, "Oh Lord, have pity on that man who is the fruit of sin that he never committed on earth, and who, to make his crime worse, married his mother after being the son of his uncle." He continued to pray and said, "Oh God, the door of penitence is always open for sinners. I vow that I will neither eat bread nor prepared dishes for all my life." He remained on the island for a great number of years and ate nothing but herbs. The *guebbeh* that he wore was torn, and his body was exposed to the cold of winter and the heat of summer. He cried out at every instant, "Have pity, oh my God, on him who is born of sin and has himself committed sin with his own mother who carried him in her womb. My God, you who know all that which is done unknowingly among men, has anyone ever committed such a sin?" The tears fell on his cheeks like drops of rain.

The patriarchs of old had at their service young clerks, from whom they chose those who had been distinguished for their good conduct. It was to those that they left the government of the patriarchy when they died. The king went to find the patriarch at his deathbed and said to him, "Tell me, oh father, the name of the one who will succeed you as patriarch." The patriarch replied, "I have examined all my young clerks, and amongst them have not found one who would be worthy of such an honor." "Advise me," replied the king, "as to what I should do." The patriarch replied, "The Lord, the Messiah, will advise you what to do, he would never leave his church without someone to direct it." As soon as the patriarch had said these words, he gave up his soul into the hands of the Lord.

Soon after, the king chose several of his attendants, gave them money and provisions and said to them, "Go amongst the monasteries; if you find a monk worthy of this post because of his good conduct, bring him here so that we may then make him the patriarch." The attendants went and applied themselves to this search, just as the king had ordered them. The Lord willed that they come to the fisherman who had taken the clothing of the king. They said to him, "Give us fish to eat!" "Gladly!" replied the fisherman. Right away, he took his net and threw it into the river. A big fish was caught without delay. The fisherman brought it right away to his wife and said to her, "Prepare it as is fitting, for we have guests." As soon as the wife had opened the stomach of the fish, she found the key to the chains there, recognized it, and spoke about it to her husband. He said, "That's the key to the fetters that I put on the feet of the king when I took him to the isle. I've only seen him very rarely; he's doubtless become a dumb savage, since he's been there a long time." The envoys of the king, having heard what the fisherman said to his wife, said to him, "We beg you, good man, to take us across the water to this isle so that we may see this man who will come to our aid." "Wait here until tomorrow," said the fisherman, "and I will arrange it so that your wish is fulfilled." He then served them the fish, which they ate with great appetite, and then they spent the night in his house.

The next morning, they crossed the sea to the isle where they found the hermit standing up, hands outstretched, busy praying to the merciful Lord that he be pardoned. He took off the rest of his *guebbeh* to cover his nudity with it. They seized him, and brought him to the king with great joy. The king had twelve bishops come, who ordained him patriarch. Thus he was saved by the good hope that he had held in the assistance of God who performs prodigies and miracles by his grace, and gave him the power to cure diseases and sicknesses.

His mother, very much grieved by what had happened to her, first through her brother, then through her son, was struck by a disease so serious that she was bound to die. This disease was accompanied by nearsightedness. Having heard the piety of the father patriarch being praised, she took several of her servants and presented herself to him, hoping to arrive at a cure, thanks to the prayers of the holy man. As soon as she presented herself before him, he recognized her. She immediately asked him for his benediction and said, "Have mercy on me father; I have great faith in your sanctity, and from the moment I saw you, I knew that your prayers would stop my sickness." The father patriarch walked toward the place of prayer, wept bitterly, and begged the Lord to cure the ills of the queen. She was soon cured, her strength returned, her eyes saw clearly, and she recovered her health. She then said to him, "Oh saint of God, I am going to return to my city. Pray to God in my favor." The father patriarch replied to her, "You should not do so before learning who I am." "No," she said, "I don't recognize your worship at all." He replied, "I am your son." As soon as she heard his words, she fainted at the feet of the patriarch. "Oh my dear mother," said he, "see the great benefice that God accords to those who do penance!" Soon after, he clothed her in the nun's habit, and she was saved because of her good thoughts. As God knew that their first and last sin had been committed involuntarily, he had pity on them, received their penitence, pardoned their sins, and for their efforts, performed signs and miracles before taking them away from this mortal world. She rejoiced greatly to see her son patriarch, and the two died together in the land of God (may He be exalted).

Know, oh brothers, that penitance still exists; despair not of the Lord. Let one who has committed an error turn to penitance; let him ask pardon for his sin; for God is merciful; He accepts sinners and pardons them. Pray that He come to our aid so that we will do what pleases Him at every instant, that He pardon our sins and our faults by the goodness of Her who intercedes, our sainted Lady, the Virgin Mary, and by the intercession of all the fathers, prophets, apostles, martyrs, all of the saints and all those who satisfied God, now and forever and forever: amen, amen, amen.

That is the end of the life of Armenios, king of Tyre, in the peace of God. Amen.

LT3 POPE GREGORY

Source: Hermann Oesterley, *Gesta Romanorum* (Berlin, 1872) ch. 81 (pp. 399-409). Translation: Charles Swan, *Gesta Romanorum: or, Entertaining Moral Stories,* . . . , rev. and corr. Wynnard Hooper (London, 1877) tale 81 (pp. 141-54).

The title, *Gesta Romanorum,* bears slight relation to the contents: tales not only of Romans and Greeks but of medieval kings, commoners, saints, and knights; beast fables; allegories; parables; in short, tales of every kind. The *Gesta,* the most popular storybook of the Middle Ages, existed in a multitude of forms. In his preface Hooper summarizes the extremely complicated history of this book thus: "What is known *par excellence* as the *Gesta Romanorum* is a collection of 181 stories, first printed about 1473. . . . But before the appearance of this collection there existed a great number of MSS. all over Western Europe, no two of which exactly resembled each other" (p. viii). Oesterley's edition contains 283 tales, the additions to the basic corpus coming from the various manuscripts and printed texts that he investigated.

Another tale of incest in the *Gesta* is chapter 13 (Oesterley, pp. 291-94; Swan-Hooper, pp. 26-29), which tells of a widowed queen who slept in the same bed with her son until he was eighteen years old, when the devil caused her to become pregnant by him. The son left the kingdom and was never heard of again. The queen killed the offspring of the incestuous union. Half of the tale deals with the queen's inability to confess her sin and the intervention of the Virgin Mary, who prompts the confessor to extract a confession from the queen. She is then absolved and dies a few days later. I have not included a translation of this tale in this collection.

The story of Gregory is known in other versions. In the one believed to be the oldest, that of a German *Volksbuch* (Karl Simrock, *Deutsche Volksbücher* 12 [Berlin, 1920]: 83-113), Gregory becomes not pope but bishop, and the motif of the key is lacking. There is an Old French version from the eleventh or twelfth century. On the date, see P. F. Baum, "The Mediaeval Legend of Judas Iscariot," *PMLA,* NS 24 (1916): 595, n. 42. For a history of the Gregory legend in the Middle Ages, see Adolf Seelisch, "Die Gregoriuslegende," *Zeitschrift für deutsch Philologie* 19 (1887): 392-99, 419-21.

The Emperor Marcus had an only son and daughter, to whom he was extremely attached. When he was much advanced in years, he was seized with a grievous sickness; and seeing his end approach, summoned into his presence the chief nobles of his empire. "My friends," said he, "know that this day my spirit will return to the God who gave it. All my concern resides in an only daughter, whom I have not yet bestowed in marriage. Therefore, do thou, my son and heir, upon my blessing, provide for her an honourable and befitting husband; and as long as thou livest, value her as thine own self." Saying these words, he turned toward the wall, and his spirit fled. The state made great lamentation, and interred him with much magnificence.

The young emperor commenced his reign with great wisdom, and in all that related to his sister strictly fulfilled his father's dying injunction. He seated her in the same chair with him at table, and assigned to her a separate couch in the same apartment that he occupied himself. Here began their unhappiness. Tempted by the devil, he gave way to the most horrible desires; and finally, in spite of the pleading of the wretched girl, violated every law both human and divine. Her tears, if tears could have retrieved the ignominy, had been enough: she wept bitterly, and refused all comfort; although the emperor attempted to console her, and evinced the excess of grief and love. About the middle of the year, as they sat at table, the brother narrowly scrutinized his sister's looks. "My beloved sister," said he, "why dost thou change colour? the upper part of thine eyelids darken." "No wonder," she returned," for I bear the weight of thy most fearful wickedness." Hearing this, the emperor felt his spirit sink within him, and turning round, wept very bitterly. "Perish," said he, "the evil day that I was born; what is to be done?" "My brother," said the lady, "hear me; we are not, alas, the first who have grievously offended God. There is, as you well know, a certain ancient knight, one of the most approved counsellors of our late father: call him hither, and, under the seal of confession, let us tell him the whole sad story; he will give us counsel how we may make atonement to God, and avoid disgrace before the world." The emperor assented— "but, said he, "let us study in the first place to be reconciled to God." They were then both confessed, and their contrition was perfect as sincere. Afterwards sending for the knight, they revealed amid a flood of tears their crime. "My lord," he replied, "since ye are reconciled to God, hear what I counsel. As well for your own sins, as for the sins of your father, hasten to the Holy Land; and before you embark, call together the noblemen of the kingdom, and explain to them your intent. And because your sister is your only heir, charge them to be obedient to her. Then, turning to me, command that she be placed under my custody; and that, as I value my life, she be securely and happily lodged. I will so provide that her parturition be kept secret, and every one remain ignorant of her fate—unless, indeed, my wife be made acquainted with it, in order to wait upon her in her necessity." "You counsel well," rejoined the king, "and I will do as you have said."

Immediately the noblemen were summoned, and preparations made for the emperor's departure to the Holy Land. His sister was conveyed to the knight's castle; and when his wife beheld her she inquired whom he had brought. He answered, "The king's sister; but, wife, swear to me by all that thou holdest sacred, on penalty of thy life, never to communicate to a living soul that which I am about to impart." She swore accordingly; and the knight then informed her of the situation of the lady, and his desire that no one might attend her but herself. The obedient spouse promised compliance, and the lady was privately introduced into the hall appointed for her residence. She was splendidly attended, and when the time of her confinement came on, she was safely delivered of a beautiful boy. As soon as the knight understood this, he entreated permission to call in a priest for the purpose of performing the rite of baptism. But she positively refused, declaring that its shameful birth forbade her to interfere, since it would expose her to detection and disgrace. "Your crime indeed is heavy," returned the knight, "but consider, should your child, therefore, perish immortally?" "My vow is registered in heaven," said the lady; "I have sworn, nor will I add perjury to my faults. Moreover, I command you to prepare an empty cask." The knight obeyed; and the lady, placing therein the cradle with the new-born boy, inscribed on small tablets the following words: "Know ye, to whomsoever chance may conduct this infant, that it is not baptized, because it is the unholy offspring of incestuous affection. For the love of God, then, cause it to be baptized. Under the child's head you will discover a quantity of gold, and with this let it be nurtured. At the feet is an equal weight of silver, designed to assist it in the future prosecution of study." This done, she deposited the tablets by the infant's side, the gold at the head, and the silver at its feet; then, enveloping it in silk garments embroidered with gold, she enclosed it in the cask, and directed the knight to cast it forthwith into the sea—trusting that, by the overruling providence of God, it might be carried into a place of safety. The knight faithfully executed the lady's wishes; he threw the cask into the sea, and, standing upon the shore, watched its progress, until it was at length lost to his sight.

As he returned to his castle, a king's messenger met him, whom he thus accosted: "Friend, whence come you?"

"From the Holy Land."

"Indeed! what rumours are abroad?"

"My lord the king is dead; and we have brought his corpse to one of his own castles."

Hearing this, the good knight could not refrain from tears. At that moment, his wife approached, and learning the unwelcome tidings, joined her tears to his. But the knight, recovering somewhat of the dejection of spirit into which the intelligence had thrown him, said to his wife, "Weep not, I pray thee, lest our mistress should perceive it, and inquire the cause. It were better to keep silence on this unwelcome subject, until she be risen from her child-bed." Saying this, the knight entered the queen's apartment, followed by his wife. But the manifest sorrow on their countenances could not escape the penetration of the lady, and she eagerly asked the occasion. "Dear lady, we are not sad," they said, "but rather joyful at your rapid recovery." "That is not true," replied she; "I conjure you, conceal nothing, be it for good or evil." "A messenger," answered the knight, "has just returned from the Holy Land, conveying intelligence of my lord, your brother."

"What does the messenger say? Let him be called hither."

This was done; and the lady asked after the king. "He is dead," said the messenger, "and we have brought the body to his own kingdom, to be buried according to the rites of his country." The lady, possessed of this fatal intelligence, fell upon the ground; and the knight and his wife, participating in her extreme grief, cast themselves beside her. For a length of time, they all three continued in this attitude; and so intense was their sorrow, that neither the sound nor sense appeared remaining. The lady arose first; tore her hair, wounded her face, and exclaimed in a shrill voice, "Woe is me! May that day perish in which I was conceived! May that night be no more remembered in which so great a wretch was born. How vast is my iniquity! In me all things are fulfilled. My hope is broken, and my strength; he was my only brother—the half of my soul. What I shall do hereafter, alas! I know not." The knight arose and said, "Dearest lady, listen to me. If you suffer yourself to be thus concerned, the whole kingdom will perish. You only are left; and you are the lawful heir. Should you destroy yourself, the nation will remain at the mercy of foreign powers. Arise, then, and direct the body to be brought hither, and honourably interred. Afterwards, we will debate concerning the prosperity of the kingdom." Quieted, if not comforted, by the knight's words, she arose, and proceeded with a noble company to the castle, where her brother's body lay. It was placed upon a bier; and no sooner had the queen entered, than she fell upon the corpse and kissed it, from the crown of his head, even to the soles of his feet. Now, the soldiers, perceiving the violent grief of their queen, drew her from the bier, and led her into the hall; and then, with great pomp, carried the body to its sepulchre.

A short period after this, a certain Duke of Burgundy sent messengers to demand the lady in marriage; but she declared her fixed determination never to marry. Irritated at her refusal, the duke observed, "If she had married me, I should indeed have been king of the country; but since it is her pleasure to despise me, she who fills the throne shall enjoy little satisfaction." Whereupon he collected his troops, and devastated every place to which he marched. He perpetrated an immensity of ill, and subdued all opposition. The queen, in this extremity, fled to a strongly fortified city, where there was a castle well appointed and defended; and here she continued many years.

Let us now return to the boy, who was thrown into the sea. The cask in which he was placed floated through many countries, until it reached, at length, a certain monastery, about the sixth festival. On that day, the abbot of the monastery proceeded to the sea-shore, and said to his fishermen, "My friends, make ready to fish"; and whilst they were preparing their nets, the vessel was tossed by the motion of the waves upon the shore. The abbot observed it, and said to his servants, "See ye that cask? open it, and find out what is within." They did so, and behold, it was a newly born boy covered with very rich clothing. No sooner had the child looked upon the abbot, than it smiled. The sight greatly concerned the worthy monk. "Oh, my God," said he, "how comes it that we find a child in his deplorable situation?" Raising it with his own hands, he perceived the tablets under its side, which the mother had placed there; and when he had read them, he discovered that it was the offspring of an incestuous bed, and not yet baptized—and saw that this sacrament was implored, for the sake of Heaven; and that gold and silver were deposited for his nurture and education. When he had read this, and observed that the cradle was ornamented with rich cloth, he saw that the boy was of noble blood. He immediately baptized and called him after his own name, Gregory. He then intrusted him to a fisherman to nurse, with the gold and silver found upon him. The boy grew up universally beloved. In his seventh year the abbot provided for his studies, which he mastered in a surprising manner; insomuch that the monks were as fond of him as though he had been of their own order. In a short time he acquired more knowledge than them all.

It happened that one day, as he played at ball with the son of the fisherman, his presumed father, by chance he struck him with the ball. The lad wept bitterly, and running home, complained to his mother that he had been struck by his brother Gregory. Instantly the angry mother issued out of doors, and harshly reproved him, exclaiming, "Audacious little vagabond, why hast thou struck my son? Thou!—of whose origin and country we know nothing—how darest thou do this?" "Dear mother," answered Gregory, "am I not your son? Why do you speak to me in this manner?" "My son!" said the woman; "no, in good troth; neither do I know whose thou art. All I know is that thou wert one day discovered in a cask, and that the abbot delivered thee to me to bring up." When the boy heard this he burst into tears, ran hastily to the superior, and said, "Oh, my lord, I have been a long time with you, and I believed that I was the fisherman's son; but I learn that it is not so: consequently, I am ignorant who my parents are. If it please you, my lord, suffer me to become a soldier, for here I will not remain." "My son," said the abbot, "think not of it. The monks all love you, and I doubt not, after my decease, will promote you to the abbacy." "My good lord," answered Gregory, "I know not my parents, and I will not continue longer than I can help in this intolerable suspense." The abbot, finding solicitation useless, entered the treasury and brought to him the tablets which he had found in the cradle. "My son," he said, "read this; and what you are will be clear to you." When he had read, he fell to the earth, and exclaimed, "Alas! are such, then, my parents? I will hasten to the Holy Land, and do battle for the sins of the unhappy authors of my being; and there I will end my life. I entreat you, therefore, my lord, without delay to make me a knight." The abbot complied, and when his departure was made known, the whole convent and neighbourhood were loud in their lamentation.

Straightway he agreed with certain sailors for his passage to the Holy Land, and embarked. But as they sailed the wind became contrary, and they were suddenly driven upon the coast of that country in which his mother's castle stood. What the state was, and who reigned there, the sailors knew not; but as Gregory entered the city a citizen met him, and said, "My lord, whither are you going?" "To seek an inn," was the reply. On which the hospitable citizen led him to his own house, and entertained him magnificently. As they sat at table Gregory inquired of his host what state it was, and who was the lord of it. "Sir," returned the other, "awhile ago we had a very powerful emperor, but he died in the Holy Land, and left his throne to his sister. The Duke of Burgundy would have married her, but she was pleased to refuse his offer. Whereupon he has forcibly made himself master of the whole kingdom, save a single city in which the queen resides." "May I," returned the young knight, "declare with safety the secret wish of my heart?"

"With the greatest safety."

"I am," continued the other, "a soldier. If it please you, go to-morrow to the palace and obtain for me a communication with the seneschal, and if he will promise to remunerate me, I will fight for this year in behalf of the lady." "I doubt not, my lord," answered the citizen, "but that he will acquiesce with alacrity. To-morrow I will do as you desire." He went accordingly, and declared the occasion of his coming. The seneschal, not a little exhilarated, immediately sent off a messenger for Gregory; and, on his arrival, presented him to the queen, who expressed herself well satisfied with her champion. She observed him closely, but had not the remotest suspicion that it was her son, for she thought him long since overwhelmed in the waves. The seneschal therefore, in the presence of his mistress, covenanted that he should serve a full year. On the morrow he prepared for war, and assembled a large host. So judicious were his movements that Gregory triumphed in every engagement, and penetrated to the very palace of the duke, whom he finally took and beheaded.

Gregory after this continued the war from day to day with constant success; and the fame of his great prowess was carried to all parts of the realm. Thus, before the completion of the year which he had covenanted to serve, he had wrested the whole kingdom from the hands of their enemies. Then he went to the seneschal, and said, "Good friend, you know in what state I found your affairs, and in what a good condition I leave them. I therefore beg you to give me my hire, for I intend to proceed to another country." "My lord," said the seneschal, "you have merited much more than our agreement stipulated; let us hasten to the queen, and there conclude as to the recompense." They went accordingly; and the seneschal thus spoke: "My dear lady, I would say something, which will be to your advantage. From the absence of a head, we have sustained many grievous afflictions. It were desirable, therefore, for you to take a husband, who is able to defend us from a return of the like troubles. Your kingdom is rich enough, so that I would not advise you to select a spouse for his wealth. And this being allowed, I know not where you could find one in every respect so suitable and beneficial to the state as my lord Gregory." The lady, as we have seen before, rejected a second marriage; but overcome by the arguments and urgency of her seneschal, appointed a day on which, after mature deliberation, she would give an answer. That day came; and in the presence of all the assembled nobles, she arose and spoke thus: "Since my lord Gregory has valiantly and effectually liberated both us and our kingdom from the thraldom of oppressive foes, I will receive him for my husband." The audience rejoiced; and an early period was fixed for the celebration of their nuptials. They were then espoused with the approbation of the whole country—the son to his own mother: but both were ignorant of the relationship. They loved each other tenderly: it happened, however, that the lord Gregory on one particular occasion went out to hunt; and a handmaid of the queen said to her, "Dear lady, have you not offended my lord in something?" "Surely not," returned she. "I believe that there is not in the whole world a married pair so mutually attached to each other as we are. But why do you ask?" "Because," said the handmaid, "every day, when the table is laid, my lord enters his private chamber in great apparent pleasure; but when he returns it is with lamentation and wailing. After that he washes his face; but why all this is done, I do not comprehend."

On hearing this, the lady immediately entered the private chamber before alluded to, and narrowly inspected every closet and crevice. At length, she came to the place wherein the tablets, inscribed with the ignominy of his birth, and which he was wont to read day by day, were deposited; and then she wept most piteously. For they were the same which she had laid in the cradle; and which, when they now started up before here, as it were, by magic, she remembered too well. She opened them, and recognized her own handwriting. "Alas!" she exclaimed, "how has he obtained this dark testimony of my crime, if he be not my son?" And then bursting into a lamentable cry, "Woe is me, that I ever saw the light of heaven—would that I had died ere I was born." The soldiers in the hall, hearing the clamour produced by the anguish and perturbation of her mind, ran into the chamber, and found her stretched upon the earth. They stood around her a considerable time before she was able to ejaculate, and when at length she could speak, she said, "If ye desire me to live, hasten immediately for my lord." The spectators hearing her wish, mounted their horses, and rode to the king. They explained to him the imminent danger of his wife; and he forthwith left the chase, returned to the castle, and entered the chamber where the queen lay. When she saw him, she said, "Oh, my lord, command us to be left alone; what I have to say is for your private ear." The room was accordingly cleared; and the lady eagerly besought him to say of what family he was. "That is a singular question," replied he, "but know that I am a native of a distant country." "Oh," returned the lady, "I solemnly vow to God that, unless you declare to me the whole truth, I am sure I shall quickly die." "I tell you," he said, "I was poor—possessed of nothing but the arms with which I freed you and the kingdom from slavery." "Only tell me," urged the lady, "from what country you came, and who are your parents; and unless you speak truly, I will never more touch food." "You shall be satisfied," said the king. "I was brought up by an abbot from my earliest age; and from him I learnt that I was found cradled in a cask." Here the queen showed him the tablets, and said, "Dost thou remember these?" He looked, and fell prostrate on the earth. "My son!" cried she, "for thou art so; my only son, and my husband, and my lord! Thou art the child of my brother and myself. Oh, my son, I deposited in the cask with thee these tablets. Woe is me! Why, O God, didst thou permit my birth, since I was born to be guilty of so much wickedness! Would that the eye which looks upon me might reduce me to ashes; would that I had passed from the womb to the grave!" Then striking her head against the wall, she cried, "Oh, thou Almighty

Being, behold my son—my husband, and the son of my brother." "I thought," replied Gregory, "to shun this danger, and I have fallen into the snares of the devil. Dismiss me, lady, to bewail my misery: woe! woe! my mother is my mistress—my wife! See how Satan hath encompassed me!" When the mother perceived the agony of her child, she said, "Dear son, for the residue of my life, I will expiate our crimes by hardships and wanderings. Thou shalt govern the kingdom." "Not so," returned he; "do you remain, my mother: you are wanted to rule the realm. I will roam about, until our sins are forgiven."

The same night he arose, broke his lance, and put on the dress of a pilgrim. He bade his mother farewell, and, with naked feet, walked till he reached the uttermost boundaries of the kingdom. Having entered a certain city, he sought out the house of a fisherman, with whom he requested permission to lodge. When the fisherman had considered him attentively, and observed the comeliness of his person and the grace of his form, he said, "Friend, you are no true pilgrim; this is evident from the elegance of your body." "Well," answered the other, "though I be not a true pilgrim, yet, for the love of God, I beseech you to give me harbourage." Now, the fisherman's wife, looking upon him, was moved with a devout feeling, and entreated that he might be sheltered. He entered therefore; but directed his bed to be made for him at the gate. Fish, with water and bread, were given to him. Amongst other things, the fisherman said "Pilgrim, if you would become holy, go into some remote place." "Sir," answered Gregory, "I would willingly follow your advice, but I know of no such place." "On the morrow," returned he, "I will myself conduct you." "May God reward you," said the pilgrim. The next morning the fisherman bade him rise, and hurried him so much that he left his tablets behind the gate where he had slept.

The fisherman, with his companion, embarked upon the sea, and sailing about sixteen miles came to a huge rock, having chains at its feet, which, without a key, could not be unloosed. After the fisherman had undone them, he cast the keys into the sea, and returned home. The pilgrim remained in that place seventeen years, with every feeling of the most perfect penitence.

About this period the pope died; and at the moment of his decease, a voice from heaven cried out, "Search after a man of God, called Gregory, and appoint him my vicar." The electors, greatly rejoiced at what they heard, sent messengers into different parts of the world to seek him. At length, some of them lodged in the house of the fisherman; and as they sat at supper, one said, "My friend, we are much harassed by journeys through town and country, in pursuit of a holy man, called Gregory, whom, when we find, we are to place in the pontificate." The fisherman, then recollecting the pilgrim, answered, "It is now seventeen years since a pilgrim named Gregory lodged in this house. I conducted him to a certain rock in the midst of the sea, and there I left him. But it is so long ago, that he may be dead." It happened that on the same day, a number of fishes were caught; and as he gutted one of them, he found the keys which seventeen years before he had cast into the sea. Immediately he shouted, "Oh, my friends, behold these keys! I cast them into the sea; and I draw from this circumstance a good omen respecting the success of your labours." The messengers were much pleased with the man's prognostication, and early in the morning desired him to bring them to the rock. He did so; and there finding Gregory, they said, "Man of God, go up with us; by the command of the Omnipotent, go up with us: for it is His will that thou shouldst be appointed His vicar upon earth." To which Gregory replied, "God's will be done;" and then followed them from the rock. As soon as he approached the city, the bells rang of their own accord, which the citizens hearing, said, "Blessed be the Most High, he cometh who shall be Christ's vicar," and hastened to meet him. St. Gregory, thus appointed, conducted himself worthily in every respect; and multitudes from every part of the world came to ask his counsel and assistance. Now, his mother, hearing of the remarkable sanctity of the reigning pope, thought that nowhere could she find help sooner than from so holy a man. But that he was her son and husband she knew not. Hastening, therefore, to Rome, she confessed herself to the vicar of God; nor was it till after confession that the pope recollected his unhappy mother. He then spoke thus: "Dearest mother and wife, and mistress, the devil dreamt of bringing us to hell; but, by the grace of God, we have evaded his toils." At these words, she fell at his feet; and even for very joy, wept bitterly. But the pope raised her up, and tenderly embraced her. He founded a monastery over which he made her abbess, and a short time afterwards, both yielded up their souls to God.

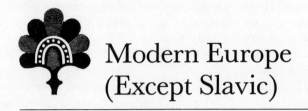 Modern Europe
(Except Slavic)

GR1 JUDAS

Source: G. Megas, "Ho Ioudas eis tas Paradoseis tou Laou," *Epetēris tou Laographikou Archeiou* 3 (1941–42): 4–5 (a French summary of the article appears on pp. 219–23). The story was collected by K. Zēsiou, who does not report where or from whom he heard this story, and was published by him as no. 10 in *Hebdomas* (1887), pp. 6–7. Translated by Margaret M. Thorne.

Once there were a man and his wife. After they were married and the woman was pregnant, she saw in a dream that she bore a flame. In the morning she told her dream to her husband, and he said to her, "Alas! poor wife, the child you are to have will be a devil. As soon as it is born we will cast it out."

As soon as his wife gave birth, the husband took the child out onto a mountain and there he abandoned it.

Nearby a goatherd pastured his flock, but one goat, the best of the herd, took to slipping away to nurse the child. The goatherd would then try to milk her, but she would have no milk. He suspected his helper of milking her, and he decided to watch.

Next day he saw the goat slipping away and he followed her, and he saw her kneel down to nurse the child. He took it immediately to his cottage, and the goat followed him.

When his wife saw how beautiful the child was, she said, "Husband, where did you find this child?" "I found him on the mountain, where the goat was nursing him." She said to him, "We shall keep him and raise him in our cottage like our other children."

When the boy was eight or ten years old, the king went out on a round. As he was passing the goatherd's cottage, he was astonished to see how beautiful was this one boy while the goatherd's other children were swarthy and ugly. He asked the goatherd why, and the goatherd told him all, and how he had found him. Then, because he had no son of his own, the king asked the goatherd to give him the boy, and he took him to the palace.

The boy's true father had leased the king's garden. When the boy was twenty years old, he took to going to the garden, cutting down the trees, and doing other damage. The gardener (that is, his own father) would say to him, "How do the trees harm you, that you should destroy them?" But the young man paid no attention, and they had words, and right away the boy drew his sword and killed him.

Then the gardener's wife (that is, the killer's mother) ran to the king, "O king, live forever! That boy of yours has killed my husband, for no reason but that he told him not to cut down the trees."

Immediately the king replied, "Since he has killed your husband, you must take him to be your husband"—that was the law in that country. And as soon as he commanded it, they married them.

One evening after they were married and the woman had become pregnant, her husband (that is, her son) began to tell her his story and how the goatherd had found him abandoned by his parents. Then his mother told him who he was, and what he was to the man he had killed and to his wife.

As soon as he heard it the young man fled, and he went to be a disciple of the Christ. Christ took him in and made him his purse bearer, that is, his treasurer—until the time came when he betrayed Him and revealed himself to be in truth "Judas Iscariot" and "the devil."

Then the narrator of this story invoked the protection of the day's saint and crossed himself, and those who had been breathlessly listening to him imitated him and spat three times into their bosoms.

GR2 JUDAS

Source: G. Megas, "Ho Ioudas eis tas Paradoseis tou Laou," *Epetēris tou Laographikou Archeiou* 3 (1941–42): 7–8 (a French summary of the article appears on pp. 219–23). The tale, in Cypriot dialect, was originally collected by K. Hadjiioannēs on Cyprus in the town of Makrosyka in the region of Famagusta, and published by him in *Kypriaka Chronika* 9 (1933): 291 ff. Translated by Margaret M. Thorne.

When Judas's mother was pregnant, she saw in her dream that the child she was to bear would do great harm to their people. She went to the king and told him the story. The king commanded that as soon as the child was born she should kill it. But when Judas was born, his mother had pity on him, and instead of killing him, she tarred a basket and cast him into the river to die by himself.

There were some shepherds, they saw the basket, they went near it, and they heard the baby cry. They opened it and took the baby out, saying, "Let us bring him up and have him help us with the flock." They took him and fed him on the milk of the goat (the accursed beast). The goat loved him and nursed him.

When he was seven years old and could have helped them a little, he became intractable. Now, his leg would hurt him, now his arm would hurt him, he did not work for them at all. So they decided to take him to the king. They brought him to the king and he took him as his servant.

One day the princess said to him, "Boy, go bring me some flowers!" So he went to the palace garden, but instead of picking flowers he began to cut off whole branches. —Oh, I forgot to tell you, in this garden were Judas's father and mother, because they had been very unlucky, and Judas himself had killed another son of theirs on the mountain, and they had come to beg the king for a living and he had granted them that garden, to tend it and to take the profits.

Well, as soon as his father saw him—now, neither did the one know the boy was his son nor did the other know the man was his father— "Boy," he said to him, "why do you cut the branches? Do I do all this work to have you come and cut down my trees?" But Judas answered arrogantly, "My mistress, the princess, told me to." But it was really out of his laziness that he did it, not for what his mistress said.

He went again another day, his mother saw him and told her husband, and he came. "Hey, boy, why are you cutting the branches again?" "Not another word!" said Judas to him, "or I will kill you as I once killed another on the mountain," and he meant his brother. They fought, and he killed his father too.

His mother was all cries and groans. The queen heard and told the king. "Boy," said the king to Judas, "marry this woman to stop her crying, or I shall cut off your head." So he married her.

One day, as Judas was going into the house, he listened and heard her mourning and telling all her woes. He questioned her, because the shepherds had told him the story of how he was in the tarred basket, and he understood that he had killed both his brother and his father and had married his mother.

So they parted on the spot and he went to find Christ and Christ accepted him.

It was because Judas was greedy of money and He knew that he would betray Him; no one else betrayed Him.

GR3 JUDAS

Source: G. Megas, "Ho Ioudas eis tas Paradoseis tou Laou," *Epetēris tou Laographikou Archeiou* 3 (1941–42): 5–7 (a French summary of the article appears on pp. 219–23). The tale was collected in 1938 on Crete, in the town of Latsida, in the district of Merabellou, by M. Lioudakēs from her father, an illiterate. Translated by Margaret M. Thorne.

When his mother was pregnant with Judas, the prophet Nathan came and said to her, "Woman, the child you are to have will be a flaming torch that shall consume the whole world!"

"What makes you say that, wife?"

"Husband, I tell you what I know."

"Then all we can do is to drown the child as soon as you have borne it."

As soon as the woman had given birth, they put the child into a small chest and cast it into the sea. But the sea threw the chest up onto a lonely shore where two donkey herders found it. They opened it and discovered the baby inside. The asses had just foaled, so they gave it to a jenny to nurse, and they raised it.

When the boy was grown, they sat him down and told him how they had found him and how they had raised him, and then they said: "Now that you are grown, it is right for you to go to work."

The young man arose and went—but where should he go? He went to be a servant in the house of his own father. His parents, however, had borne and raised another son.

One day the two boys came to blows, and Judas killed his little brother. Straightway he arose and went, and he became a servant in the palace of the king.

When the parents saw their son dead, they tore their cheeks in grief, but what were they to do? In time they comforted each other, and one day Judas's father said to the mother, "My poor wife! We cast away one child, our servant slew the other, and we are left like a light that has been put out. Let's go. What are we to do living here any longer?"

So straightway they arose and went, and they became gardeners on an estate, and there they lived and cultivated flowers.

Suddenly one day the king said to his servant, "Boy! I want a bunch of roses. Go and fetch them." Judas rose to go, but where should he go? He went to the garden where his father worked. He went in and called high and low for the gardener, but the gardener did not appear, so he began picking the roses himself. As he was about to leave, behold! the gardener came and took him to task for gathering the roses. In a rage Judas killed his father and went and told the king: "I quarreled with the gardener, and I killed him."

"Wretch of a boy, what have you done? Now you must take his widow for your wife."

So he went and took his mother as his wife.

One day, mother and son were sitting and talking, and she asked him, "Where are you from, and how did you come here?"

"I do not know who my parents were. Some donkey herders found me in a little box, and they brought me up." And he told her his whole history.

"Wretch that you are! You are my son, and we are both damned, since we have become man and wife. Go! Go and follow that man who they say saves sinners."

So he went away and became a disciple of the Christ.

KV1(GR) RIVERBOY

Source: G. Megas, "Ho peri Oidipodos Mythos," *Epetēris tou Laographi-kou Archeiou* 3 (1941–42): 198–200 (a French summary of the article appears on pp. 219–23). The tale, which was collected in the mountains of Epirus, is in the Folklore Archive in Athens. The tale was told in Koutsovlach (Wallachian), the language of the nomadic shepherds of the Balkans. Megas gives a Greek translation, from which the English translation here is made. Translated by Margaret M. Thorne. A very similar version in Macedo-Romanian, collected in Cules din Turia, Epirus, was published by P. N. Papahagi, *Basme Aromâne* (Bucharest, 1905), no. 110 (pp. 360–62).

Once there was a time—but there was not.

Once in the olden days, it must have been a hundred years ago, there lived at the edge of the world a man and his wife, and they had nine children. After the ninth child, the wife became pregnant again, and her time came.

Three nights after the child was born, the Fates came to tell its destiny.

The mother already had nine children, and she did not look forward to this one eagerly. So on the third evening she put out neither food nor drink, and did not even set the table.

When the Fates came and found no table set for them, they were very angry and destined the child to a life of sorrow. They said, "Your father shall die, and your nine brothers and sisters shall die, you will be left a wretched orphan, and when the time comes for you to marry, you shall take your mother for your wife."

When the unhappy mother heard what the Fates ordained, her very shirt began to tremble on her, and she did not sleep till dawn. She thought and she thought, "What shall I do?" In the end, she thought of a way to avoid the evil.

She took the child and went to the river to drown it. But, poor mother! As a mother she ached for the child, and she could not bring herself to throw it in. So she left it on the riverbank and went away.

No sooner had the mother gone than a man came by who lived in another village. When he heard the baby cry, he picked it up and carried it to his own house and called it Riverboy.

Time passed, and Riverboy grew up in that man's house and became tall and strong, and when his mind was mature and he began to think, he asked his father one day, "Why do you call me Riverboy?" At first the father refused to say, but in the end, plagued by the constant, "Why? Why? Why?" he told him that he had found him as a baby, abandoned beside the river.

The boy was deeply troubled when he heard it, and wondered what to do. So he put a piece of bread into his satchel and set out to find his parents.

He came to his father's village, but as he had been taken as an infant from the cradle he did not know his family. He went to an old woman who had no children, and she kept asking and asking, and she found that he had no parents. Then she urged him and urged him to let her adopt him as her son, and she would marry him to a beautiful widow. The old woman told him that the woman was rich, that she had had nine children but that they had all died, poor things, and afterwards her husband had died too, and she was left alone and unhappy. She told him further that no man had set foot in the widow's house since then, and that if he wished he might marry her.

By talking and talking the old woman persuaded the young man, and he married the widow.

Years had passed and the unhappy widow, who was his mother, had forgotten the Fates' decreee. But after they were married, she asked the young man who his parents were. And Riverboy sat down and told her all he had learned from the man who had reared him: how the man had found him years ago beside the river and brought him up, and how when the boy grew up and began to think, he wanted to know the reason for his name, and all the rest.

As Riverboy talked and talked, the poor woman grew paler and paler, and her blood went cold in her veins. When the boy finished speaking, she shrieked, "You are my son!" and fell fainting to the ground.

And so what the Fates had said came true.

AL1 THE FAIRY'S CURSE

Source: Margaret Hasluck, "Oedipus Rex in Albania," *Folk-Lore* 60
(1949): 341–43. The original Albanian can be found in S. E. Mann, *A
Short Albanian Grammar* (London, 1932), pp. 90–92. Mann gives
an English translation, differing considerably from Hasluck's, on
pp. 136–38. The tale comes from a Dukagjin tribe in North Albania.
Hasluck comments that it "was first published in the Catholic periodi-
cal *Hylli i Dritës* ("Morning Star") about 1929" (p. 341).

A man once went at the crack of dawn to an alp to cut some boards
for a cradle, because his wife was about to be given a child by Our Lord.
As he was chopping up a spruce-tree, he heard a fairy calling to her
mate from that very mountain.

"Bless me!" she said, "that poor fellow has got a son. What name
shall we give it?"

"Oh, never mind, dear," the other replied. "I haven't time to bother
my head about all the people that are born."

But the one who first spoke would not let her be so lightly. She called
two or three times more to her, and then in exasperation she replied:

"May he kill his father and marry his mother!"

When the man heard the fairy's curse, he got a shock at first. Then he
paid no more attention to it and went on with his work.

After making the cradle he took it home and there found the child
born. The mother laid it in the cradle and put the usual necklet on its
neck as a token.

When the child had grown a little, the father, unable to put the fairy's
curse out of his mind, talked things over with his wife and decided to
expose the boy. So he made a box and putting the child inside, cast it
into the sea.

The waves caught it up, bore it far, far away, and at last washed it
ashore. There Our Lord provided a goat which came every day and let
the boy suck her.

One fine day a passing traveller came on the child and pitying him,
took him to his home. There he kept him as one of his own family.

When the boy grew to be a stripling of sixteen or so, he took it into
his head that he was a King's son. So he refused to stay any longer with
his benefactor and went wandering the world over to see if he could discover which king he was the son of—so as to go and live with his father.

A good many years passed while he wandered. Then he happened to
light on a country where the inhabitants were murmuring very much
against their king. As he knew himself to be very able, he joined the
party in opposition to the king, thinking to find a way of thrusting him
out of this world with his own hand and taking his place.

As he passed day after day wondering how he could carry out his

wish, he encountered three carriages a little outside the town, quite unexpectedly. After some people had pointed out which the king was in,
he went up as though he wanted to say something to him. When he
came close, he struck him with his mace and killed him. He then got
into the carriage, put the horses to a gallop, and entered the town. Without more ado the people elected him king and gave him the widowed
queen to wife as they liked each other.

Before a year had passed, Our Lord gave them a son, and they seemed
happy. But there was one thing which worried them. Whenever the husband talked to his wife, he had a way of calling her "mother," and she
had a way of calling her husband "son"! In order to discover what was
portended by this business, which they could never understand however
much they pondered it, they sent to inquire of a spaewife. She replied
that they must be kith and kin to each other.

After being told this by the spaewife, they began one day to talk over
their lives at great length. Especially because the husband showed his
wife the necklet which his mother had put round his neck as a token of
identity when he was small, they realised that they were indeed mother
and son, and that he had unwittingly killed his father. In his despair the
husband plunged his knife into his wife's heart first of all, then into his
son's, and last of all into his own.

As his wife rendered up her spirit, she sang to her dying child:

Hush thee, hush thee, son!
Son of my son!
Son of my daughter-in-law!
Born to thy father-in-law!

Looking about her, she saw that the house was falling down and burying them.

RM1(GM) SALAMON PREMUNDE

Source: Franz Obert, "Rumänische Märchen und Sagen aus Siebenbürgen," *Archiv des Vereins für siebenbürgische Landeskunde,* NF 42
(1924), no. 46 (pp. 454-55). My translation.

An emperor's daughter had a child, but unexpectedly. In order not
to be disgraced, she placed it in a chest and threw it in the water. The
chest floated to a mill. There it lodged under a wheel, obstructed it, and
was pulled out by the miller. He opened the chest, saw the boy, and
since one had been borne to him the previous night, he adopted him
and had him brought up with the other and named him Salamon
Premunde. But the gold that was in the chest he laid by for the boy. In

school the boy learned more quickly than the other and was generally so able that the miller grew as fond of him as if he were his own. When the boy was seventeen years old, he fell into a quarrel with the miller's son, whom he had always considered his brother, and since this one insulted him as a vagabond bastard, he ran as quickly as he could to the miller, inquired about his origins, had his gold given him, and departed thence. After he had gone some distance, an angel met him and said: "Do not go into the city, or, if you must, take care not to show yourself to the emperor's daughter, since she will desire you for her husband, though she is your mother." Salamon Premunde would not heed the words of the angel but went to the city, where the emperor's daughter saw him and became so fond of him that she desired him for her husband. He complied with her demand, but would not share the bed with her. So she cursed him and had him driven from the city. Salamon Premunde accepted this and was not angry with the emperor's daughter, since he knew that she was his mother. But he regretted that he had married her and he wandered around for a very long time, until finally he came into the underworld (*Jaad*), whence he freed his grandfather and grandmother.

RM2(GM) URSITORI

Source: Pauline Schullerus, "Rumänische Volksmärchen aus dem mittleren Harbachtale," *Archiv des Vereins für siebenbürgische Landeskunde,* NF 33 (1905), no. 67 (pp. 531-34). Schullerus explains that Ursitori are spirits visible only at midnight that place the fates of newborn children in their cradles. This tale came from Nicolae Duda of Alzen. My translation.

There were once two persons who had no children, but were well enough off. Often they prayed God for a child. But when they did not get one, they asked one another for whom they should work—they had no one. When they had formed this opinion, they had a son and were overjoyed with him. No one had ever seen such affection lavished on a child. By night the old grandmother sat by the cradle. At midnight, there came, as to all unbaptized children, the Ursitori, and laid this in his cradle: "When he grows up, he shall shoot his father dead and marry his mother." The grandmother beside the cradle was not asleep and heard everything the spirits had laid in the child's cradle. And it is the way, since the world began, that one cannot—though many try—preserve oneself from that which the Ursitori lay in the cradle at life's beginning, whether it is good or bad. When the Rumanian woman awoke in the morning, she immediately took the child into her arms and kissed it and kissed it and was so happy. Then said the old grandmother: "If you only knew what you will experience with this child, you wouldn't kiss him any longer. Last night I heard what the Ursitori laid in his cradle. They said that when the boy is ready to marry, he will shoot his father dead and marry his mother. At this the parents were aghast and determined to do away with the child, though they loved it so much, since they had to protect it from this sin. They took a small chest, laid the child therein, the mother hung her ring around his neck, shut the chest and bore it to the water. The chest floated down the water for sixteen years. At this time two men came to this water to fish. Then they saw a chest in the water and said to one another: "What can be in it?" One of these persons was poor and had many children, the other had none and was rich. Now they wished to get hold of this chest and see what was in it. If it was gold, the poor man should have it; if it was a child, the rich would keep it. They went into the water and brought the chest to the bank, but it was very heavy. When they opened it, a boy leapt out, and since he now had room, he stretched himself and lengthened himself, and now one saw that he was a lad of sixteen years. The rich man without children was very glad and immediately took him as his own child. Well and good. After some time had passed, as time will pass, the lad said "Father, I'd like to go out into the world, hire myself out as a farmhand, to see how things are in other places." "Go, my son," said his foster father, and he went, and came right to his real parents. You can't preserve yourself from that which the Ursitori lay in your cradle, even if you die immediately. This was an honorable lad and did his work. His father was John and had a vineyard. Now it was the custom in autumn to take turns keeping watch, and when John's turn came, his wife said, "Send the hired man in your place—what do you have him for?—and rest at home." Well and good. He gave the hired man the gun and said, "If you hear anyone, ask three times who it is. If he doesn't answer, then shoot." The hired man went. After a time, the master said he should just make sure that the hired man had courage, and he went into the vineyard and there broke a plum branch, to scare the guard, but he only called once without fear, "Who are you?" No answer. He asked again, and also a third time. No answer. So he took the rifle and shot his master, his father. When the wife saw that her husband did not come home, she followed him to the vineyard and found him lying there dead. She no longer thought of the Ursitori. She retained the hired man, and when she saw that he was a reliable sort, she married him and they got along well, though she was much older. After a year they had a son, too, and were happy. Once they went together to the field and took the child with them. But it kept whining and the mother would often go and soothe it. Since it now began to whine again, she said to her husband, "You go to the child, too, for once." He went, and then he recalled his ring, which he had carried in his belt for as long as he could remember. He took it out and gave it to the child to play with, and he whined no more. His mother was astonished that he was so calm and went to have a look at him. When she caught sight of the ring, she was so terrified that she grew faint. Whatever the Ursitori place in your cradle, from this you cannot preserve yourself, no matter what it is. The poor woman thought that her son had perished, and now she saw that, in spite of her concern, what these spirits willed had been brought to pass. When she came to herself again, she discussed the matter with her husband and said that he should leave her, in order that their sins might not become greater; perhaps he might yet find another happiness. He said he would go, but first would seek the Ursitori, that they might tell him what they should do. And he went and went, until he came into the forest of these spirits. There he met a blind man who ate *palukes* made of three spoons full of flour. The young man sat down beside him and ate with him. Then the old man sensed him there and said "Who are you? If you are a good man, tell me, so I may in future make *palukes* for you, too." He told the old man why he had come into this forest—to seek the Ursitori. After they had eaten, the old man told him which way he must go. He went this way, and came into their dwelling. He went in, but there was no one at home. He crept behind the oven. It happened that a few came home, while the others had gone to the unbaptized. They smelled around in the room and smelled a man of the soil and said that if it was a good man, he should come forth and they would do him no harm; but if it was a bad man, they would kill him. He came out and told them why he had come to them. It had fared with him just as they had foretold; now they should counsel him what he must do next to find another happiness in this world. They said that it was good that he had left his mother; now he should go a bit farther, until he met a couple who mowed a wheat field with their daughter. He should enter into a conversation with the people; one word would lead to another; he should marry this girl; this would be his happiness, but so long as he lived, he should never say of anything that it belonged to him, always that it belonged to his wife, or else it would burn up. He thanked them, and went and went until he came to the wheat field, in which the parents and their daughter were mowing. He wished them good-day and asked for a little water. Meanwhile he had a look at the girl. She was pretty. When he had drunk, he helped them with their work and chatted with the daughter until evening came; and they fell in love and soon held a wedding and all was well. After the wedding he went one day at dawn to another field, to begin the mowing, and thought he should see if what the spirits had foretold to him was true. When the first person who passed by asked him whose field it was, he answered, "Mine," and immediately the sheaves began to burn, and half the field burned up. Then he quickly called, "It belongs to my wife." Then the fire went out and he worked in peace again, until his father-in-law came. He was astonished that half the field had burned and asked how it had happened. The son answered that he had lit a cigar; apparently a spark must have fallen into the straw. After that, he never again said that anything belonged to him, and thus he had no further misfortune and lived well with his wife and lives perhaps to this very day. I haven't heard that they have died.

HU1(GM) JANOS THE CRANE

Source: Elisabet Róna-Sklarek, *Ungarische Volksmärchen,* NF (Leipzig, 1909), no. 28 (pp. 269–71). The Hungarian original appears in János Berze Nagy, *Népmesék* in *Magyar Népköltési Gyüjtemény,* NS 9 (1907), no. 59. (pp. 411–14). The tale comes from the counties of Besenyötelek and Heves, and was told by Tinger Jóska, the blacksmith, December 1903. My translation.

Once upon a time there was on earth a king who had an only daughter. All her life this maiden never saw anyone. However, in order that she might somehow pass the time, her father had a large, golden crane made, with music in it, so that she might amuse herself when the fancy struck her.

While the goldsmith was making the golden crane, a soldier saw him. He asked what it was to be. The master answered that such gay music was to go inside the crane for the king's daughter.

In the evening, when all were now asleep, the soldier formed a plan and slipped into the golden crane.

Early the next day the crane was brought to the king and was forthwith placed in the maiden's room. The maiden was very pleased with it, and she could not leave it for joy.

The soldier only waited for night. When he noticed that there was calm and knew from the striking of the clock that midnight had come, he crept out of the crane, and went straight to the maiden's bed. And there they did what they did. To make a long story short, soon thereafter the princess had a son.

The matter was most vexatious to the princess. How should she do away with the boy? She took resolve, had a golden chest made, laid the boy therein, and with him much gold and a sword. Then she had him placed in the Danube.

The chest floated away. Somewhere downstream a fisherman caught it. He had just become the father of a child. "Well, mother," he said, "we already have a child, now there are two; well, there's no harm. If

God brought him here, let's raise him too." And they had both the young ones baptized together.

When the boys were older, they often came to blows. The true son rebuked the other: "What do you mean, you who were brought by the wind, borne by the water?" That hurt the boy deeply. He went right to his father, and asked if what the other youth had said was true. His father, or rather the fisherman, confirmed it: "In truth, you are not my child, I only fished you out of the Danube in a chest."

Thereupon the boy was aggrieved. He stayed no longer in the fisherman's house. He thanked them for their kindness, and straightway he departed and went out into the world.

First of all he came to a large city. There he stopped on a street before a palace with gleaming windows. He thought to himself: "What can be there, to cause such radiance? O, how I'd like to get in there!" He had hardly spoken, when suddenly he was in the window, as if he had sprouted wings. There in the room a wondrously pretty young woman was undressing. She caught sight of Janos the Crane. "Come hither, my dearest, to bed. Let's sleep together," she called. But Janos the Crane answered that he wouldn't come. He was already very tired and weak from his trip. The young woman entreated him until he lay down in bed. Janos the Crane placed a sword between them. It was as if there was nothing there. They had soon dealt with one another.

In the morning the woman began to ask the lad where he came from, for she saw that he was handsome and of noble manner. Janos the Crane told her that he himself didn't know, but he had in his pocket a letter from which one could find out. All he knew, he said, was that a fisherman had caught him up in a chest.

The woman read through the letter. Then she turned pale and put it aside. "Woe is me, what have I done?" she sobbed aloud.

"Well, what have you done?" asked Janos the Crane.

"Know that I am your mother!"

"I didn't know that. Well, then, if we have commited such sins, let us go to the pope. Yet perhaps even there we shall find no forgiveness."

They made their way to the pope. For penance it was imposed upon Janos the Crane that for seven years and seven moments he should carry water in his mouth to the root of a dry hazelnut bush. It was the mother's punishment to be locked in a church, and its key to be thrown into the sea.

When the time of Janos the Crane was completed, the seven years and seven moments, then the hazelnut bush bloomed and he was absolved. Then he wandered forth, to seek his mother. But they told him that she was locked in a church and that they had thrown the key into the sea.

Straightway he went thither. He blew into a pipe. The fish came immediately and gave him the key. He opened the church and sought his mother. But he found no one. On the altar fluttered a beautiful white dove. That was his mother. She was holy now too.

He went home; married, and became so happy, that.... He is still alive if he is not dead.

HU2 ANDREW THE ABANDONED CHILD

Source: Lajos Kálmány, *Hagyományok: Mesék és Rokonnemüek,* vol. 1 (Vácz,1914), no. 24, pp. 96–99. From Hódmezö-Vásárhely. Translated by Joseph Falaky Nagy.

Once in the world there was a count who had a wondrously beautiful daughter. The count's wife had died, and the count did not pay much attention to his daughter. The king [*sic*] had a horseman who taught the girl how to ride: she got impregnated by him. So she went to another city, saying she was going to visit relatives—her father would not notice anyway. She gave birth to a boy and arranged for him to be brought up; she herself returned to her father's castle and remained a maiden. No one discovered her secret except the horseman, who shot himself; his six children were taken care of by the count. Only later did the count's daughter have a suitor; he was an officer, and they were married. She had been sending money to her son's nurse, but once she. married, she did not think of her son and did not send anything. The drunken nurse, unwilling to raise the child for nothing, tied a rope around his neck and put him out onto the street.

Dogs surrounded the little child, but a large dog did not allow them to approach the infant. All the dogs were barking in front of a house inside of which was a couple whose own child was just dying. The wife said to the husband: "Look outside, what are the dogs barking about?" The man looked outside and saw the dogs tugging on a little child. He picked up the child and brought it inside, showing it to his wife and saying, "Look, wife, at what I saw on the street; some heartless mother must have abandoned him, but this is good for us, our own son just died today." So they adopted the child, called him Andrew, and sent him to school; he was an outstanding student. Once when Andrew was quarreling with a schoolmate, the latter said: "If only the dogs had torn you apart on the street." Andrew was depressed by this remark; after he came home from school, his parents asked him: "Why are you so sad?" "Mother, it's because of what the Jewish leaseholder's son said, that it would have been better had I been torn apart by the dogs on the street." Then his mother explained to him that he was adopted but was loved by his foster parents as much as if he was their real son. This revelation motivated Andrew to study all the more, until, years later, he passed the ministerial exam. Meanwhile, a girl was born to his foster parents; Andrew taught her and found a suitor for her—she married a teacher. Andrew also helped his foster parents; he loved them as if they were his real parents.

Now let's get back to the officer's wife, Andrew's mother. She was continually disconsolate until she went to visit the woman to whom she had entrusted her child. She asked the nurse where her son was, but the nurse said that he had died and that she had buried him—she showed the mother the burial site. The officer's wife went to church, had a mass said for her dead son, and mourned him. Once her husband noticed her grief and asked what was it that was always bothering her; she did not tell him the truth; she claimed she just had a headache.

One day the officer's wife was at home, and the chambermaid came to her saying, "My lady, the nurse is asking for you; she wants to tell you a secret." Immediately the officer's wife went to the nurse, who was barely alive. The latter said, "Forgive me, my lady, your son is not dead, but I put him out on the street, since I wasn't getting paid and so I couldn't keep him." The mother fainted when she heard this; when she came to, the nurse was dead, and the mother had no idea where her son was or what had happened to him. From then on she was even more disconsolate and would not tell her husband what was wrong. She went to confession where there was a young priest. The husband noticed his wife's frequent confessions; he went to the priest and asked why his wife went so often. The priest answered, because she has sins. The officer went home and threw himself out of the upper story. When people carried him inside, all he said to his wife was, "You could have confided more in me." He then died.

The wife buried her husband and continued to pray for her son and go to confession, but the priest, who already had heard her story, told her to go to the minister in Bánát and tell her sins to him, because if he forgives her, the Lord will too. The mother took a covered carriage and went to this minister; she brought along her niece. The widow left her in the carriage while she went in to the minister. He was just in his room when she came, saying, "I have come to confess, Reverend." He replied: "Our denomination doesn't do confessions, so go to the Catholic priest, he hears confessions." "But *he* sent me—so please give me absolution, I have no peace," said the woman, who kneeled and began to implore the minister. "Well, get up, my good woman, let me hear what your sin is." "I lost my mother early, and my father didn't bother with me—he was always in the cardgame room. We had a riding instructor, a really handsome man, but married, with six children. I used to ride with him into the forest, and I fell in love with him—I bore him a son. No one knew about it, since I found a nurse for my son while I was visiting a relative; I returned to my father's castle and remained single. Later I married an officer. When I became a wife, I stopped sending money to the nurse; afterwards I heard that my son had died, and I was happy. But once the chambermaid comes all of a sudden and says the nurse wants to speak with me—on her deathbed she admitted that she had put the child out on the street . . . oh, that I never gave that child a mother's kiss! The street dogs tore him apart!" The reverend said: "They would have torn him apart, madam, had there not been good people; so get up, mother, and give me my first mother's kiss." The mother leapt up and smothered her son with kisses and thanked God that she had found her lost son.

The girl in the carriage, tired of waiting, said to the driver, "Isn't Aunt Annie taking long!" She opened the door and shouted, "Aren't you long at confessing, Aunt Annie! But now let's rush home; night is approaching, and I've caught a cold." But her aunt said, "No, we are not going anywhere since I have found the one I was looking for." The girl got out of the carriage and went into the room, while the minister sent for his foster parents and told his real mother, "If these good people had not come, the dogs would have eaten me." The lady thanked the foster parents for their goodness and built a nice palace for them, where they lived till they died. The reverend fell in love with the girl [his mother's niece] and married her.

HU3 THE PROPHECY

Source: László Juhász, "Népmese: A jövendeöleis," *Magyar Nyelvőr* 25 (1896): 572–74. Collected in Otrokocs in the county of Gömör. Translated by Gregory Nagy.

There was once a time when there was, when there was not. There was a judge, and the judge had a beautiful young wife. Then once upon a time the wife became pregnant. When they lay down in the evening, so that the wife might give birth, there was a knock on the window. So the judge looked out and what should he see but two young artisans, who asked for lodgings. The judge was kindhearted but said he could not give them lodgings now because his wife was in sickbed. But if they didn't mind, they could lie down on the porch, since the house had a beautiful porch. And that's what happened. The young artisans put their pouches under their heads and lay down in the hay, because this was the growing season, and that's where the hay was stacked, right next to the wall. In the morning, the little child had already been born, and the child cried a bit. He cried so loud that you'd think the pants of Samu[1] were on him. The two young artisans got up; they went into the judge's place to thank him for the lodgings. The judge asked them where they lived and in what direction they were heading. The two young artisans recounted where they were going. "But wait just a second," the judge said, "I'll not let you go until you eat a bit of breakfast." So he invited them into the forehouse. The young artisans sat down. The judge reached into the pantry. He took out a bottle of brandy and a portion of food [*porciaos*] and invited them to partake. They have a drink. Then he goes out into the chamber, and he brings in a big piece of bread and a pound of bacon with paprika, and they eat. When they had had enough, the judge brought the small child, the one who had been born that morning, over to them. Both the young artisans take a look at it. Meanwhile the father goes out to give water to the livestock. While he is gone, one of the two young artisans writes on a scrap of paper: "Let my lord the judge beware of this child, because he will in the future marry his mother and kill his father." And he put this scrap of paper in the pantry. He again sat down at the head of the table. Then they said good-bye. They went away, while the judge stayed at home. Then came the time when the child was eighteen years old. He was very beautiful. If he ever went down the street with his father, who was still the judge, everybody would point at them from every gate. Even the curator said about them that they were like a beautiful pair of oxen. It was sheer wonderment to look at them. But then later the judge became very rich and he wanted to build a new house and he wanted to bring in the old furniture and this particular scrap of paper fell into his hands. He reads it, and then he up and goes off roaming and doesn't say anything to anybody. He doesn't even say, "God give." He just goes away. When the woman comes home from the field, she sees that her husband is not at home. She has the whole village go out and look for him; and then she goes off roaming. She doesn't say anything to anybody. She doesn't even say, "God give." She just goes away. Then, next day, when the boy comes home from the marketplace, he sees that there is no father, no mother. He has the whole village go out and look for them, but they don't find them. So he goes off roaming. He doesn't say anything to anybody. He doesn't even say, "God give." He just goes away. He went and went. It had already been five years that he was looking for his father and mother. He even got used to the idea that he was an orphan, but he still looked for them. Well then, once he came into the middle of a forest, up mountain, down mountain, and he noticed a wildcat in a

---

1. Samu is apparently an archetypal bad little boy who is always getting into trouble and being punished.

tree, but he wasn't afraid of it. The wildcat jumps down, gets on his head, and says to him that he shouldn't go that way because there will be a beautiful maiden and there will be trouble from it. But the boy didn't heed the wildcat, just went on. He went and went, and sure enough, it happened exactly as the wildcat said. A gorgeous, beautiful maiden was sitting there. As soon as the boy, who was now twenty-three years old, saw her, he straightway forgot even what the wildcat had said, and also even that he was looking for his mother and his father. For straightway the maiden sat next to him and he started hugging her. But the maiden also forgot that to her too a wildcat had said that if she sat down somewhere, there would be trouble from it, [and she forgot] that she was looking for her husband and that she was looking for her son. For she felt a beautiful young man next to her. So she started hugging him. In a word, they got to loving each other. They went off to a *puszta* [nonagricultural land], and the boy became a shepherd and the maiden, his wife, she became a shepherdess. One day the shepherd goes out to guard the flock, but comes home for a snack and sees that there is a man lying in his wife's bed. He thought that his wife was cheating on him. He grabbed his *fokos*[2] and killed the man, who was his own father. Then his wife comes in and as soon as she sees the man she straightway faints, because he was her first husband. One glance and the young man was totally disgusted. In the window jumped two wildcats. "You see, I told you so—not to go in that direction. You went there anyway, and now you've up and killed your father and your mother, because, for her, her heart broke, as soon as she found out that, sure enough, it was her former husband."

"So that was my father?"

"It sure was," said the two wildcats simultaneously.

"Oh!" says the shepherd, son of the former judge, "Is it really true?"

"It sure is," say the two wildcats simultaneously, "and your wife was your own mother."

"Oh!" says the boy and goes up to his father and started kissing him, and he even cried. Then he went over to his mother, to that certain maiden whom he met in the forest underneath the tree, the one who then became his wife. He started kissing her, and he even cried. Then he ran out. He would have gone roaming, but meanwhile under that certain tree, there jumped in front of him those two cats. The boy by now knew why, but even the two cats told him anyway that: You have sinned so great a sin that you have to hang yourself right here. And, sure enough, the boy hanged himself. So the prophecy of the two young artisans was fulfilled. That is how God punished him.

2. A small axe on a long helve or at the end of a walking stick.

IT1(GM) CRIVÒLIU

Source: Laura Gonzenbach, *Sicilianische Märchen aus dem Volksmund gesammelt*, pt. 2 (Leipzig, 1870), no. 85 (pp. 159-62). My translation.

There were once a brother and sister who had neither father nor mother and lived alone together. Since they loved one another so much, they committed a sin that they ought not to have committed. When the time came, the sister gave birth to a boy, and the brother had him secretly baptized. Then he etched a cross on his shoulder with the words: "Crivòliu, who has been baptized; son of a brother and sister." When the child had been marked thus, he laid it in a chest and threw the chest out into the sea.

Now it happened that a fisherman had gone out to fish and saw the chest floating around in the sea. "A ship must have sunk somewhere," he thought, "I will fetch the chest, perhaps there's something useful in it." He rowed to the chest and took it. But when he opened it and saw the fine boy, he took pity on the guiltless child, brought it home to his wife and said, "Our youngest child is now old enough to be weaned—in its place nurse this poor guiltless child." So the wife took little Crivòliu and nursed him and loved him as if he were her own child. The boy grew up and throve, and became daily bigger and stronger.

But the sons of the fisherman were jealous that their parents loved the little foundling as much as them, and when they played with Crivòliu and quarreled, they called him a foundling. Then the boy was troubled at heart and went to his foster parents and said, "Dear parents, tell me, am I really not your son?" But the fisherman's wife said, "How should you not be my son? I nursed you at my breast." The fisherman strictly forbade the children to call little Crivòliu foundling.

When the boy was bigger, the fisherman sent him with his sons to school. But since their father could not hear them, the children began again to mock little Crivòliu and to call him foundling, and the other children in the school did likewise. So Crivòliu went again to his foster parents and asked them if he was not their son. But they cut him short and put him off until he was fourteen years old. Since he could no longer endure to be called foundling, he went to the fisherman and his wife and said, "I implore you, tell me if I am your son or not." Then the fisherman told him how he had found him and what could be read on his shoulder. "Then will I depart and do penance for the sins of my parents," said Crivòliu. The fisherman's wife wept and moaned and did not want to let him go. But Crivòliu would not be stopped and went away into the wide world.

After he had wandered a long time, he came at last one day into a lonely region and there stood an inn. He asked the hostess, "Tell me, good lady, is there perchance here in the vicinity a cave, to which you alone know the entrance?" She answered, "Yes, my fair youth, I know such a cave and will gladly take you there." Crivòliu took two loaves of bread and a small pitcher of water, and had the hostess show him to the cave. It was rather far from the inn, and the entrance was so covered with thorns and briers that he could hardly get in. Then he sent the hostess back, crept into the cave, laid the bread and the pitcher on the ground, knelt, and thus with crossed arms did penance for the sins of his parents.

Thus many, many years passed—I don't know how many—but so many that his knees took root and he grew fast to the ground.

Now it happened that in Rome the pope died, and a new one was to be chosen. All the cardinals gathered and a white dove was loosed, since the one upon whom it alighted was to be pope. The dove circled a few times in the air but did not descend on any of the cardinals. Then all the archbishops and the bishops were called, the dove was again loosed, but did not descend on any of them. Then all priests, monks, and hermits were gathered, but the white dove would not choose any of them. The people were greatly bewildered, and the cardinals had to go out and search in the whole land to see if anywhere there was still a hermit who could be found, and many of the people accompanied them.

So they too came finally to the inn in the lonely region and asked the hostess if she perchance knew of a hermit or a penitent who was yet unknown. The hostess answered, "Many years ago a sad young man came hither who had me lead him to a cave to do penance. But he must be long since dead, for he took with him only two loaves of bread and a pitcher of water." But the cardinals said, "We would like to see, however, if he is still alive; lead us to him." So the hostess led them to the cave, but the entrance could hardly be recognized any longer, so densely was it overgrown with thorns, and the servants had to clear the thorns and briers with axes before anyone could enter. When they now came in, they saw Crivòliu kneeling in the cave with crossed arms, and his beard had grown so long that it reached to the ground, and still before him lay the bread and next to it still stood the pitcher of water, since through all the years he had eaten and drunk nothing. When the white dove was now loosed, she flew around for a moment in a circle and then alighted on the head of the penitent. So the cardinals recognized that he was a saint and bade him consent to come with them and be their pope. But when they tried to lift him up, they noticed that his knees had grown fast to the ground, and they had to cut the roots first. Then they took him with them to Rome and he became pope.

Now it happened that at the same time the sister said to her brother, "Dear brother, when we were young we committed a sin that we have not yet confessed, since only the pope can absolve us of it. So let us go to Rome before death overtakes us and there confess our sin. So they prepared to go to Rome, and when they arrived they went into a church where the pope sat in the confessional.

But when they had confessed in a loud voice (since one always confesses publicly before the pope), the pope said, "Behold, I am your son, since upon my shoulder is the sign of which you speak. For your sin have I done penance many years, until it has been forgiven you. So I absolve you of your sin, and you are to dwell with me and be at ease." So they stayed with him, and when the time came, the Lord called them all three to His heavenly kingdom.

IT2 VERGOGNA

Source: Alessandro d'Ancona, *La Leggenda di Vergogna, etc.* (Bologna, 1869), pp. 2–29. D'Ancona says of his source: "We give an early, unpublished text taken from cod. palatine-panchiatichian n. 75, somewhat different from that which has already been published by the indefatigable Cav. Commend. Francesco Zambrini under the title, *Novella d'un barrone di Faraona* [Lucca, 1853; 33 pages; edition of eighty copies]." D'Ancona also publishes in this volume a version of the Vergogna tale in verse. A note in the manuscript attributes this poem to a fifteenth-century Florentine. Note: in d'Ancona's volume, there are two separate paginations: the introduction (pp. 5–113), including an appendix by D. Comparetti (pp. 115–29), and the tales (pp. 1–100). Translated by Carmela V. Franklin.

In the kingdom of Faragona there was a great baron whose wife was one of the most beautiful women in the whole kingdom, and the wisest. She was also a great friend of God, and it pleased God that this woman should have a most serious disease that caused her to depart from this life. Realizing that she was so sick that she could not get well, she called her husband and told him: "My lord and mate, I am going to the next world as it is the pleasure of Jesus Christ, my Lord, that I should not stay any longer in this wretched one. Thus, I recommend to you above everything else the safety of your soul so that when God will call you to him you will not be afraid to appear in his presence. And next, I recommend to you our daughter. Watch over her and take great care of her, because, as you see, God gave her great beauty that she should struggle more. And if she will be able to defend herself in the struggle of the flesh when she is young, she will receive a great crown in heaven. But I doubt and am fearful that she will not be able to defend herself in the struggle of human nature: take care of her wisely and protect her purely." When she had finished speaking these words, she asked for the girl. She made the sign of the cross on her forehead and blessed her, asking God to bestow his grace and love upon her and to give her the virtue needed to save her soul. And when she had finished, the woman, as it pleased God's will, departed from this life in holy peace.

Her husband was filled with grief because he loved his wife very much. And because of what she had said, he began to watch over his daughter and care for her with great diligence. He found, in fact, three nannies to feed and nurse her so that she might be better taken care of. And behold, as the girl grew older, she became so beautiful that everybody who saw her was astonished, and many women and girls of the kingdom of Faragona would go to see her as if she was a marvel, and they would say to each other: "Truly, she is the most beautiful girl ever born in the kingdom of Faragona."

The girl was fifteen years old and was indeed the most beautiful girl ever seen. The kingdom's counts and barons asked for her hand because of her beauty. Her father, however, would in no way consent to marry her off but, on the contrary, considered her a great enjoyment and thought that she was his paradise on earth. As the baron was so disposed, Lucifer, the leader of Hell, tempted him to sin with his daughter and fought and battled with him so much that the baron finally succumbed and was ruined. He took her and made her pregnant.

When the girl saw that she was pregnant by her father, she could not stop crying and thought of herself as the most wretched, most unhappy, most unfortunate woman ever born into this world. The father, seeing his daughter crying and grieving asked her: "What is wrong with you my daughter? Why do you never stop crying and moaning?" The daughter answered: "I have more reason to cry than any other unfortunate woman ever born in this world because I am pregnant by you who are my father. I want to be buried alive or drowned. I do not want to live in this world anymore because my hard fate has led me to this mean and wicked state. What is my life worth to me now that I have lost the grace and love of him who created me? Now that I have lost my good name, my good reputation, and my purity?" The father replied: "I am the most unhappy and wretched sinner who was ever born into this world. I let the infernal enemy be too successful over me. However, take comfort, my daughter, and lessen your sorrow, because from this sin that we have committed, we shall return to God's mercy, and he will forgive us out of his great kindness. Conceal this sin, for otherwise too much dishonor would befall us. We shall make our peace with God." The girl replied: "I shall do all this. But I pray the King of Glory that he make me die during childbirth so that I won't have to live this wretched life anymore. What is my life worth to me now that I made myself an enemy to him who brought me into this world and who must take me out of it again and whose grace and love I have now lost?" The father answered: "St. Mary Magdalen was greater after her sin than before. The same is true of many saints who were sinners and God's enemies until they did penance and returned to his mercy. God forgave them, and they are now in Heaven. Thus, do not despair, my daughter."

And behold, her time came, and she gave birth to a male child, the most beautiful child ever seen. During labor, the father alone was present to provide whatever was necessary and to deliver the child. The girl asked for the baby, took it in her arms, made the sign of the cross on his forehead, and blessed it. She prayed God to give him His grace and His love and then she started to wail: "O my son, what will become of you, born from such filthy sin, and of me who conceived you?" And thus saying, she wetted her son's face with her tears. The father, seeing his daughter crying and grieving, told her: "Be quiet, my daughter; do not trouble yourself so much. I would rather have the sin than dishonor in the eyes of the world. I want to put this child in a small boat at sea. His fate will be determined by God who created him and who will bestow His grace on him." They had him baptized secretly and named him Vergogna [Shame] because they were putting him to sea to hide their shame. They wrapped him in a beautiful golden cloth and tied around his neck an inscription that said: "This child has been baptized and named Vergogna. He is the son of a noble baron and a noble lady." And then, one early morning, he got up, put the baby in the small boat, blessed him, and abandoned him to his fate.

As it pleased God's will, a favorable wind arose that brought the little boat to Egypt's port. Some fishermen who were fishing found the boat with the beautiful baby in it. They immediately brought him to the lord king and queen of Egypt as a marvel. When the king and queen saw him, they were extremely happy because they had no children either male or female. They sent for two nannies so that he might be well nursed and taken care of. As the boy was growing, he was so handsome that everyone who saw him was astonished. The king loved him as his own son, and the queen also loved him as though she had borne him herself. The boy was now fifteen and was considered the most handsome youth in the whole kingdom. Everybody at court loved him for his beauty and his goodness, and everybody in the city honored and revered him as if he were the son of the king and queen.

And it pleased the king and queen to change his name and call him Girardo Aventuroso. And so he was called. Now, let us leave his account and return to his parents, who never stopped crying, neither during the day nor at night, because they had fallen into such sordid sin. One day, being in great misery, the father said: "Daughter, I have decided to go on a pilgrimage to Jerusalem for the good of my soul. I want to visit the holy places where our Lord Jesus Christ suffered his passion for us and all of mankind. I want to make this pilgrimage for the remission of your sins and mine, that they be forgiven by Jesus Christ." And immediately he ordered and prepared his equipage for the pilgrimage. Before he went, he took his daughter to a monastery of holy women, friends of God, whose abbess was the baron's sister. She was a woman of holy life. When he had disposed of all his business at home and given all necessary instructions, he took his staff and his purse and started his trip to Jerusalem in God's honor. When he arrived, he made a thorough confession of all his sins. For penance, he was told to mortify his body by fasting, praying, and keeping vigil and by living a holy and angelic life. The girl was staying at the convent, leading a good and holy life. And this lasted a good while. As it pleased God, the baron fell gravely sick and passed away in great peace. He had lived a righteous life so consistently that God forgave him his sins. Before he died, he asked that after his death the news be sent to his daughter. As soon as he was buried, a messenger was sent to his daughter with letters to announce his death.

And so, while the girl was still with the holy women, the messenger arrived bearing the letters that recounted how her father had died and how his body was buried in Jerusalem. When they heard that he had died in holy peace, the girl and the abbess praised God and His power.

When the barons of the country heard the news of the father's death in Jerusalem, they informed the girl that they wanted to give her a husband. The girl refused to marry under any circumstances. She wanted to stay with those holy women instead and to make penance for her sins. The barons, as they could not induce her to marry, took away from her all her castles and cities with all her belongings and took possession of them themselves. The girl had nothing left to live on. When she saw herself reduced to such a condition, she started to cry and call herself the most wretched, unfortunate creature ever born. Thus crying and wailing, she went before the image of our Lord Jesus Christ and humbly begged him not to abandon her and to advise her on what to do. While praying, she fell asleep in front of Christ's image. During her sleep, she saw a vision that told her: "I am the Angel sent to you by God the Father to tell you that he has heard your prayers. He wants you to go without delay to the room where your father used to sleep. Search the boxes and chests kept there and you will find a great quantity of gold and silver coins. As soon as you have found them, send for your closest relatives and tell them what I say. Tell them to hire as many people as they can and to start a war against those barons who have occupied your castles and cities. And I tell you that you will have in your service someone who will get your castles and cities back for you." As soon as these words were uttered, the angel disappeared. The woman woke up and without delay went to the abbess, who was her father's sister, and told her secretly of her vision. The abbess decided to go with her and took along the two nuns who were closest to her and were great friends of God. They reached the above-mentioned place and unlocked all chests, coffers, boxes, and any other container they found there. They found the money as the angel had said and in such quantity that a large number of knights and foot soldiers could be hired.

Without delay, they sent for the woman's closest friends and relatives. They showed them the treasure they had found, and the girl reported all the angel had said. They thus announced that any knight or foot soldier who wanted to be hired should come to such and such a place. In a short time they had many soldiers and started a big and pressing war against the barons who had occupied her castles and cities.

The news reached the kingdom of Egypt that one of the most beautiful girls in the world was warring against the barons of Faragona and was offering money to foot soldiers and knights and that the war was rough and hard. When Vergogna heard this, he felt a great desire to go see her, not knowing that she was his mother or his sister.

Thus one day, he went to the king and said: "Lord, I beg of you to give me arms and horse. I hear that a noble lady of the kingdom of Faragona is fighting against the barons of that country and is offering good money to foot soldiers and knights. If it is agreeable to you, I would like to go and try my valor at war." The king and queen were very grieved at Vergogna's desire to go because they loved him as their own son. But because this was the first time he had asked anything, the king did not want to refuse him. He told him: "Son, this trip could bring you good fortune and great wealth. Take the best arms I have and the best horses from my stables. Furthermore, I want to give you fifty youths, all sons of counts and great barons, to accompany you. Take as much gold and silver as you please so that you will be well provided for in your trip. Go with God's blessing and mine. Because this is the first gift and favor you have asked me, I do not wish to deny you. But this I want to order you, that for my sake you return as soon as possible." Vergogna answered: "Lord, I will surely do this, if it be God's will."

On the next day, Vergogna took his leave from the king, the queen, and the entire court. He and his fifty companions mounted their horses and started to gallop towards the kingdom of Faragona. They went so far by land and sea until, as it pleased God, they reached safe and sound the kingdom of Faragona. When they arrived in the city where his mother lived, they immediately went to her palace, in front of which was a young man posted to guard the door. Vergogna told him: "Please go to your lady and tell her that fifty knights have come from the kingdom of Egypt to be hired by her whenever she pleases. Tell her that we are all sons of counts and great barons and we boast that we can give her certain victory."

The young man went immediately to his lady and gave her Vergogna's message. She told him to let them come up, as she wanted to see them and talk to them immediately. The young man went back and led them where the lady was. Vergogna and his companions knelt before her and greeted her with great reverence, and she returned the greeting. Vergogna said: "Lady, my companions and I are from the kingdom of Egypt and have come here to be hired in your service whenever it may please you. We are all sons of counts and great barons, and we boast that we can give you certain victory."

The lady then said that they were welcome and honored. She had them given great pay. And as soon as she saw Vergogna, she was smitten with love for him, not knowing that he was her son and her brother. And he similarly, as soon as he saw her, also fell in love with her, not knowing that she was his mother and sister.

On the next day, Vergogna and his companions rode where the army of the woman's enemies was encamped. As soon as he arrived, he asked for his father's flag, he arranged his troops and fighters, and then fought bravely with his comrades. The battle was rough and hard, but finally, as it pleased God, the woman's enemies were defeated with all their people, two of whom were taken captive. In a short while they recovered all the castles and cities that those barons had taken away from the woman.

The woman's friends, seeing such beauty and valor and good sense in Vergogna, consulted among themselves, and each said to the other: "We all see that because of this noble youth we have been victorious in this war. And thus it seems to me that we should give him our relative for a wife. Otherwise, if we allow him to go, we shall have greater war with them than we had before." All agreed to this. Forthwith, they went to the woman and explained their plan to her. She answered that she was ready to do whatever they wanted. They then went to Vergogna, and he agreed to it. And thus, they gave him for a wife his mother and sister.

Living together, they enjoyed each other and led a very good life together because each enjoyed the other. He had himself called Girardo Aventuroso. They had lived together for a while in mutual love and affection when, one day, being very hot, as they were spending the afternoon in amusement and merriment with each other in their room, the woman said: "My love, mate and husband, I would like to know at your convenience about your background, your family, and your place of birth." Vergogna answered her by saying: "Noble lady, my life and hope, I don't know anything about my family or how or when I was born or whose child I am. I know only this about my background, that I was found, wrapped in a golden cloth in a small boat with an inscription around my neck that said: 'This child has been baptized, and his name is Vergogna. He is the son of a noble baron and a noble lady.' Some fishermen who were fishing on the sea took the little boat where I was and brought me to the king and queen of Egypt. They fed me, brought me up, and raised me to very great honor. I stayed with them until the day I left to come here into your service. I do not know what else to tell you, lady, of my family and birth."

When the woman heard this, she felt such pain in her heart that she fell unconscious to the floor, and it was a long time before she revived. When she came to, she started tearing her clothing from her breast to her feet, and crying profusely, told him: "Surely you are my son, and son of my father who conceived you in me, miserable, wretched creature! Out of shame we put you in that little boat where you were found and left you to your fate. Now I see that in this world there is no good fortune, but only misfortune and great danger and pain. O my son, what a horrible situation do we—you and I—find ourselves in! O wicked world! O sin! O sweet flesh, how were you deceived? O God, lord omnipotent, why did you allow such power and license to the infernal enemy over this miserable, wretched, unfortunate creature? O Lord, you who have created me, please do not abandon me! You have slammed Heaven's doors against me, tied with the chains of sin because of my beauty! Alas, cursed beauty, how bitter you have become for me! Happy are you girls and women who have no beauty, for beauty gets you nothing but a trip to hell and an unending battle against the flesh. You do not realize the favor God has bestowed on you!" Thus the woman grieved and lamented. Vergogna hearing such laments from his mother, wife, and sister, told her: "Mother, do not cry and exhaust your soul and body, because God's mercy is greater than our wickedness, his kindness greater than our sins. God demands nothing but the heart of the sinner, and if our heart repents of the sin we have committed, God will forgive us out of his kindness. Thus, mother, I want us to sell all that we own and give it to Christ's poor for God's sake. Then, I want us to go to Rome to the holy pope, vicar of God. We shall confess all of our sins to him and do with good courage whatever penance he will assign to us."

The woman said: "Son, I agree to it." Immediately they sold their possessions and gave them to Christ's poor. They then started their trip to Rome to the holy pope. On their way, everyone gazed at the woman's face because it was so beautiful and pleasing. She, seeing that every man stared at her told her son: "Son, I am afraid that I may be dishonored and that you may be harmed and shamed because of me. I want to wear a helmet and man's clothes so that we may travel safely." This was immediately done, and they made their trip without impediment. As it pleased God, they reached Rome and immediately went to the holy pope and made a thorough and diligent confession of all their sins. The pope recognizing that the deed was done inadvertently, made the sign of the cross, blessed them, forgave them all their sins, and gave them this penance: Vergogna should become a monk in the monastery of St. Presedia in Rome and the mother should enter the convent of St. Chiara in Rome and they should never see each other. Vergogna, living in the monastery with the holy monks, friends of God, began to practice great abstinence by keeping fasts and vigils, by praying and living an angelic life. He lived in this way pleasing to God for eleven years. At the end of eleven years he was stricken by a very grave disease, and he passed to heaven in great peace.

The mother survived him by eighteen months, and then she passed away in great peace. As her son, who led a holy and good life, she too conducted herself so well that at her death she gained heaven. Before she died, she begged her abbess to do her the favor of going to the pope and begging him to allow her body to be buried in the tomb of her blessed son. The abbess went to the pope and asked for the favor. The pope, hearing that both had died in holy peace, granted her wish and thus gave great honor to her body. And such perfume came from it that it seemed as though all the nutmeg trees in the world were in bloom. The pope had the following words written in golden letters on the tomb in which they were both buried:

"Here lie two dead bodies, mother and son, sister and brother, wife and husband, born of a great baron in the kingdom of Faragona, who are now in heaven."

Let whoever goes to Rome go to the monastery of St. Presedia, and he will see these words written in gold on the tomb where these two blessed bodies are buried.

IT3 SALVATORE

Source: Hermann Knust, "Italienische Märchen," *Jahrbuch für romanische und englische Literatur* 7 (1866): 398–401 = Allessandro d'Ancona, *La Leggenda di Vergogna . . .* (Bologna, 1869), pp. 69–77. Knust and a motley group of travelers heard these tales from an old, illiterate *guardia marina* who boarded their ship at Leghorn and remained during a three-day quarantine in the harbor of Genoa. Each evening he told tales on deck. Knust later went to Leghorn and had the man tell him the tales again (pp. 381–82). Translated by Carmela V. Franklin.

Once upon a time there were a husband and wife who had two children, a boy and a girl. They had so much money that they did not know what to do with it. On his deathbed, the father calls his wife and tells her: "Wife, before you die, be sure to make your will." And he dies. His wife becomes sick and says to her son and her daughter: "Son, I am sick. Today or tomorrow God will call me to him. All this money, all these riches—keep them in the house." The son replies: "Don't worry about it. Be certain that we will do what you say." The mother dies, and the brother and sister are left. When they grow up, the brother wants to take a wife and the sister a husband. But according to the will that their mother had left, neither the gold nor the silver nor the money could be touched. The brother then tells his sister: "Let us take our pleasure in each other." The sister becomes pregnant and gives birth to a son with a beautiful tress of red hair. They put him in a small box and throw him in a river. The current carries him out towards an island. There happens to be a lord jumping into the sea who sees the box. He takes it, opens it to see what there is inside, and sees a very beautiful babe. He picks him up and takes him home, where he tells his wife: "Wife, I have found this baby on the sea. Give him some milk, some julep, and we will act as if he were our son."

They raise him up, and when he is eight years old, they send him to school to learn to read and write. They had also another child, who always told him: "You are not my brother; my father found you on the sea." The other cries and says: "Lord, my brother injures and mistreats me. He says you are not my father. Give me your blessing: I want to go and find my parents."

And so, this poor eight-year-old child begins to wander and is forced to beg. And while traveling through a city, the wretch enters a shop and begs for a little charity. In this shop were the brother and sister who were moved to pity. "We have no son, we have nobody. Let's invite this poor child to our house. Let us give him food and drink." They keep him at home for a good eight years. The child is now sixteen. Then, one day, the brother says to his sister: "Listen, let us give up our sin. We have eaten together for many years. We have had this youth in our house now for eight years. Take him for your husband." She replies: "Yes, brother, you have thought well." And thus, when they are eating together in the evening, he says: "Salvatore, would you marry my sister? You will lack nothing: there is lots of money, gold and silver: you will be a lord."—"If you are satisfied, so am I." They were married on Sunday. There is great mirth. At night they ate and then went to bed to sleep. The bride wakes up: "Treason!" The brother gets up, rushes in and asks: "What is wrong?"—"Brother, I recognized that this is my son; I recognized the braid of hair. A great sin has been committed." The youth wakes up: "What is the matter?"—"Son, I embrace you and kiss you as a son and as husband you are in great sin towards me."—"What? You are my mother? He is my father? I, your son, have committed a great sin against you. But do not despair. I am going to expiate my sins against you. Dear mother, dear father, give me your holy blessing. I want to go and be a wanderer in the world." He went into a thicket and began to eat wild grass and drink water from a well. And he nourished himself with this. He beat his breast with a stone in his hand and prayed incessantly to God. He lived this holy life for two years. His hair was long and so was his beard: he looked like a bandit. And behold, the holy father dies in Rome. A pilgrim is wanted for pope. All of Rome's cardinals searched in all the woods and thus found him in a grotto while he was entrusting his soul to God. The people asked him: "Who are you?" He answers: "I am a Christian through the grace of God."—"Why are you here?"—"Because of my great sins." They put him on a balda-chin, carry him to the church in Rome, and make him forthwith Holy Father. He published a ban that whatever sins a person had committed, he should come to him and would be forgiven. The sister tells her brother: "We have a great sin on our conscience, and we are old. Let us go to the pope of Rome and see if he will forgive us the great sins we have committed against each other."—"You are right, sister. Let us go." They start for Rome, and while on the road they see the Holy Father in a procession. The brother and sister kneel on the ground and begin to shout: "Holy Father, forgive us!" The pope turns around, recognizes them, and tells them: "Go to the church. When I have finished the pro-cession, I shall come and confess you." He finished the procession, went to church, gave his holy blessing, and went to the confessional. He calls the man and says to him: "Tell me your sins."—"I had a son from my sister, and I had the courage to throw him into the sea." The Holy Father says: "Dear father, I am your son. I forgive you all the sins you have committed until now." And he blesses him. Then he turns to his mother: "Tell me your sins."—"Holy Father, I gave birth to my brother's son. I threw him into the sea. I saw a poor young beggar. I brought him up for eight years and then married him. When I married him, I realized that he was my son. Father, forgive me."—"Dear mother, yes, I forgive you."—"Son, now I am happy and die happy because you are pope." And while saying these words, all three embraced together. They raise their eyes on high and say: "God, you have forgiven us. Now we shall go to heaven's eternal glory." And they died embraced together. They are put in a tomb that is still in the church of St. Peter in Rome.

SP1 RIDDLE TALE*

Source: Aurelio M. Espinosa, *Cuentos Populares Españoles,* vol. 1 (Madrid, 1946), no. 19 (p. 46). For a brief discussion and list of parallels, see ibid., 2: 149-51. Translated by Susan T. Edmunds.

I bring with me, Holy Father,
Three sins of ignorance
For this woman whom I bring here
Is my wife, my daughter, and my sister.

There once was a maid who served a lady. The lady's son made amorous advances toward the maid, and she said to the lady,

"Mistress, I shall leave tomorrow, because your son makes amorous advances toward me."

Then the mistress said,

"I shall lie in your bed."

Then the son got into the bed, thinking that it was the maid, and he made his mother pregnant. She gave birth to a daughter, with whom, after a number of years, the son fell in love, without knowing it was his daughter, and he married her. When he found out to whom he was married, he went to Rome to ask pardon from the pope.

FI1 THE MAN WHO WATERED THE TREE STUMP

Source: Suomalaisen Kirjallisuuden Seura (Association of Finnish Literature), Helsinki, collected by Nikolai Ruusunen. Told by Herman Ketonen, born 1875, parish of Messuklyä; he heard it from a Russian pedlar in the village of Heikkilä, Arkangeli. Translated by Marja Heinonen.

There were two apostles walking around the world, and one evening they arrived at an inn and asked for lodgings. But as the innkeeper saw that they came on foot, he did not let them have a room but sent them to the bakery. The women had been baking all day, so the apostles could not have asked for a better place, and they climbed on the big oven and lay down.

In the night they heard moans and screams from the bedroom next to the bakery. And from the stables they heard pitiful bleating. So the younger apostle asked the older one: "What is happening in the stable?"

"There is a ewe lambing, and she is in great pain," the older apostle answered.

"Why don't you help her out of this suffering?" the younger one said.

"It would not be of much good, because they will be eaten by a wolf anyway, both the ewe and the lamb."

"Even so, help them now."

The innkeeper had overheard all this talk, and he shook his head thinking, now how could you possibly know that?

"Then the younger apostle started again and asked: "What is happening in the bedroom?"

"The innkeeper's wife is having a child, and she is in great pain."

"So why don't you help her?"

"It would be better not to help, but to let them die. That would prevent great sins, the mother's sins and the boy's."

"What sins?" the younger one asked.

"Murder and incest."

"How would those be committed?" the other one kept asking.

"The boy that would be born, would kill his father and marry his mother."

"Even so, help the mother now," the younger apostle insisted. So the older apostle let the child be born, and it was a boy. Now the innkeeper had heard all this too, and he started planning how he could prevent the predictions from coming true. So when the boy was to be christened, he made it a big feast and had both the ewe and the lamb slaughtered. When the roasts were done, they were put on the window to cool, and since it was winter and the wolves were starving and therefore very bold, one of the pack came and snatched the meat from the window. And when the people came to fetch the meat, they looked out and saw a wolf gnawing the last bones of the sheep. The innkeeper was really frightened now that the first prediction had already come true. And he thought and thought how he best could escape the other.

In the spring he took the child to the river and threw him, swaddled, into the water: that boy was never to come and kill him or to marry his mother.

The infant boy drifted for miles with the current, and a gentleman who was rowing on the river happened to see him. The swaddling clothes had kept him afloat. And the man took him to his house and he lived there for eighteen years. On his chest the boy had a black mark that did not wash off: it was as if he was meant to have it, and he had had it from his birth.

Then the gentleman died, and the boy had to leave the house. He started wandering around looking for work where he could find it. At last he came to his parents' house. His mother was there, a handsome woman who did not look like her age but almost seemed like a young girl.

She told the boy that they could certainly use a farmhand, as the farmer himself was getting old and could no longer manage all the work by himself. But she did not dare to promise anything until her husband came home; he was out just now.

The evening came, and there was no sign of the farmer.

Now the wife told the boy that they had had trouble with thieves coming to their storehouse [*aitta*] and that it would please her very much if the boy went there with a gun to watch for the night. He was to shoot at once if any one tried to break in. It was midwinter and a beautiful full moon.

Well, the boy sat on watch and waited. Then he saw someone come out from the woods. The man had a long bar on his shoulder, he walked straight to the storehouse, kneeled before the door, and then pushed the bar under the door. The boy felt that this must be a thief, and he shot the man to death.

Then he went to tell the farmer's wife that he had shot a thief, and together they went to see who the man was.

The wife, of course, recognized her own husband immediately: he had meant to repair the floor of the storehouse and had been trying to push in a new log through the cathole in the door. The wife wept and cried, but then understood that it did not help. And she comforted herself by thinking how old her husband had been: maybe he would not have had a much longer life anyway.

The farmhand stayed in the house, and as time passed, he became very close with the woman, and they lived together as any couple and slept in the same bed.

One day in the sauna, the woman noticed the black mark on the man's chest and asked how he got it. The man said that he had had it all his life and told her how this gentleman had found him in the river. Now the woman realized that he could only be her own son, and she remembered the apostles' prediction, which had now become true. They were much anguished and went to the priest to tell him what had happened. Even the priest was alarmed, and he wrote to the bishop, asking for advice. The bishop summoned all priests to a meeting. For three months they were assembled and then came to a decision: the man was to find a spring and from that spring carry water with a sieve to an age-old tree stump. The mother was to sit near by, a black sheep in her lap. This they had to do until leaves began to shoot forth from the tar of the stump and until the black sheep had turned white. The boy started to carry water with the sieve and the mother sat beside him, and for twelve years he watered the stump, but it never showed a sprout.

About once a year a big fat prelate used to pass by, driving a cart. He always had a big sack full of money, and he laughed at the boy and his mother and scorned their futile effort.

When this happened for the twelfth time, the boy was enraged, and he stood up and killed the prelate. As he then came back to water the stump, it was suddenly full of green sprouts, and the black sheep had turned white.

Now they went to the priest again to tell him that the stump had shot new leaves and that the black sheep had turned white.

The priest was amazed, because he had counted on three more years of penitence for them, and he asked what other good works the boy had done to his merit. The boy said that he had done nothing good, on the contrary, he had again committed a crime and a sin. He had killed the fat prelate, but soon afterwards the stump had shot forth all these leaves and the sheep had turned white.

So the priest said that he, in fact, had done good by killing the prelate: that man never preached, but he took the curates' pay, and that was all he ever did in his life.

FI2 KILLED HIS FATHER AND MARRIED HIS MOTHER

Source: Suomalaisen Kirjallisuuden Seura (Association of Finnish Literature), Helsinki, collected by Juho Karvinen, in 1935, in Sortavala. Translated by Marja Heinonen.

In a farmhouse the farmer's wife was lying in fearful labor pains and at the very same time the ewe was lambing and she was also having trouble. A traveling stranger passed by, and the farmer asked him to come in and told him about their troubles.

The stranger said: "You poor man. Even if the ewe has a lamb, it will be of little good, because the wolf is going to eat it. And if your wife has a child, he will kill his father and marry his mother." Then a boy was born, and he was their first son. And the ewe got a lamb, and it was a ram.

The farmer and his wife were quite alarmed because of the stranger's predictions. The lamb was watched over very carefully so that the wolf could not get it, and when it was grown up and fattened, they slaughtered it, to be once and for all rid of these fears. The farmer killed it, skinned it, opened the stomach and cleaned it, and finally hung the carcass in an open shed.

Then he ran to his wife and said: "Now we do not have to worry any longer. No wolf ever got the lamb. Come and see how fat he is. Now we can celebrate and make a really good dinner."

Together they went over to see the slaughtered ram. They came to the shed, and to their horror they see a wolf running across the yard with the carcass.

The mother starts moaning: "Oh, almighty heavens, what shall we do with the boy? He will kill you and then marry me."

"What shall we do? I have to kill him. With this knife I killed the ram; with the same knife I will cut his throat." The farmer stepped in the house and went straight to the child to kill him, but his wife ran after him and said: "No, we cannot kill him. Oh, now you already wounded him."

"He will not die of a wound like this. But what can we do? He is going to kill me and then marry you. We have to get rid of him."

"We could tie him to a board and push him to sea: maybe a pharoah's daughter will find him and make him another Moses."

So they bandaged the boy's wound and then tied him to the board and threw him to sea.

The waves carried him along, and one day a big ship spotted him and he was taken on board. Then, at the first port in England, they stopped and left the child to the authorities. There he was taken care of, and he grew up to be a man. He wanted to see the world, and so he started traveling and finally came to the country where he was born. He went to a restaurant, and his father happened to be there. Now the father recognized him because of the likeness and the scar on his throat. And he feigned to make friends with the boy and then lured him to a steep cliff at the sea.

"Now, you scoundrel and knave, now you will die. Nothing will save you this time," the father said and grabbed his son. But the boy was quicker, and in the struggle he pushed the father over the cliff into the sea, where he soon drowned.

The boy went on wandering around the country, and one evening he stayed for the night in the house of his parents.

The woman of the house told him that she had been alone for a whole year already: her husband had gone to town and then disappeared, and no one knew where he had gone.

"You look like an honest man. I wonder if you could stay. I am doing quite well, but I need somebody to do the man's work. And a good man I will consider as the master of the house."

"That is fine," the boy said. "I have no ties. I am an orphan, no father or mother or home."

"So you will stay?"

"I will."

The time passed. The woman had already fallen in love with the young man, and he, on the other hand, had thought of proposing to her. She was, after all, a handsome woman, and if they married, he would get the farm. One day as they were having supper, the woman said: "Haven't you ever thought of marrying?"

"Who would care for a poor tramp like me?"

"Who? Well, all the girls seem to be after you, so is the neighbor's widow. And, for that matter, I myself would not mind having you either."

The boy jumped up, quite overwhelmed, and they embraced and lay down on the bench, kissing each other and full of love.

"We will have to go to the vicar," the woman said. "Next Sunday we can have the banns called."

They did so and were married, and they lived together for a while. Then the wife happened to notice the scar on her husband's throat and asked how he got it.

The man explained: "I was found in the sea with this wound, and I was tied on a board. A big ship spotted me, and they saved my life." His wife embraced him and said, with joy and sorrow: "You are my son—you are my husband—my son. We have sinned, in a horrible way."

"So you are my mother?"

"You were to kill your father, that is what the stranger said even before you were born. Have you ever killed a man?"

"Yes, I have. In town a man pretended to be my friend, and he took me to the cliff and tried to push me over and he said: "Nothing can save you this time." But I was quicker, and in the fight I pushed him over to the sea and he drowned."

FI3 OEDIPUS TALE*

Source: Suomalaisen Kirjallisuuden Seura (Association of Finnish Literature), Helsinki, collected by A. V. Koskimies, in Pielavesi. Set down in the 1880s by Heikki Väätänen, who had heard the tale thirty-two years earlier from a man then sixty years of age. Translated by Marja Heinonen.

Quite a long time must be gone since all this happened, and I think it happened somewhere along the coast of the Gulf of Finland. At that time people were rather backward and did not know much about civilization. So there was this man and his wife, and the wife, in the course of nature, became pregnant. So did one of the sheep. Now two wizards came to the house, one of them the master wizard and the other the apprentice. It was the time of lambing for the ewe, and she had great pain, and even as they were resting in the house, the wizards knew what was happening. So the younger one said to his master that they should help the ewe, but the master answered that their help would be no good because what was going to be born was a ram, and that ram would be eaten up by a wolf. The farmer heard this, and his wife heard this: she herself was in labor. And the apprentice once again said that they should help the poor woman as she was in great pain, but again the master said that their help would be of no good, because the child that would be born would be a boy who would kill his father and marry his mother. The farmer heard all this and kept it in his mind. Half a year went by, and, autumn coming, the ram was slaughtered. They cooked the meat and set it out on the window to cool. But while they were eating the broth, a wolf came and snatched the meat. After they had finished the broth, they went to fetch the bowl of meat, and all they saw was a fresh wolf track, just outside. Now the farmer remembered what the two wizards had predicted, and he took the child from the cradle and his knife from the wall and slashed the baby's chest, wanting to kill him. But his wife, the mother, stopped him and said that they should not kill him but take him elsewhere. They thought for a while, and then the mother said that she could put him out to sea in a big milk can. This was agreed upon, and the mother then took a wooden milk vessel and put the boy inside and threw him into the sea. The wind was from the north and very gusty, and in no time it carried the boy to the shores of Estonia. There some people were fishing and they found the poor child. They must have been good Christians, because they fed the boy and brought him up until he was something like fifteen or sixteen years old. At that time there was no telegraph or telephone and very few newspapers, so that even an incident like this [lacuna in the text]. But the boy grew restless and wanted to travel. He did not know where: the only thing he had heard was that he had been brought to Estonia by a northerly wind. But he was quick and smart and started wandering by land, working for his living. For three years he traveled like this, working here and there until he happened to come to the house where he was to get married. When he first arrived at the farm, he asked for work, and as the farmer was not at home, the farmer's wife hired him, gave him a bow and arrow, sent him to guard the turnip field, and told him to shoot anyone who came there. The boy went to the field. The farmer, however, happened to be in the forest looking for wood for some tools he needed, and as he walked around, he crossed the turnip field. The boy did not know the farmer, and obeying his orders, he shot him, then went on watching and came home when it was already dark. In the house they still waited for the farmer, but nobody had seen him. Then the morning came, and the farmer's wife went with the boy to the field to see the dead man. She saw that it was her husband, but there was nothing she could do. She herself had told the boy to shoot whoever came. So life went on in the house, the boy stayed there as a farmhand. But when a couple of years had passed, they began to think of marriage. And so it happened that they went to the vicar and had their banns called, and then they were married and lived together for many years. Once as they went bathing, the wife happened to notice the long scar on the man's chest, and she asked how he got it. The man said that his family had told him that they had found him as a child in a milk vessel in the sea, and even then he had had this wound. Now the wife remembered the two wizards' prediction, and word by word she told it to the man. Now they started to live as mother and son, and then later they set off on the road to confess and do penance. They walked and they walked, and one day they met an old monastery man with a Bible under his arm. They said to him: "We are great sinners and evildoers, and I have killed my father and married my mother. Such is our sin and can we ever be set free?" The monk looks in his Bible, and after a while tells them that there is no remittance for their sin. Now the boy's heart, which is already tormented by grief, gets inflamed and he hits the monk and kills him. They started walking again, mother and son, and they walked and walked. Then they meet another monk, this one also has a Bible under his arm. The boy tells him about his sins and also confesses killing the monk. The old one consults his book and says that such sins cannot be remitted. Hearing this, the boy kills him. They went on walking, and they happened to meet a doctor of the New Teaching,[1] and they confessed to him and also told him about the killing of the two monks. The professor consulted his books very seriously and said that there was no sin that could not be remitted if the penitence was right. Then he said: "This is what you have to do. You have to dig a well into such and such a cliff and your mother has to sit by, a black sheep in her arms. And when that sheep turns white, you shall be free." So they worked there for some weeks. Then a man of the world goes by grinning and laughing, a real Lord Big Pants drives by in a carriage with six horses all glittering with silver. He asked what the boy was doing. The boy answered and honestly told him what he had done and then, in turn, asked who the other man was. And Big Pants said: "I am a man who makes crooked things straight and straight things crooked." Now the boy got sick and mad at heart, and he hit the man with his hammer and killed him. And at the same time water leapt up from the rock, and the sheep in his mother's lap turned white. So they went once again to the learned professor to tell him what had happened. He was surprised to hear that it had all happened so soon, as he had expected at least six weeks to pass, but as he studied the matter, he said that it might have helped them that the boy had taken the worldly man's life; the blessing had truly happened, and so they could go on living as mother and son.

FI4 OEDIPUS TALE*

Source: Suomalaisen Kirjallisuuden Seura (Association of Finnish Literature), Helsinki, collected by K. Saari, in 1890, in Lehtimäki. Told by Vilhe Takala, age twenty-five, who heard the tale from Juha Leppänen, also of Lehtimäki. Translated by Marja Heinonen. Ladoga, the body of water mentioned in the tale, is the so-called Karelian Sea in the east of Finland; Turku is the old capital, in the west.

1. Capitalized in the manuscript; it is not clear what this New Teaching is.

Three sorcerers from the North were traveling in the Turku country, and they came to a farmhouse to stay for the night. When they lay there on the bench, one of them said: "The good woman of this house will have a child, but that will be of little good, because the boy will kill his father and marry his mother." The second sorcerer said: "The sheep will have a lamb, but that will be of no good, because a wolf will eat it." In the morning they left and went their way. But the old mother-in-law [*muori*] had heard their talk, and she told the farmer and his wife. And when the wife then got a child, the farmer said: "Better kill that boy so that whatever the northerners knew will be in vain." And he took a knife and had already cut a wound on the boy's chest, but the mother begged him to stop: "Let us not kill him, better put him on a board and take him to the Ladoga." So they threw him into the sea. Then the sheep lambed, but they decided to wait till autumn, and then at threshing time they made a big feast and slaughtered the lamb. The meat was cooked and put on the porch to cool. But a wolf came and took the meat. Now they realized that the sorcerers had been right. The wind carried the board and the boy upon it to an island of the sea, and there was a house on that island. The boys of the house were fetching water from the sea when they saw the boy, and they took him home. He was brought up and taken good care of, but the other boys always scorned him and said: "You are not one of us, you are nothing, we found you in the Ladoga, on a piece of wood." Once the boy asked his father: "Did you really find me in the sea?" And the father said: "Yes, we did." So the boy said: "Give me three marks and a boat, as I would rather go away and look for work elsewhere." The father gave him the money and the boat, and the boy left. He came to a farmhouse and asked for work. The farmer's wife promised to hire him, and she gave him a gun and a sword and said that the first thing he had to do was to go and guard the potato pit. "If anyone comes there at night and does not talk to you, you had better kill him," she said. The boy went to the pit. After a while a man came there and never uttered a word, and so the boy shot him dead. Then he went to tell the woman that he had now killed a man. Only then did it occur to the woman that it might well be her husband. They ran to the pit, and she saw that the man was indeed her husband. Together they wondered what to do and decided to bury the dead farmer in the swamp. The boy then took the farmer's place and married his wife. Once in the sauna the wife saw the scar on the boy's chest and she asked: "Where do you come from and where was your home?" The boy answered: "I was found on a board in the Ladoga sea." The woman said: "You are my son, and you have killed your father and now you have married me." She remembered what the northern sorcerers had predicted. And they went to Turku to see a high priest and to make a confession. And the priest said to the boy: "You are to hammer a rock until water spurts out, and then you shall be free." And to the mother he said: "You are to sit with a black sheep in your lap until the sheep turns white, and then you shall be free." Well, on the first day the boy hammered his rock, and in the morning he saw an old lawyer who went singing and dancing towards Turku and then returned in the evening weeping and crying. The boy went to ask why he was crying, but the man was too quick for him and just passed by. On the second day the boy was there again hammering, and the same lawyer passed him dancing and singing on his way to Turku. In the evening he returned weeping, but once again he was too quick for the boy. The third day came and the boy hammered the rock. The lawyer went towards Turku singing and dancing, but in the evening came back weeping. Now the boy asked: "Why are you crying?" The man answered: "To see you work on that rock makes me cry, because where you hammer you will never get a drop of water." Then he showed the boy another spot in the rock, and as the boy hit it three times, water spurted out, and in this manner he was set free. He went home and there the black sheep in his mother's lap had turned white.

The boy then took himself a wife from the village and they had a big wedding and celebrated for three days, and I was there, too. And afterwards I had a bad hangover and found myself sleeping with a kitchen maid. The young couple were sleeping in the bedroom. In the morning the maid got up to make coffee, and I asked if I could have some too. The maid said: "You will have yours in a minute, I have to serve the young couple first." And she opened the door and peeped in, and there they were in their bed and very busy. She waited a while and then peeped in again, and there they were at it again. And that is why I never got my coffee.

That's the end of the story.

FI5 OEDIPUS TALE*

Source: Suomalaisen Kirjallisuuden Seura (Association of Finnish Literature), Helsinki, collected by K. Krohn in 1884. Told by Juhana Ahonen, age seventeen, of Lehtimäki farm, village of Paajala. Translated by Marja Heinonen.

The wise men came to the house, and the people told them that their sheep was lambing and in great pain, and that she should be helped. But the wise men said that their help would be of no use, because both the sheep and the lamb would be eaten up by the wolf anyway. Still they helped the ewe. In the morning, as the woman lay in labor and was in great pain, the wise men said the same thing: helping her was not of much use, because the child was lost anyway. Still, they helped the mother but said once again that the child that was born would kill his father and marry his mother. When the father heard this, he got up at once, took his knife, and slashed the face of his newborn child. But the mother begged him not to kill the baby. Then she tied the child onto a board and pushed him into the sea, where the winds carried him near a big town. There somebody found him and, seeing that he was alive, took him up. He became a sea captain and he went to sea sailing, and came to the place where his mother and father lived. So he said: "Is there any work for me? The sea is rough now, and it is no time for sailing." So the woman of the house gave him a bow and arrow and told him to go and guard the turnip field, saying: "Whoever comes there, you shoot straight away." So a man came from the woods, the boy's own father, and the boy shot him. And since the old man died, the boy married the widow. Then one day the woman happened to notice the scar on his face and she asked how he had hurt himself like that. He said: "When I was a child, my father wanted to kill me, but my mother saved me and put me to sea, and in the harbor of a big town I was picked up." So the woman understood that here was her own son. Now the boy took a Bible under his arm and started wandering along the roads. And walking there he met a prophet who also carried a Bible. He asked him whether anyone who had killed his father and married his mother could be forgiven, and the other one said no. He met another prophet, again carrying a Bible, and he asked him if a man who had killed his father and married his mother could be forgiven, and this one also said no, there was no way. Then a third prophet came along the road with a Bible under his arm, and the boy asked again if there was forgiveness for a man who had killed his father and married his mother. The prophet told him that indeed there was. So the boy said: "I am the man, what should I do?" The other one said: "You dig a well into that big rock, and your sins will be forgiven the day when water spurts up from your well, and when the black sheep that you shall tie on the edge of the well turns white."

And one day there was water flowing in that well.

I went away and (I was shot, and still today it hurts) [these words appear in parentheses in the manuscript].

FI6 OEDIPUS TALE*

Source: Suomalaisen Kirjallisuuden Seura (Association of Finnish Literature), Helsinki, collected by A. Käki, in 1891, in Viipuri. Translated by Marja Heinonen.

Two wizards came to the farm in the evening, and they spent the night in the hayloft. That night the farmer's wife had a child, and that same night the ewe had a lamb. In the morning the farmer was out and walking, and he heard the strangers talking. One of them asked the other what he thought would become of the boy who was born during the night. The other one said: "That boy will kill his father and marry his mother." "And what do you think will become of the lamb that was born?" the first man asked. The other one answered: "That lamb will be eaten up by a wolf." The farmer was much grieved, and he went to his wife and said: "This boy will one day kill me and marry you." And he took his knife and went to his child to kill him. The mother ran after him and snatched the child from his hands, but already there was a long wound in the boy's chest. Then the autumn came, and it was time to slaughter the sheep. The farmer remembered what the wizards had predicted, and he said that it had all been a lie: no wolf had touched the lamb, here it was slaughtered and ready to be roasted. So they put the lamb into a big pot, and when the meat was cooked, the farmer opened the window and put the roast there to cool. But a wolf came and stole the meat. Now the farmer took fright: the wizards had been right after all. And he rushed to the child, meaning to kill him. But once again the mother managed to save the child. They sat down to think, and then agreed that it was better not to kill the boy. As they lived by a lake, they took a wooden board, and with ropes they tied the child on that board and then set him adrift thinking: now where he goes, he goes. The water carried the boy to an island, and there were people living on that island, and they took care of him until he was sixteen years old, and never once did they let him out of the island. But he longed to go out: he wanted to go back to the mainland. So finally they let him go. He came to a village and to a farm and asked if they needed a farmhand. The people said that they did not need help, as they had men enough, but that the neighboring farm might well use him, because there was only one man in that house. So he went to that house and asked for work. The farmer's wife said that they certainly needed help, but she could not promise anything, as the farmer himself was away, at the mill. Nevertheless she asked him to go to the turnip field in the woods. And she gave him a gun and told him to guard the field well: if he saw a thief, he was to shoot. The boy sat there all day keeping watch, and nobody came, but late at night a thief came, and as he started to carry away his load, the boy shot him dead. The boy went home and told the farmer's wife that a thief came and that he shot him and left him lying in the woods. They had their supper and slept the night, and still there was no sign of the farmer. Now the wife got alarmed: what if the boy had shot her husband? They went to the field to see, and there, indeed, was the farmer. As there were no men in the house, the woman asked the boy to stay there and help her. And he stayed as a farmhand. A year passed, and the woman started suggesting that they could just as well get married. So they did. And the woman heated the sauna, and they went there together, and it was then that she noticed the scar on his chest, and she asked where he had been wounded like that. The man said that when he was very small, his father wanted to kill him and had already slashed a wound in his chest, but his mother had managed to save him. Now the woman struck her breast and cried out: "So the prediction was true, a wolf came and ate the lamb, and the boy killed his father and married his mother." Then they went to see the wizard to ask him what they should do. And the wizard said: "There is no forgiveness for a sin like yours unless you do this. With a sieve you shall carry water into the hollow of a tar-filled stump [*tervaskanto*] until it brings forth green sprouts. When it shoots leaves, you shall be free." So they worked and toiled and did all they could to fill the hollow of the stump. But it was only after it got very cold and the sieve was frozen that they managed to fill the hollow. And the next spring the stump was shooting forth new green leaves.

That is the end of the story.

FI7 OEDIPUS TALE*

Source: Suomalaisen Kirjallisuuden Seura (Association of Finnish Literature), collected by A. Ahlqvist, in 1846 in North Karelia. For the place, the SKS MS adds Ilomantsi in parentheses, with a question mark. Translated by Marja Heinonen. It happens that a tale practically identical to this one, published by Erik Rudbeck in 1854, was collected in Ilomantsi. Rudbeck's tale, entitled "Ennustukset" (The predictions), appears in Erik Rudbeck [Eero Salmelainen, pseudonym], *Suomalaisen Kirjallisuuden Toimituksia*, vol. 17 = *Suomen Kansan Satuja Ja Tarinoita*, vol. 2 (Helsinki, 1854), pp. 81-89. Only these differences occur: the predictions are made by two wizards instead of Jesus and Peter; and the boy is exposed only after the lamb is eaten by the wolf at Michaelmas. The style of the Rudbeck tale is repetitive and embroidered.

This happened when Jesus was walking around this land, and he had Peter as his apprentice. They came to a farm. There was an ewe just lambing. Peter says to Jesus: "That ewe is in too much pain, it should be helped." Jesus says: "So it should, but whatever we do, the lamb will be eaten up by a wolf." The farm people hear all this. But then Jesus said: "Let the ewe be delivered," and so she was, and a lamb was born. The farmer's wife was expecting a child, and she was in labor pain also. So Peter asks Jesus to deliver her. "Of course we can help her," says Jesus, "but the boy who will be born will kill his father and marry his mother." The farm people hear all this. But Jesus helped the woman, and a boy was born. The two men stayed for the night, and in the morning they went their way. The farmer says: "You heard what Jesus said: this lamb will be taken by a wolf, and this boy will kill me and marry his mother." What is there to do except kill a child like this? The father is there, a knife in his hand, all ready to kill the boy. The mother says: "Better put him to sea on a board. Let him drift where he may." So the father puts away his knife, but already there is a wound on the boy's chest. They put the child on a board, wrap some clothes around him, push him into the sea. The boy drifts and drifts, the waves push him, carry him ashore at a monastery. There are workmen on the shore, they take the child to the monastery, to their master.

Well, at home, on the farm, when autumn came and Michaelmas, they slaughtered the lamb and made a big stew. When it was ready, they put the meat on the window: an open window such as they were in the old times, with only shutters. They start with the broth, sit there eating and talking about the two men who had said that a wolf would eat the lamb. Whoever they were, they certainly lied: here was the lamb made to a stew. They eat, finish the broth; it is time to have the meat. They go to fetch the bowl; the bowl is outside on the ground, and a wolf stands there gnawing the last bones.—So the prediction came true, after all (It may be that it was only now that they put the boy to sea).—

The boy was taken to the monastery and he grew up and became a man, a good honest man. But when he became of age, he grew tired of his life at the monastery and longed to get out to see the world. He asked the master if he could go. "Well, if you long for it that much, go." He sets off, starts walking, looking for work and food, then comes to a farm. The farmer is out in the woods, but his wife is there. She asks: "Who are you and what do you do?" "I am just a wanderer looking for work and food." "Well, there is work for you here: go guard the turnip field, and we have had robbers there; if anyone comes, you shoot." She gave him a gun, and he went to the field. He sits on guard, waits: then he sees an old man climbing over the fence. The man picks turnips, takes all he can carry; as he turns to leave, the boy shoots, and the old one falls down. The boy goes home and tells what happened. That was that—the farmer has not come yet, no sign of him; it is getting dark. The wife is suddenly alarmed: what if it was he who was shot? They go and see: there is the farmer, dead in the field. The wife could not blame anyone, as she herself had told the boy to shoot whoever came. The farmer was buried, and the wife married the boy. And why not, a wanderer as he was, alone, no ties? They lived together, lived well. Once they go together to bathe. The wife sees a big red scar on the man's chest and asks how he got it. "I don't know," he answers, "maybe I was born with it or maybe got it as a child." "Where were you born?" "Even that I do not know, I grew up in the monastery, they found me in the sea, on a board." "Then you must be our son, and the prediction came true after all: the wolf ate the lamb, and here we are married, and you killed your old father." They are very troubled and begin to wonder how they can ever be forgiven. So the mother says: "You had better go and talk to the learned and ask them how we can be set free." The boy sets off, walks along. Then he meets an old monk and asks him. The monk looks in his books, finds nothing: "You poor man, for such a sin there is no forgiveness." The boy is cruelly pained by this, and he hits the monk and kills him. Then he walks on and meets another monk, even older than the first. Again he confesses his sins and also tells about the monk whom he had killed (the same thing happened with his one). He walks on, grieved and remorseful: why did he have to kill these two? Then he meets a third monk, a very old one, quite grey. He says: "This I have done: I killed my father, then married my mother, and on the way here I killed two monks when they told me that I could never be forgiven." The old one looks in his book, then says: "There is no sin so big that it could not be remitted, if only there is true repentance. You both have to go to that cliff. You are to dig a well in the rock until you reach water, and your mother is to sit by and hold a black sheep in her arms until the sheep turns white." The boy went home. Then they go together to the cliff. The boy starts hammering the rock; the mother sits beside him with the black sheep. There is a road going by that cliff, and all kinds of people pass by, good and bad. On the third day a big lord drives by, bells jingling, carriage glittering. He asks the boy what he is doing. The boy explains. Then the other one tells him: "Well, I am a man who can make right come out wrong and wrong come out right: all this for good money, of course. Actually it is to the court that I am going even now. I am ready to help you if you pay me well." It hurt the boy sorely to realize that while he himself was toiling as he was, the other one lived by swindling. And he hit the man on the forehead with his hammer and killed him. At the same time a well opened in the rock and water came up, and the black sheep turned white. Now the boy had new cause for worry, however, and he went back to the monk, the same old monk. "This is what happened: there is water in the well, and the sheep turned white." "How did that happen," the monk wonders, "it should have been only after six weeks." "A man, this big lord, passed by, and I killed him." "So much the better: killing that man was to the good. All his life he cheated and swindled and he sinned against God far more than you ever did." In this manner they were set free, and they could live together again, as mother and son.

FI8 OEDIPUS TALE*

Source: Suomalaisen Kirjallisuuden Seura (Association of Finnish
Literature), Helsinki, collected by V. Alava, in 1889, in Virolahti.
Told by Tanel Hyypiä, age thirty, of Vaalimaa. Translated by Marja
Heinonen.

There was an old woman in our village who used to tell this, and she
said it had all really happened. A couple had had a child, and when he
was born, two wizards came to the house. The younger one asked the
other one what he thought would become of the child. The older
wizard answered that the boy would grow into a man who would kill
his father and marry his mother. The parents happened to hear all this,
and they did not feel like keeping the child any longer, and they tied
him on a big wooden board and put him into the sea, thinking that
death would soon take him. But the sea took the child to some other
shore. How far away it was, I do not know. Well, on that other shore
people found the child on this piece of wood, and they took him in and
took care of him. So he grew up, and when he became a man, he started
traveling to see the world. Then he happened to come to the country
and to the house whence he had been sent out as a child. He, of course,
did not know that it had happened here, he only knew that he had been
put into the sea and then found. So he came to that house and asked
for work. The farmer was not at home, but his wife was there, and she
sent the man to the woods where they had a turnip field. And she told
him to watch it carefully and gave him a gun, saying that he was to warn
thieves off, and if they did not obey, he had to shoot. Well, the man
watched. Then the farmer comes to the field, the owner himself. The
man does not know him, warns him, shouts; the other one does not
listen. So the man shoots him. In the evening he went home: there was
no going home for the farmer, as he had been killed. And the man told
the farmer's wife that there had been a thief who never listened to him
however hard he had tried to warn him and that then he could only
shoot and there the stranger was dead in the field. The wife wondered
who the thief might have been and wanted to go and see. So they went
to the field together, and there the farmer, her husband, lay dead. But
she could not really blame the man who had shot him, because she herself had given the orders, and the man had only done what she had asked
him to do. So the man stayed at the farm to help her and they lived
there quite a while. As time passed, she started thinking that they might
just as well get married. And that is what they did, and they began to
live together as husband and wife. Then once when they were talking
about this and that, the man started to tell her about his life, how he
had grown up and that he had been found in such and such a place and

picked up from the sea. And now the woman understood that he was
her own son, the one she had had and then put into the sea. And she
realized that the wizards had predicted it all and—that is the end of the
story.

FI9 NOBODY CAN ESCAPE HIS FATE

Source: Suomalaisen Kirjallisuuden Seura (Association of Finnish
Literature), Helsinki, collected by Ulla Mannonen, in 1939, and told
by Helena Suni, age eighty-two, of Rakkola, Säkkijärvi. Translated
by Marja Heinonen.

In the old times people used to tell this story. Two men came to a
farm to stay for the night, and as they lay on their beds on the floor, a
boy was born to the farmer and his wife. So one of the men said to the
other: "Now you who are the wizard, why don't you predict the fate of
that child." The other man answered: "When that child grows up, he
will kill his father and take his own mother as his wife." The parents
heard this prediction, and they decided not to let the boy grow into a
murderer and an adulterer: it was better to kill him now. So they tied
the child onto a board with ropes, took a knife and drew a sign of the
cross on his chest, and pushed him into the river.

Well, the boy drifted with the current for many kilometers and came
to an island. There some people found him and brought him up. As a
grown man he got tired of his life on the island; he wanted to see the
world. So he left and started traveling, and one day he happened to
come to the house of his parents. Only the woman was at home. The
boy asked if there was any work for him. "There is work all right," the
woman answered. "You see that club at the door. Take it with you and
go guard the turnip field, we have had thieves there." The boy took the
club and went to the field. He sits there a while and waits: now an old
man comes and starts throwing turnips into a big sack. The boy hit him
on the head with the club and killed him. They buried the old man, and
the wife told him that it was her husband but that there was nothing to
be done about an accident. So the boy stayed in the house and later on
married the woman. Once they were in the sauna together, and as they
were sitting there naked, the wife happened to notice the cross-shaped
scar on the man's chest. "Where did you get that mark?" she asks. The
boy says that he does not know: all he knows is that as a child he had
been found in the river on a wooden board. The woman is terrified and
says: "So the prediction came true after all. Nobody can escape the fate
that is his from birth."

FI10 OEDIPUS

Source: Suomalaisen Kirjallisuuden Seura (Association of Finnish Literature), Helsinki, collected by K. Krohn, in Sievi in 1884. Told by Antii Kangaskovski, age twenty-two. Translated by Marja Heinonen.

Once there had been a traveling stranger who had come to a farm. In the house there were only a man and his wife and a small child, and there was also a sheep inside the house with the people. The child had been crying, and the stranger had said: "He is crying now, that boy is, but one day he will kill his father and marry his mother. And as to that sheep, it will be eaten up by a wolf." The farmer kept these words in his mind, and the next thing he did was to slaughter the sheep. The meat was cooked and the cooked meat sliced and chopped into a big bowl, and the bowl was put on the windowsill, the window being just an opening in the wall. But a wolf came and took the meat so that the sheep was eaten then and there. Now the farmer wanted to kill the child too. He had already slashed the baby's chest when the mother said that they really should not kill him, there were other ways. So they put the little boy into a barrel and pushed the barrel into the sea. The winds carried the barrel over the ocean, and there some people found it and found the boy inside. They fed him and brought him up until he was big enough to go begging for his living, and so he began wandering around the world. Then, as it happened, he came to the house of his father and his mother. The father was not at home, but the woman in the house gave the beggar boy some food and then sent him to watch the turnip field, which was in the woods. She gave him a loaded gun and said: whoever dares to come there, you shoot him. So the farmer himself— the boy's own father—walked to the field, and the boy shot and killed him. Then he came home, and the woman asked if he had seen anyone. He told her that indeed he had seen a stranger, but that he had used the gun straightway, so the trespasser had been taken care of. The woman went to the field and saw her husband dead. They decided to keep secret what had happened, and as time passed, they started to live together as husband and wife. The boy never knew that the woman really was his mother. Then one night, in the sauna, the woman happened to notice a big scar on the boy's chest, and she asked what had happened to him. The boy said that he did not know: the only thing he knew was that as a baby he had been found in a barrel in the sea. Now this became very clear to the woman, and she said: "You must be my own son." They went together to see the priest, to hear what he had to say about their sin. Well, the priest said that such a sin could not be forgiven at all. Hearing this, the boy, as he had a violent temper, struck and killed the priest. Then they went to see another priest, and this one told them that they could indeed be forgiven, but to repent they had to go to a far-away graveyard, and there they had to sit on a grave, and each was to hold a black sheep in his lap. And they were to sit there until the sheep had turned white.

FI11 ABOUT A BOY WHO KILLED HIS FATHER AND MARRIED HIS MOTHER

Source: Suomalaisen Kirjallisuuden Seura (Association of Finnish Literature), Helsinki, collected by A. Rytkönen in 1893. Told by Juho Silander, age thirty-five, of Taipale. Translated by Marja Heinonen.

Once there was a rich shopkeeper who had only one son. When this boy was born, the parents went to see all sorcerers and wizards to learn what was to become of their boy. But the wizards all told them that he would grow up to be a man who would kill his father and then marry his mother. The parents were quite stricken by this, and the mother finally decided that it was better not to let the boy grow up to be such a sinner. And she made a basket for him of rushes and reeds, and slit his belly open with a sharp razor and then put him into the basket and threw it into the river. The basket drifted with the current and came to a water mill and there it was caught in the wheels of the mill. Now the miller felt that there was something wrong, and he stopped his work and went to see the wheels. There was a basket there and a little child crying in the basket. The miller took him in and brought him up. Nobody knew where he came from. When the boy grew up, he wanted to see the world, and he worked in country shops to earn his living. Then he came to work in the shop that was owned by his father. Neither of them knew that they were related. He stayed there as an assistant and became very close with the shopkeeper's wife. They plotted and planned how they could get rid of the old man so that they could get together and also have the shop. So one day the assistant got enraged and killed the shopkeeper. He talked with the wife, and they decided to keep the whole thing secret. If the killing was not reported, they could start living as husband and wife. Once as they were sleeping together, the woman saw a scar on the man's belly, and she asked what iron had wounded him like that. The man said that he was a foundling who had been found at the mill in a basket and that the miller had brought him up. The mother realized that he could be no other than her own son, and she was numb with terror remembering the prediction that had come true: here was the boy who had killed his father and then married his mother. And she was so grieved that soon afterwards she died.

FI12 OEDIPUS TALE*

Source: Suomalaisen Kirjallisuuden Seura (Association of Finnish
Literature), Helsinki, collected by D.E.D. Europaeus in 1845, in Aunus.
Translated by Marja Heinonen.

There was a maiden in the house. A gypsy read her hand and said:
"When you are wed, your first child is a boy. The boy will marry you
and kill his father." When a son was born to her, they tied him to a
board, marked him with a knife, and pushed him into the sea. The boy
came across the sea, and there was a girl working on shore. She saw him
and picked him up, and when she saw that he was alive, she took him
home. A priest christened him. Board-Boy was the name that they gave
him. He grew up, went to sea, and one day arrived at his home farm.
The farmer hired him to guard the turnip field, gave him a gun, and said:
"If thieves and robbers come, you shoot." He spent his time at the field,
and on Saturday, when it was already getting dark, the farmer went to
check if he really was there and working. The farmer looks around,
listens; does not see or hear anything. The boy sits on guard on the
shore side. So the farmer picks some turnips, and just as he is leaving,
the guard shoots. The boy goes home now and asks for the farmer. The
wife says: "how come you did not see him, he left for the field." The
boy answers: "all I saw was a thief, and I shot him." "Oh no, poor boy,
you shot my husband." They went to the field to see, and there the
farmer lay dead. Now people came and priests, and they buried the
corpse, but there was nothing they could do about the boy, because he
had only done what the farmer had told him to do. So he stayed in the
house as a farmhand, and then later married the farmer's wife. In the
sauna the wife saw a long red scar on his body and asked how he got it.
They sent me out on a board and knifed me, the boy explains. Then
you are my son, says the woman. They went to the priest to confess.
The priest ordered men to dig a grave, full nine fathoms deep, and they
put them both in, mother and son. Three men were there filling the
grave with rocks, but the boy rose up stepping on the stones and was
not hurt. The mother was buried thereunder.

FI13 THE STORY OF JUDAS ISCARIOT

Source: Suomalaisen Kirjallisuuden Seura (Association of Finnish
Literature), Helsinki, collected by Heikki Meriläinen, in 1888. Told
by Esaias Kalliokoski, in Sotkamo, who heard the tale in his childhood
from his father. Translated by Marja Heinonen.

Judas Iscariot's parents were poor farmers. Once his father had to go
to the village to work, and the mother was left home alone with seven
children. An old witch happened to come to the house, and the mother

asked her to look after her children while she went on some errands. Iscariot was the youngest of the children; he was only six months old and called Judas. The witch sat rocking the boy, and she looked at his hands and his feet and saw that he was going to grow up into a criminal. So as soon as the mother came back, she said to her: "It is no use bringing up this one. When he grows up, he will be an evildoer, so cruel and bad that there has never been his like, because he will kill his father and marry his mother and then afterwards betray the Savior who is now born." This made the mother very sad, and when her husband came home from the village, she told him what the witch had said. He told her not to worry: he could take care of the boy, just kill him and get rid of him for good. But the mother had a dream in which she was warned not to kill/not to stain her hands with blood [thus in the manuscript]. So the father said: "I will make an ark and we will throw him into the sea and the winds, live he then or die." But the winds carried him to an island, and the island was called "Iscariot." Now the royal family happened to be strolling there, and on the beach they found the boy crying but still alive. So the king's wife took him up and hired a nurse for him, and he was brought up together with the king's own children. He grew fast and became very strong, and as soon as he was old enough to play with the others, he showed his temper and always hurt them, breaking their arms and legs. So the king gave him a good scolding and said: "You, boy, you are just a foundling and only live here becasue we took pity on you, and if you do not know how to behave, we will take you back to where we first found you." So the boy went to the queen, whom he thought to be his mother, and asked her where he was from, as the king had called him a foundling. And the queen told him that he was from an island and was named after that place, because that island was called Iscariot. The boy was too proud to stay in his home as a foundling, and he went away and started wandering, asking for work and food. And finally he came to Pontius Pilate of Syria, who hired him as an errand boy. He lived there for a long time, and when he grew up, he worked as a foreman. Pontius Pilate had a large orchard with all sorts of fruit trees, and there was a couple, man and wife, taking care of the trees. The boy always quarreled with the gardeners, and one day, when he went there for apples, he had a fight with the gardener and he killed the man. Pilate kept his secret so that the boy was not punished by law. But Pilate said to him that since it was his doing that the widow now lived without help or protection, he should marry her. The boy did so and married the widow. Once they were talking together about this and that and were also speaking about children. The wife told him that she had seven children with her first husband, but the youngest was no longer alive. A witch had predicted a very bad life for him, and so they had put him to sea in an ark. The boy's name had been Judas: where the wind had carried him, nobody knew. So the boy said that the witch's prediction was, in fact, true; he must be the same Judas, he had been found on an island in an ark such as the woman told him they had used. And now he had killed his father and married his mother. And Judas Iscariot felt remorse and went to be a disciple of the Savior, whom he then betrayed and sold for thirty silver pennies. And afterwards he hanged himself and that was it, a good ending to the good.

FI14 PREDICTION: KILLED HIS FATHER, MARRIED HIS MOTHER: JUDAS ISCARIOT

Source: Suomalaisen Kirjallisuuden Seura (Association of Finnish Literature), Helsinki, collected by Ellen Fabritius in 1889. Told by Puavo Pekkanen, age seventy-three, in the village of Pitkälahti, Anttola. Translated by Marja Heinonen.

Iscariot was the son of the king of Nääsi, and when he was born, a great wizard was asked to predict his future. The wizard said: "This boy will kill his father and marry his mother." When the king heard this, he went in grief to his wife. Together they thought and reasoned, and the king had a wooden chest made, and they put the boy inside and set the chest adrift.

The boy drifted and drifted, and the waves carried him across the sea before another king's house. There the king's servants found him, and they came running to the queen and told her that there was an infant boy in the chest. The queen said: "Whoever he is, we have to save him and take care of him." Then they went to tell the king that he had a son, and he was very pleased. But two weeks later the king was told that the queen had just given birth to his child, a boy, and that the first boy had been a foundling. The king said: "Let him be, whoever, he is, we will take care of him." So the boys grew up together, thinking they were brothers. Then one day the parents told their own son that the other boy was not his real brother but a foundling. Iscariot was much troubled at heart, and he said: "Why does my brother call me a foundling and a stranger? Am I not your son just as he is?" So they had to tell him the truth. When Iscariot heard this, he felt he had to leave, and he left and went out to the world. There he became a soldier. Soon afterwards they raised a war against the king of Nääsi. The generals wanted chickens, but there were not any except in the garden of the king of Nääsi, and no one dared to go there because the king himself was guarding them. But Iscariot went there, and in the king's garden he killed his father. Then the war ended, and he went back home. Now everyone urged him to go and marry the queen of Nääsi, as he certainly had had more success than the others. So he went and took the queen to be his wife. One day the two of them were talking together, and suddenly the queen said to him: "You must be my son whom I believed dead, and so the old wizard's prediction was true: here we are married and you did kill your father." When Iscariot heard all of this, he left her and went away to become one of the disciples of Jesus. What happened to him afterwards, everybody knows.

FI15 OEDIPUS

Source: Suomalaisen Kirjallisuuden Seura (Association of Finnish Literature), Helsinki, collected by K. Krohn in 1884, in Pyhäjärvi, Vöyri. Told by Martti Haapapuro, age twenty-nine, who heard it from his father, who came from Vöyri and was Swedish-speaking. Translated by Marja Heinonen.

There was a woman who lived in Vaasa on the coast, and she had her fortune told. They said that her son would kill his father and marry his mother. When she then had a child, she put him in a chest; the father made a solid chest of wood, and they put the boy therein and pushed him to sea. The wind carried him to the coast of Sweden. And the chest came ashore, and there were some maids washing clothes. They were servants of a big manor house. They picked up the chest and took it in to show the lady and gentleman. They opened it and there was a child inside, still alive. So they took the child into the family and raised him. But the gentleman had a son of his own, and one day the boys had a fight and the foundling boy killed the other one, and when he then heard that in truth he was only a foundling, he ran away and came back to Vaasa coast. /As he came ashore, he killed his father/[1] His mother was now a widow. And he married her, his own mother. Afterwards he learned where he had come from, and he fled back to Sweden. There they took him prisoner.

FI16 OEDIPUS

Source: Suomalaisen Kirjallisuuden Seura (Association of Finnish Literature), Helsinki, collected by K. Krohn in Pyhäjärvi, in 1884. Told by Paavo Hukkonen, age thirty-five, who heard the tale from old people in Kiuruvesi. Translated by Marja Heinonen.

Once there was a traveler who came in the evening to a farm to stay for the night. He lay down on the bench and slept there. During the night the farmer's wife gave birth to a son, and the ewe had a lamb, a ram it was. In the morning the traveler began telling his dreams. He said

---

1. These slash marks are in the manuscript.

he had dreamt that the boy was born into the family and that the ewe also had a newborn ram; and that this boy would kill his father and that the ram would be eaten by a wolf. Well, the whole long summer the little ram followed his mother in the meadows, but wolves no one saw. Then the summer passed, and at Michaelmas the farmer slaughtered the ram and it was roasted. When the meat was done, they put it in a big bowl on the window. In the old times they had no glass in their windows, so it was only an opening, all wood. So the meat was put there to cool. Now a wolf happened to pass by, and he knocked the bowl down and ate the meat. When the people saw this, they remembered what the traveler had said: this was the ram, that was a fact, and now it had been eaten by a wolf. They started pondering and wondering about the boy, trying to think how they could prevent him from killing his father. Finally it came to them that the only way was to put the child on a wooden board and push the board out on the lake and let it drift with the winds. They did not have the heart to murder the boy. So the boy was driven along by the wind and the waves, no one knew where, across the sea, and he was found by some good people. They took care of him until he was a grown man. Then he started traveling and he came to the country and to the house where he had been born. There the people wanted to know who he was and where he came from. And he explained that he did not know his country or his home, as he was a foundling from the sea. His parents rejoiced: this grown man could only be their son. They were so happy that they wanted the boy to stay with them again: who would any longer fear him killing his father? They had a big turnip field in the woods, and as they had had trouble with thieves coming there at night time, the boy went to the field in the dark and took a gun with him. He sat there guarding, and at night the father happened to cross the field. The boy shot him and killed him. So it all came true, as it had happened in the traveler's dream. The wolf ate the ram, and the boy killed his father.

FI17 THE BOY WHO MARRIED HIS MOTHER*

Source: Suomalaisen Kirjallisuuden Seura (Association of Finnish Literature), Helsinki, collected by Savokarjalainen Osakunta (an association of students from Savokarjala) in 1887. Told by Petter Falk, age twenty-eight, in Sääminki, Varparanta, who had heard the tale in his village. Translated by Marja Heinonen.

A father was maddened, wanted to kill his son, slashed him across the waist. The mother wanted to save the boy, put him on a piece of wood, then set him adrift. He came ashore. Someone found and raised him. Then he traveled around and came to his old home. The father had died. The boy fell in love with his mother and married her. Once, in the sauna, they learned the truth. The mother fainted.

KR1 JUDAS

Source: Suomalaisen Kirjallisuuden Seura (Folklore Archives of the Finnish Literature Society), Helsinki, collected by Kaarle Krohn in 1884. Told by Ilja Ignatjof, age fifty-one, of the village of Kaitajärvi. Translated by Anna-Liisa Scharf.

There were once a man and a woman who had not had any children. An old man came to stay with them for the night. They show him the hand of the mistress of the house. He looks at her hand and says to her, "a son will be born to you. The son will receive the name Iuda, he will marry you and kill his father. There are forty maidens at a convent; he will ravish them all. That's the kind of son that will be born to you." The old man leaves. They live on, time passes, and the mistress becomes pregnant. When the time came, she gave birth to a baby boy. They summoned a minister to christen the child. The minister came and began looking for a name. He looks in his books for a name; the name Iuda falls to the boy. They are sad that Iuda is not a good name, but the name remains. The minister does not have any other name, so they have to accept Iuda. Thus, Iuda was taken for his name.

Sadness begins to grow in their minds; "this boy was not born for our good." They make a two-headed barrel, which is bound with iron bands, and put the boy into the barrel. With a knife they slash open a part of the boy's chest, seal the barrel, and push the barrel with the child into the sea, go wherever it may. The wind begins to carry the barrel with the child over the sea. He traveled, traveled over the sea until he landed on the shores of a convent. One of the maidens came to get some water; the crying of a newborn child could be heard from the barrel. She brought the news to the older girls that a child's crying could be heard from a barrel that was washed up on the shore. All the maidens go to the shore. What a strange thing that a child's crying comes from a barrel. They open the barrel; there is a child with his chest slashed open. They sew the child's chest with silk thread. They take him to the convent. They feed him for a year, for two, for three years, and up to his eighth year. They teach him to write, and he becomes a very good penman. He grows into a full man of seventeen years, and he becomes quite a charmer.

He starts fooling around with the maidens; he has already ravished one, then a second and third one, until he raped all forty of them. As he ravished the oldest maiden, she felt remorse. She thinks: "How can we now worship the Holy God here all our lives, but we fall in sin like this young man? He must be sent back the way he came." They again make a two-headed barrel and put the young man into it. Go wherever you may end up, and they push the barrel into the sea. A wave begins to carry him with the barrel downwind. It brings him to the shore of a settlement. People from the town go there to get water. A man's voice is heard from inside the barrel. The thing inside the barrel says: "Whoever you are, Christian, let me out!" He is let out of the barrel. They look over the young man; quite a good and sensible boy. He is taken to work for a man and he is put guarding the orchard. The master says, "If somebody comes, yell: Don't touch; yell a second time: Don't touch; but if he comes after your third call, you may shoot him." He guards the orchard at night. There are apples on the trees. They keep a bit of a guard on the apples. The master thinks to himself: I have to go and see whether he guards at night or not. He goes to look; he opens the gate to the orchard. The boy yells: Don't come into the orchard! A second time he yells: Don't come here! Third time he yells: Don't come! The master just goes in. The boy shot him. Then he runs to the master's house. "Three times I called; a man came to the orchard. I shot him, whoever it was." The mistress looks; the master is not at home. They went to look; the guard had shot the master. He is being questioned in court about the matter. "I," he says, "called three times as he came, and then I shot." Nothing was done to him.

He is a very capable young man. The widow is still young and lonely. He takes the widow as his bride. They go to the bathhouse together, and they undress. The widow begins to look; there are stitches on his chest. "Why do you have stitches on your chest?" "I was told that my father and mother cast me off in a barrel and cut open my chest. I grew up in a convent of young girls; from there I was sent back." Then the mother found out. "You are my son," she said, and then they were separated.

KR2 JUDAS

Source: Suomalaisen Kirjallisuuden Seura (Folklore Archives of the Finnish Literature Society), Helsinki, collected by Kaarle Krohn in Suojärvi, 1884. Told by Ilja Glim, age thirty-seven, who heard the story from Katšku Hilippa in Hautavaara. Translated by Anna-Liisa Scharf.

Once there was an emperor to whom a son was born. When he was being christened, the name Iuda was drawn all twelve times that the book was opened, so he had to be named Iuda. As he grew to a boy, there came a monk, a very holy man and very wise. The emperor said, "Look, God gave us this son." He said, "The son is good, but he will kill his own father." The emperor spoke to the empress: "Why should we let our son kill us? We better kill him ourselves." The empress said: "We are not going to kill the boy; we will not shed our own blood." "What do we do with him?" She said: "It is better to put him into a two-headed barrel and push it to go wherever it will go; he will die there too." So they take a two-headed barrel, put the boy into it, and push the barrel into the sea. Soldiers were told to push it into the sea. As they did it, the barrel rolled and floated up on the sea and came to other lands, other kingdoms. Then he ended up at a castle. There lived an emperor who ate Christians. Every day he had to have a Christian to eat. The boy came to the shore. The daughters of the tsar came to the shore to wash clothes. A message was taken to the emperor that a barrel had come over the sea along the shore. "Go and bring to the courtyard whatever is inside the barrel." The barrel was brought to the courtyard and opened, and there was a small child alive. "Look," the emperor said to the empress, "we have received a titbit to eat from over the sea." "No," said the empress, "what comes over the sea is not for eating. This one we are not going to eat; we don't have a son, so we'll take him as our son." The emperor thinks about it; they adopt the boy. He has to be named. The name Iuda is drawn twelve times, so it cannot be anything else, only Iuda.

After they took the boy, the empress became pregnant and had another son. So they had two sons, one adopted and one of their own. They are being brought up together. Their own son is clumsier; the adopted one is cleverer. They go for walks together. The adopted son hits the natural son and makes him cry every day. When he comes home at night, the natural son complains that the other one hits him. He is being punished. He makes a plan: once when the brothers go together, the adopted son kills the real son. He walks and walks and thinks: What shall I say now that I killed my brother? He decides to go wherever God is going to lead him. He runs away, walks, walks about until he is eighteen years old. Then he gets to the same castle where he was put into the barrel. When he goes there, he walks on shopping streets. An old man in a shop calls him: "Come here." He goes there, and the man says: "Aren't you a clever man, wouldn't you become a salesman for us? We are looking for one, if we had the luck to get one." He begins to sell; the business is doing very well. Soon the old man lets him do everything, both buying and selling. He is trading at home.

The emperor has an orchard in which all kinds of berries and apples are growing. He starts to go there to steal. He goes there at night and eats apples whenever he has the opportunity to leave the shop. The orchard is being guarded, but they are not able to get the thief. Berries are being eaten at night in the orchard, and a message is brought to the emperor that there is somebody eating the apples. The emperor says: "Why can't you men take care of guarding? I must go and guard it myself." He puts his clothes on and goes to guard and stands at the place where the thief has come over the gate. The boy comes and jumps over the gate. The emperor grabs him around the chest; he struggles and struggles here and there. The boy picks a rock from the ground. He hits the emperor behind his ear with the rock. The emperor falls down on his back and dies. The boy ran away quickly and came home. They slept one night. In the morning, bells are tolled, because the emperor has been killed. I do not know who did it. The emperor had to be buried, so he was buried and the empress was a widow. But the shopkeeper (the old man in whose shop he is a salesman) and the empress used to visit each other. One time when visiting, he says: "The emperor just died and left you. Can you reign in the realm?" "No, I cannot," she answers. "Now I should have a husband to reign." "If you take a husband, we have a salesman who is very clever and quick-witted. He could reign but he does not own anything." "I wouldn't take him for property; with the help of God we would have property enough." "If you take him, we will come to propose." They go to propose, and they have a wedding, and the salesman takes the empress as his bride. They live together for nine days. One night they start to play cards to pass the time. They play and play. "Say, my dear man, of what race are you, what family?" "My dear, I don't know myself." "Tell as much as you know." "I only know that as a small boy I was found in a barrel. Then the emperor took me as his son. The empress got another son. Then we went walking, and I killed my brother. Because I killed, I had to run away. After I ran away, I got to this castle." But he does not tell her that he killed her husband. "Well, how old are you?" "Eighteen years have gone by since that time." The empress grabs a book: see, this is my own son. She puts her hands on her hips and said: "My own son it is, and we lived for nine days together." "Now, since I am your own son, we must part. I'll leave at night; don't know me anymore." He runs away at night; he looks for his clothes and shakes his mother's hand. He left with sad feelings but cannot be angry. Well, he thinks, oh Lord, now if I would meet the son of Mary, the Savior, either he would cut my head off or he would absolve my sins. I cannot live on this earth any more. As he walks on, he meets the Savior, with his eleven apostles. He falls down on his knees in front of the Savior. "Oh Lord," he says, "absolve my sins or cut my head off, I cannot live on this earth any more." "Tell me the sins you have committed, that I may absolve you and we don't cut your head off." He starts to confess his sins; he tells everything, all the sins he committed. How I killed my own brother, my own father. How I lived with my own mother for nine days as a married couple. The Savior absolves him, says a prayer and blesses him. "Now," he says, "go join the group and become an apostle." He took him into the group of apostles. They walk together. Iuda helps the Savior with all kinds of things. He is a quick-witted, clever man.

They walk, and one day they get to a wide, open swamp. Heavenly bells were tolled for them there. The Savior stopped and said, "Brothers, we'll have a festival here." So they sat down on the wide swamp to have a festival. They are sitting there, but they don't have anything to eat. "Go, Iuda," asks Mary's son, "go and look for something to eat. There is a castle in the forest, it belongs to bad people." So he goes to the castle. The bad people also have their festival. "No, they say, today we are not selling anything. What kind of people are you?" they ask. "We are the people of Mary's son." Then they offer him liquor. He gets drunk and starts talking too much. "Eat with us," they say. "Then we'll give you something to take along." They eat; he is being fed and given drink several times and he gets quite drunk. He talks a lot. "Couldn't you tell us, since you are one of his group, show us who is Mary's son. How much do you want for it?" "If you give me thirty gold pieces I'll tell you." They collect thirty gold pieces for him. "Well, where can we see him?" "Well, we twelve men look alike," he says. "Next week Thursday we shall go to so-and-so place visiting. When we sit down to eat, he will sit at the middle of the table. When he dips his bread into the salt basket, a fly will land on his nose. That is Mary's son; otherwise you cannot distinguish among us; we look alike." Then they gave him thirty gold coins. He left to bring the food to the others. They asked: "Did you get something to eat?" "I did," he said. They started to eat. "Are you coming to eat, Iuda?" "I already ate, they offered me." "Good," they said. The others ate. Mary's son said: "Now there is a traitor among us." Iuda jumps up: "Who is the traitor? Among us there should be no traitors." Iuda grabs a sword. "Soon his head will fall, whoever is the traitor," he says. Mary's son says: "Let it be, don't swing that sword. We'll see this coming Thursday who is a traitor and who is not." Iuda feels displeasure finding out they realize he is the guilty one. Soon he is as before, but without any joy. It came Thursday. The Savior said: "As it was predicted, it will happen." They start eating the midday meal. The yard is filling up with people. Lots of bad people are coming. They are eating. The Savior opens the window and says: "Look, brothers, who the traitor is and who isn't." Iuda is eating at the lower end of the table. Look, lots of bad people are here. He ran away quickly. The door remained open. They go on eating. The Savior sighed at the window: "Eating time is the time of peace," he said. They all must kneel down. Then they ate. While they were eating, he talked. He said: "Now, brothers, we'll have to part." Michael, Paul, and Peter said: "We are not going to part from you. Whatever happens to you, happens to us." "Oh, brothers, brothers, when an hour goes by you won't know nor recall me," he said. For an hour, they ate in peace. Then he opened the window wide again. He called: "Do what you came for." The bad people rushed into the room. "Who are you," he asked.

They look: all the men look alike; they cannot tell who is Mary's son. Mary's son says: "It is I." They grab him, one tries to hit him, another to wound him with a spear, another with a strap. Peter, Paul, and Michael are coming after them. The bad people are in trees. "More people of Mary's son are coming, catch those men." "We don't know him. We'll help you." They were set free. Then he [the Savior] was tortured. Then he was buried. Then the brothers gathered together, but Iuda ran away. Mary's son calls: "Iuda, Iuda, come back here." He looked back; he was ashamed. The old brothers saw him running quickly away ashamed. He didn't look back any more. And then he happened to fall into the arms of the chained devil, and in his arms he is still sitting on this very day.

KR3 OEDIPUS TALE*

Source: Suomalaisen Kirjallisuuden Seura (Folklore Archives of the Finnish Literature Society), Helsinki, collected by Kaarle Krohn in Salmi in 1884. Told by Anni Zivoi, about thirty years old, of the village of Tunninen. Translated by Anna-Liisa Scharf.

There was a very wealthy man and a woman, and they did not have a child. Then a fortune-teller came. The husband asked her to tell why they could not have a child. She said: "Now the mistress is pregnant, but don't get excited or scared, because this boy is going to bring you death." So the wife carries for nine months, and she gives birth to a baby boy. The man brings an aspen log to the yard, splits it into two and makes a chest. He opens the boy's stomach with a knife, puts him into the chest, and nails it up. Then he goes to the seashore, throws the container into the sea. Let it go wherever it will. So the chest "walks" in the sea, floats who knows for how long. There is a hermit on the shore in a hut, and it comes to the hermit. The man goes to the shore to get water with a cup. He looks; there is a new chest. He takes it, brings it to the hut, and pulls the nails out. He says to himself, wait, I want to look what is inside this chest. He opens it, looks, there is a real newborn soul with stomach opened. He sews the child's stomach up with silk thread and brings him up for twenty years. Then the boy is let out of the hut, and he thinks, now I am not going to stay here anymore now that I am out. He goes back into the hut and bids farewell to the hermit. "I am not going to stay here anymore," he says. The boy leaves and wanders all over the world. He comes to a rich man's house. He asks for permission to stay overnight. "Take me in for the night, master," he says. The master takes him in. Then he begins to hire him as a guardian for the garden; he says: "Start guarding the garden." And then the master says: "If you see someone coming to steal in the garden at night, yell: don't come, I'll shoot! The second time yell: don't come, I'll shoot. Third time yell, don't come, I'll shoot. If the thief comes into the garden, you may shoot and nothing will happen to you for it." So the fellow goes to the garden and guards it at night. Nobody comes. He stands guard the second night; nobody comes. He guards the third night; nobody comes. The master thinks, let me go and see secretly if the boy is guarding faithfully or if he is sleeping. The master does not go in the garden through the gate, but he climbs up the wall. The boy yells: "Go away, don't come!" He does not say anything, but climbs, and the boy yells a second time: "Go away, don't come!" He still climbs without saying anything, and the boy yells a third time: "Go away, don't come!" but he does not answer. He starts getting down into the garden, and the boy shot him; he died on the spot. The mistress is waiting in the house, but the master does not come back. Why does he not come back? The mistress wonders if everything is all right, "Wait, I'll go and see," and she goes through the gate to the boy and asks him: "Didn't you see the master, he left for the garden? I wonder what is taking so long." The boy said: "I didn't see the master. Somebody, whoever it was, was climbing over the wall, and I shot him. Perhaps it was the master." And when they went together to look, there was the master. So they buried him since he was dead, for a dead one cannot be alive any more.

The mistress proposes to the boy, and he takes her as his bride. So they have a wedding and sleep together as man and wife for three nights. Then they take a sauna bath; the bathhouse is heated for them. They go in; the mistress gets undressed and goes up to the bench, but the boy does not undress. The mistress says to her husband: "Why don't you [polite form] get undressed?" Her husband answers: "I don't want to; I am ashamed because I have a seam in my stomach." The mistress remembers: oh yes, I had a child, and the master opened his stomach and put him into the sea; maybe this is he. She asks: "How did you get the seam in your stomach?" The boy answers: "I don't know, but I had been put into a chest and my stomach had been opened when I was a small boy. And I floated in the chest to a hermit's shore, and he took me and brought me up until now." The mistress realized that now she had her own son as husband. She said: "You are certainly my own son." He put a hat on his head and took farewell, because "you, mother, were my wife." So he leaves and goes along.

He goes to a priest and says: "Father, absolve me." The priest says: "What is your sin, my son?" The boy answers: "I killed my father and married my mother." The priest says: "I won't absolve you, go on, you have sinned a lot." He kills the priest and walks on, until he meets another priest. He says: "Father, absolve me." The priest says "What is

your sin, my son?" "My sin is this: I killed a priest, I killed my father,
I married my mother." The priest says: "I won't absolve you, go on,
you have sinned a lot." So he kills the second priest and goes to a third
priest and says the same thing: "Father, absolve me." The priest says:
"What is your sin, my son?" He says: "I killed two priests and my father
and married my mother." "I absolve you," he says. And then the priest
hires ten men to dig a well in the yard. He puts the boy in a separate
room for the night. After the night he comes out on his knees. The
priest asks him: "What did you see while you were lying there?" "What
did I see? The Gods came there and I was beaten with iron weapons so
that I cannot even move." The priest said: "That's how you paid, by
being beaten." The following day the men dig the well, and the priest
puts the boy in that separated room for the second night. On the following day, he crawls out, and the priest asks: "What did you see, my son,
while you were lying there?" "Gods came; I was beaten with iron
weapons so that I cannot even move." "That's how you paid, by being
beaten." On the third day, he has ten men digging the well again, and
he puts the boy into that room for the third night. After the third night,
he comes out. The priest says: "What did you see, my son, while you
were lying there?" "What did I see, the Gods came, I was being beaten
with iron bars and could not move."

The well is finished, and the men take him and put him into the well
and lock it. They go to the sea and throw the key into the water.
"Whenever this key gets in somebody's hands, you will get out of the
well." The priest lives who knows how long and forgets even whether
the boy was put there or not. Then the priest gets a strong craving for
fish. The seine-haulers of that lake come, and the priest sends a helper
to buy fish from them, as much as they have. When the helper goes to
the fishermen, the priest says: "Call the fish." When they haul the seine
in there is only one pike in it. So the helper says to the fishermen: "Sell
this pike to the priest." The seine-haulers say: "We really shouldn't sell
it, but we'll sell it to the priest." They sell the pike to the helper to take
it to the priest. When the helper brings the pike, the priest says: "Open
it." He starts to open it. There is a key in the pike's stomach, and the
helper gives it to the priest. He ponders over it: what kind of a key is
this now? Then he tries to remember and recalls: I put a boy into a well
a long time ago. And he again hires men to look for it. Grass has grown
all over the yard. He does not remember any more where it could be,
and they look and look around the yard. They find a well cover, and
the priest sees that there is a lock on it. He tries to open it with the key.
It opens the lock, and when the priest raised the cover, the man's hair
had grown up to it and they saw him suddenly fly into the sky.

LP1(NG) THE BOY THAT MARRIED HIS MOTHER

Source: J. Qvigstad, *Lappiske Eventyr og Sagn,* vol. 1 (Oslo, 1927), no. 29 (pp. 143–44). The tale was collected for Qvigstad in Varanger in 1891 by Isak Persen Saba, a schoolteacher. The present translation is from the Norwegian. The Lappish original also appears in the cited volume as no. 29 (pp. 142–43). Translated by Annette Voth.

Once upon a time there were two sorcerers [*noaide*] who wandered from place to place making prophecies about this and that. Once they came to a farm, and on that farm a ewe was about to give birth to a lamb. The one says, "Why do we not help that ewe?" The other answers, "We should probably help it; but the wolf will eat the lamb." The ewe gave birth to the lamb, and the lamb lived until autumn. When autumn came, the people on the farm slaughtered the lamb. Then the two sorcerers came again to that same farm. At that time the wife was giving birth to a child. The people asked the two sorcerers to help the woman; but they said, "We should probably help her, but he will kill his father, you know, and marry his mother." The father and mother did not believe it; for they saw that the prophecy about the lamb had not come true.

So they cooked the meat of the lamb, which the sorcerers had foretold would be eaten by the wolf. When they had cooked the meat, they set the cauldron outside to cool and themselves went inside. Then the wolf came and ate all the meat and thereafter drank the bree. Then they said, "Certainly it is true, that which the sorcerers said; it can well happen also that our child will turn out as they said." And so the father took a knife and slashed the child on the breast with it (he wanted to kill the child); but the mother said: "It is not necessary to kill the child; but make a basket which is watertight, put the child in it, and throw it into the sea!" The man did so. The child was put in a basket and thrown into the sea. The basket drifted to an island and was found by a man who took the child and reared it.

When the child became full grown, he gave himself to wandering and came to a farm. There he became a farmhand. One time the wife gave him a gun and said, "Go out tonight and guard the field, and if anyone comes into the field, it is a thief, and you must shoot him." The boy did that. When he had been there a while, he saw someone walking in the field; he shot at once. It was the farmer he shot; for the farmer had not been there when the wife set the boy to watching the field. The wife became a widow, and the boy married her.

One time they were in the sauna; the woman became aware of the wound on the man's breast and asked, "Why do you have a wound on your breast?" The man told why he had a wound on his breast, and about his whole life. For the first time the mother understood that it was her son she had married.

LI1 STORIES OF FATHER AND SON

Source: LMD III 161 (58). (LMD = Lietuvių mokslo draugijos tautosakos rankrasciai LTSR Mokslų akademijos Lietuvių kalbos ir literatūros instituto, i.e., Lithuanian National Academy of Manuscripts.) This
tale was copied down by Leonas Kairys in 1933, in the village of
Aidukus, state of Švenčionys, province of Švenčionys. Translated by
Michael J. Connelly.

There was an old man and his wife, and to them came to stay overnight an angel of God and Jesus. The old man said, "It would be no
bother to take you in, but there is no place to sleep." "You know, sir,
it would be good even to be upon the barn hearth."[1] The old man said,
"Go and climb up on the barn hearth, then." So they went and climbed
up upon it. But the old man was afraid of them, and kept watch, lest
they do anything wrong. Now his wife was sick.[2] So God let the angel
guard at which of two moments the birth would take place. For there
were those who said that if he were born at one moment, he would be a
great tailor,[3] but if he were born at another moment, he would shoot
his own father. The father came to the hut and said, "You know, wife,
that we have heard people say that if he is born at one minute, he will
be a great tailor, and that if he is born at another minute, he will shoot
me." The old man continued, "I will take him and put him in the sea."
The woman said, "Take him, old husband." He took him and brought
him and placed him in the ocean. Now a great wave came up, and you,
O child, were tossed back to the shore. Now not far from there happened to be an estate, and the lord was walking by the shore—the sun
was very hot. And when he came close by to see what was there [on the
shore], he saw that it was a small infant. He took you, O child, and
carried you home and brought you up there, and gave him[4] a gun and
said, "Guard the estate, lest anyone steal the apple tree; ask three times,
and the fourth time, shoot." Now as he listened, he thought he heard
someone climbing the apple tree. He called out once. Just silence. He
called out again. Still silence. He said, "Answer, or I'll shoot." Still
silence. So he took aim and fired.

1. *Tvarto,* a sort of brick stove to heat up the barn; or simply a table or a bench.
2. *Sirgo*—not specifically labor pains.
3. In old Lithuanian culture, a tailor was especially honored, since he didn't have
to do the manual labor of the old peasants.
4. A sudden shift from apostrophe to third person.

LI2 STORIES OF FATHER AND SON

Source: LTR 1550 (74). (LTR = LTSR Mokslų akademijos Lietuvių kalbos ir literatūros instituto Lietuvių tautosakos rankraštynas, i.e,, Lithuanian Academy of Language and Literature.) Told by Mykolo
Lisausko, age seventy-five, and written down by Bronius Abelevičius,
1938, in the village of Navikys, state of Salako, province of Zarasai.
Translated by Michael J. Connelly.

The men came to a house of lodging, and they foretold future fortunes, to one man giving one prophecy, another to another, just as
something would happen to each one. Now to a certain lord there would
be born a child, and he would kill his father. Then the child's birth
occurred. He thinks to himself what he should do with the child,
whether to kill him or let him go. He thought that he would make a
raft and let him go into the water with the raft. He let him into the
water upon the raft. Now for the lord. Now there was another man riding by on a road and he saw something floating along, and told the
coachman to fetch it out. And he took the child home with him. He
brought him up and brought him up and brought him up until he was
twenty years old, and then let him go out into the world to seek his
livelihood. So he went on his way, and came to an estate to guard. And
as he was guarding the estate, the lord came into the estate to find out
if he was guarding it diligently. For it had been agreed that whoever
entered the estate, he should shoot them. So when he came in, the
guard said "Stop," but he did not, so he fell and the guard shot him.
And when you were shot, oh lord, you were buried—there's nothing
you can do about it—it was arranged that it would happen. Now this
guard was very appealing to the lord's wife, and she married him. And
when they went to the priest for confession, he refused them absolution, and the reason he refused was that he knew that [the guard] had
married his own mother. And when they went to the bishop for confession, he told them each to go on his separate way. This is what they did,
and parted.

LI3 STORIES OF FATHER AND SON

Source: LTR 1550 (119). (For the abbreviation LTR, see the headnotes
to the preceding tale.) Told by Antano Lisausko, age forty-five, and
written down by Bronius Abelevičius, in 1938, in the village of Čigon-
iškiai, state of Salako, province of Zarasai. Translated by Michael J.
Connelly.

There was a married lord. And there came to him Jesus with the
twelve apostles asking for lodging. He let them into the linen barn to
lodge. Then the lord went away and thought what he was going to do

with them. And a priest came to him who foretold fortune and misfortune. To this lord he foretold that a son would be born and he would shoot his father and marry his own mother. And at the very moment he said this, a son was born, and the lord, knowing what had been foretold, took and baptized the child, and making a raft, put his son on it and wrote his name on it, and that he had been baptized by his own parents, and then with the raft, put the child into the sea.

A king was riding by and saw that there was something bobbing in the sea and so told his coachman to swim out and find out what it was. He told the king that it was a very small infant, and the king told him to take up the living foundling.

And when the child had grown up in years, and when there was a war, he, as if the king's son, happened to go back to his own country. And he came to a certain house and asked for night lodging. He was told to go into the estate and keep watch and guard, lest anyone steal the apple tree. Now he was greatly appealing to the lord's wife, so much so that she fell in love with him. And the lady told the lord to find out whether he was watching or sleeping. For he had been directly told to guard well: "If you see anyone loitering, ask three times, and if there is no reply, shoot."

The lord, thinking the guard was asleep, said nothing, so the guard in anger shot him. Now frightened that he had shot the lord, he came and told the lady, but the lady did not cry too much about it. Indeed, the situation was pleasing to her, and she said, "It's no big thing; we'll bury him."

After the burial, she married the guard. After the marriage, he journeyed back to his own king. He took his papers and journeyed back to his own people. And when he looked over the papers, it appears that this was his mother, and that it was written that he was baptized by his father.

"What are we sinners to do? We will sell the homestead and divide it up among the poor, and we will take bread for the journey, and will part and go our separate ways." And as they went along praying, they were remembering their sins.

Now when he had lived with the king, it had been offered to him to go to the holy city, where the holy father is selected. So now he went to the holy city, and there he stood and was selected as the holy father.

But his mother, the greatest sinner, went to the holy father and sought absolution, and during the absolution, it appeared to her that this was her son. And so living with her son, she came to die, and he buried her as if he were the greatest sinner.

LA1 A TALE ABOUT HOW RIDDLES CAME INTO EXISTENCE

Source: I. J. Niedre, ed. *Latviešu Pasakas* (Riga, 1948), 2: 89. Written down by A. Rimdžuna in Rundale, Bauska (central southern Latvia). Translated by Juris Rozìtis.

A son was born to a king. In a dream, the king was told that his son would slay his father and marry his mother. For this reason, the king had his son thrown into a river. Some boatmen were passing by, and they took the king's son and carried him away to foreign lands. There he grew up as a tramp. The strangers told him, however, whence he had been brought. The son said he would go to seek his fortune, and began wandering.

It happened that in a narrow mountain pass, he met some grand lords driving by. Not being able to get past, he killed the lords and went away. He went on and on, and came to a city where a queen lived (his former mother). Before the city stood a wizard-monster: half-animal, half-human. He asked riddles. Whosoever could not answer his riddles, was mauled on the spot.

The king's son's turn to answer the riddles came. The wizard asked him this riddle: "Who walks on all fours in the morning, on two legs in the afternoon, and on three legs in the evening?"

The prince guessed correctly and was thus saved. The monster disappeared. The queen had the guesser of the riddle brought to her. As a reward she married him, because he had saved the whole city from the wizard's terror.

Finally, it came to light that the prophecy the king had dreamt had come true.

Thus from that time on, riddles came to be.

IR1 THE STORY OF JUDAS

Source: Irish Folklore Collections, Dublin, MS. Vol. 73, pp. 297–306. Collected or told by [record ambiguous] Pádraic O'Maoláin of Eoghanacht, Aran, County Galway, November 11, 1932. Translated by Kenneth E. Nilsen.

A poor scholar was traveling about long, long ago, and he came to a house, and a young child, a boy, had just been born in that house. The poor scholar told the child's mother and those who were gathered in the house that a hard fate was in store for the child who had just been born, that he would go through many tribulations and that he would cause a great deal of destruction when he grew up. He told them that it would come to pass that he would kill his own father, that he would marry his mother, and that he would crucify the Savior. In any case, the child was baptized, and he was named Judas, and it was noticed at that time that he had a black cross on his back between his shoulder blades.

The child's mother continued to think about the poor scholar's conversation, and it worried her a great deal. Finally, she became afraid of the child, and she decided to rid herself of him. She prepared a coffin for him, and she put him in it, and she put some food or milk in it, and she threw the coffin into the river or sea that was near the house. The coffin was moving along with the wind and the current until it reached land in a far-off country. A man was walking along the shore, and he found the coffin and opened it and found the child in it. He brought the child to the house of a gentleman, and when the gentleman saw the child, he decided to keep him and to raise him together with his own children. This situation continued for a number of years until Judas was a grown boy approaching manhood. One day, he and the gentleman's children were hitting a ball when Judas hit one of the gentleman's children with a stick and accidentally broke his leg. He was severely reprimanded, and someone told him that he had been found washed ashore and that no one knew who he was or who his family was. Judas had not known until then that he was not one of the gentleman's children. When he got that information, he took off, and at last he came to the house where there was a young couple. He told the man of the house that he was looking for work, and the man of the house said that he needed a workman, and they settled with each other. Judas spent a number of years working for him without any mishap.

The man of the house had an apple orchard, and people used to come at night and steal apples. One night Judas was placed on guard in the orchard, and he climbed up to the top of a tree, and he took a load of stones with him. Some time late in the night a man came into the orchard and stood under the tree that Judas was in, and he started shaking it so that the apples would fall down to him. Judas threw a stone at him, and he managed to hit him on the top of his head and killed him. He did not know at that time what man he had killed, and he did not wait to find out either but he left the district the next day before he could be pursued for having killed the man.

He traveled along not knowing where he was going, but when he thought he was far enough from the place where he had done the killing, he hired himself out to a farmer. He spent a number of years working for him and things went along quite well. The farmer was rather fond of him, and the farmer, hoping to improve Judas's lot, started advising him to marry a widow who was living near them. He mentioned it so often that Judas finally said that he was willing to marry her if she would marry him. The farmer and he went to ask for her one night, the marriage was arranged, and Judas and the widow were married without much delay. That was fine until one day Judas was changing wet clothes he had on, and his wife saw the black cross between his shoulder blades. Her soul almost fell out of her with fear when she saw it, because she immediately recognized that it was her own son that she had as a husband. Judas did not know any of this until she told him all about his birth and what the poor scholar had said and everything else. From the story it came out that it was his own father that Judas had killed with a rock in the apple orchard and that much of the poor scholar's talk was true. Anyway, "He killed his father and he married his mother."

Then Judas went away sad, brokenhearted, and ashamed because of all the destruction he had caused, and he walked along until he came to the place where our Savior was going about teaching the people. He often went along in Jesus' company, and at least he was accepted as one of the disciples. He was all right for a while and very repentant for all that he had done, but gradually greed and deceit started to increase in his heart. He found fault with Mary Magdalene because she put a box of ointment on the feet of our Savior, making out that it was more proper to give money to the poor. In the end he became so bad that he arranged to betray Jesus for money, and after doing that he went to the Last Supper along with the other disciples. When our Lord said that one of his disciples was going to betray him, Judas, as well as the others, asked Him, "Am I the one, lord?" Unbeknownst to the others, our Lord told him that he was the one. A short time after this Judas left the room and was struck by regret for what he had done. He went to the leaders from whom he had gotten the money for betraying Jesus, and he threw the money back at them and said that what he had done was wrong. He received little satisfaction from them, but they put the money aside to buy a place in which to bury strangers. Judas went away from them, and with the burden of grief, regret, and heartbreak that was on him, he went and hanged himself with a rope from a tree.

A number of years after this some monks were sailing on the sea as if they were fishing west of the Breanndain,[1] and they saw what they thought was a small little island rising out of the sea. They made for it, and as they came near it, they saw that it was an island of ice and that there was one man on it. They came close enough to be able to talk to him and ask him who he was and what he was doing in such a place. He told them that he was Judas. "I am Judas," he said, "who betrayed Christ, and I am damned in Hell forever except that I get one day a year to come here to cool myself off. I have been here since the sun rose

1. A place name; the place is not readily identifiable.

today, and when the sun goes down this evening a group of devils from Hell will come to take me back with them." The monks felt so sorry for him that they started to pray to God to see if He would give him an extra day. The sun was about ready to go down at that time, and the monks saw a group of devils coming through the sea like a school of porpoises or whales, but they could not land on the island of ice because Judas had received an extension until sunset the next day as a result of the prayers of the monks. When the monks saw this, they raised their sail and headed for home.

IR2 JUDAS

Source: Irish Folklore Collections, Dublin, MS. Vol. 605, pp. 66-71. From County Galway, Barony of Moycullen, Parish of Cill Chuimín. Written down February 10, 1959 by Proinsias De Búrca (Francis Burke) from the recitation of Pádhraic Ó hIoláin, age eighty, a farmer, living in the townland of Gort Riabhach, born and raised in Moycullen. He heard the story years ago from old people who lived in Moycullen. Translated by Kenneth E. Nilsen.

A poor scholar was once going around asking for alms, and he came to the house of a well-to-do man. But in the night the woman of the house was about to have a child, and there was a "nurse" taking care of her, if "nurse" is the right thing to call her or a "midwife," one of them, it is all the same. But in any case, late at night she told the man of the house and the poor scholar to go outside, and they went out. It was a fine night, and the poor scholar was looking at the stars. And he said to the man of the house, "you had better go in," he said, "and if the child is not born yet," he said, "try to delay him for a few minutes." He went in and soon came out and told the poor scholar that the child had been born. "O, there is no harm in it," said the poor scholar. "Well," said the man, "you have to give me some explanation for it," he said, "before you leave here." "Ah, well," said he [the scholar], "there is no particular harm in the story," he said, "leave it as it is." "O, you will not leave this place," he said [the man of the house], "you have to give an explanation for it." "Well," said the poor scholar, said he, "go in," he said, "and if the likeness of a lamb's tail is not growing between his shoulder blades, you can say that I am a liar."

He went in, and he found things as the poor scholar had said, and he came out again. "Well," he said, "you have not given me a good explantion yet," he said. "You have to give me an explanation," he said, "about this story." "It would be better for you," said the poor scholar, "to forget about it, much better." But in spite of this, he frightened the poor scholar so much that he said, "Well now," he said, "he will kill you," he said, "and he will be married to his mother," he said, "and he will betray Christ." "O," the man said. He could not stop until he had told the mother, and of course she took fright, and she asked what should be done with him. "It is best to burn him," she said. "O, we will not burn him," he said, "but we will make a little box for him, and we will put him in it, and we will throw it into the sea." The little box was made, and the child was put into the little box with a lot of cotton around him; he was wrapped up and the little box was thrown into the sea. The little box went along and did not stop until it came on the top of a wave to the land of a gentleman, the "demesne" of a gentleman. Well, that was fine, the servant girl ran in, she had been outside, and she told the gentleman that a small box was coming in on top of the wave and that it would soon be in. The gentleman sent a messenger out, and the little box was taken in, and Judas was found in the box, and when it was opened he was perspiring. The child was taken out, and he was cared for in every way as he grew up. When he was hardy enough, he started going to school together with the gentleman's children. Well, one day, on their way home from school they were on a bridge looking down at the river below them, and Judas took hold of the legs of one of the gentleman's children, lifted him up, and threw him into the river, and he drifted with the current and was drowned. They came home, and the other school children told what had happened.

"I said," said the gentleman's wife, "that it was not for any good that he came. What will be done with him now?" she said. "He will be driven away," he said, "and he can wander about aimlessly," he said. "I believe that is how he came."

Judas was sent away, and he wandered about like a poor scholar who would be here for a while and there for a while, and in the end he was asking for alms in order to pay for books. Judas grew up to be a fine man and a very learned man, and he traveled throughout the country. He came in to his mother and father and asked if he could have lodging until morning, and they told him that he could and why couldn't he. He stayed there, and they thought him quite good-looking when they saw him the next morning. But the father was out and he was up in a tree knocking down apples, and Judas took one of the apples and threw it and hit the father, and the father fell down out of the tree dead cold, and he [Judas] came in and told it to the mother. They went out together, and they found the father dead in the big field. Well, when the father was buried and everything done, Judas stayed together with the mother in the house, and she was very fond of him. Finally, Judas married his mother, and at night as they went to sleep, when he took off his clothes she noticed the likeness of a lamb's tail growing between his shoulder blades. She yelled, and she told him the story. Judas wandered off and he continued to roam about and learn, becoming a very clever man, until finally he joined the twelve apostles, and he was highly respected. And one day the Jews were hunting after the Son of God so that they could hang him and crucify him. And Judas spied on the Son of God, and he told them (the Jews) to come the next day and that there would be no red-haired man in the group except the Son of God. They came the next day, and all of the apostles had the same color hair. Well, they told Judas that he was leading them astray. He said that he was not, but that they should come the next day and that none of the apostles was exactly six feet tall but the Son of God. They came and they measured the men, and all of them were exactly six feet tall. They reproached Judas again.

"Well, come tomorrow," he said, "and I will go up to him, and I will kiss him, and then you can seize him and take him away."

They came the third day, and Judas went up to the Son of God and kissed him, and the Jews came and seized him so that they could hang him and crucify him.

"Oh, Judas," he said, "that was a treacherous kiss." That is how they found out.

IR3 A SON WHO KILLED HIS FATHER

Source: Irish Folklore Collections, Dublin, MS. Vol. 258, pp. 288–92. From County Galway, 1967. Written down by Proinsias De Búrca (Francis Burke). Translated by Kenneth E. Nilsen.

There was a king in Ireland a long time ago. I suppose it was three or four hundred years ago, anyway. He had only one son. Well, the day his wife was giving birth to the son, who should come there but a poor scholar. He came in. When he had been there for a while, he started reading his book, and he asked the "nurses" who were running around the house what was the matter. "The queen," they said, "is about to give birth." "Tell them," he said, "to try to delay it for five minutes." They went away, and they soon came back and said that it could not be done. "That cannot be helped then," he said.

By God, the child was born, and it was a son. But when the poor scholar was leaving in the morning, the king asked him why he had been trying to delay the child's birth the night before. "Ah, do not worry about it," he said, "maybe you ought not to worry about it." "It is no use," the king said, "you have to tell me." "Well," he said, "I was trying to delay him because when he grows up and is twenty-one years old, he is going to kill you. He will kill you then. There will be no man in the world as strong as he." "That is rather bad," the king said.

The poor scholar left and they discussed the matter for two or three days. They said it would be best to kill him before he could grow up and kill his father. Well, they got a box; they fixed it up; they put him into the box, closed it on him, and threw it out into the river.

The box moved along until it had gone about a half mile. The king had a steward who watched over things for him. The steward found the box on land. He opened the box and found the child inside perspiring.

"It is a great shame to let a fine child like you die if it can be prevented," he said.

He took him home to his wife. He had one or two sons of his own. He took very good care of him, raised him well and sent him to school. He went to school for a good while and became a very fine man. Well, when he and the steward's son were young lads, the steward's son said to him that they should go to the king's garden, that it was full of apples, and try to steal a bunch of apples at night. The two of them went off together and went into the garden. The king was on the lookout. They had not been in the garden long when they heard the king coming toward them. His own son, who did not know who he was, grabbed a stone, struck the king with the stone, and killed him. Away with the two of them then, and they took off until they came to the steward's house.

Well, the king was found dead, and it was not known what had happened to him. The next night, then, the king's son asked the steward's son if he would go to the wake. He said that he would go lest people should think that they were responsible. This way no one would take any notice of them. They went there and spent the night at the king's wake. The king's wife saw this one [her son]. She thought that she had never seen a more handsome man, and she said that she would have him for herself if she could. She sent for him two days later, and he came. She told him that he might as well marry her. He said that he was not willing to marry her because he was too young. But it was no use. The day they were going to get married, he was outside washing himself and getting himself ready for the wedding. And what should she see on his back but a mole that she had seen on the back of her child when he was born. She was certain that he was her son.

"O," she said, "I recognize him well. You are my son. You are the one who killed your father."

"It may be that I am," he said.

Away with him and off he went. He went away, and he was not seen again. He went into the forest and wandered until he came to another kingdom. He spent some time traveling around in this kingdom. He met a young queen and she fell in love with him. He was a very good-looking man. She went up to him and asked him what he thought of marrying her.

"Oh well," he said, "I do not think that you will marry me."

"Oh, I will," she said, "If you are willing to marry me."

"Well," he said, "in that case we might as well make the arrangements."

They did, and he married the young queen, and she took him to live with her in the castle. She was all her father had, and they lived happily in the castle forever after. I do not know what happened to them from then on.

IR4 A BOY WHO KILLED HIS FATHER AND WAS INTIMATE WITH HIS MOTHER

Source: Irish Folklore Collections, Dublin, MS. Vol. 186, pp. 478-79. From County Donegal, Barony of South Raphoe, Parish of Cill Taobhóg. Written down by Lian MacMeanman (William McMenamon) on May 8, 1936, from the recitation of Heddy Va Muighe (O'Moy), age eighty-one, a farmer, living in the townland of Glaiseach Beag, born and raised in the same place. He heard the story forty years earlier from Séumas Mhac Gaoithín (James MacGeehin), age eighty-five, who lived at that time in Srath an Airbhir, Parish of Inis Cael. Translated by Kenneth E. Nilsen.

Well, a man was traveling around a long time ago, and whenever a child was born, if he was there, he was able to say what was in store for him. Once he was in a place where a male child was born, and it was the child's fate to kill his father and to be intimate with his mother. They took the child off and put him into a box and threw it into the sea. It happened that fishermen were going by, and they found the box.

The child was raised. Then he got a job with a gentleman guarding his apple orchard. His father was going around one day, and he went in to pick apples. He shot him and killed him. When he came his mother was there—he came and he stayed—he said that he would stay with her, since he had killed his father. He stayed with his mother. He stayed with his mother for a very long time. Then he was intimate with his mother. The story turned out to be true.

IR5 A SON WHO KILLED HIS FATHER AND MARRIED HIS MOTHER

Source: Irish Folklore Collections, Dublin, MS. Vol. 166, pp. 514-16. From County Galway, the Barony and the Parish at Ros. Written down by Proinsias De Búrca (Francis Burke) on January 1, 1936, from the recitation of Proinsias De Búrca. The records of the Irish Folklore Collections are evidently in error here, and a second hand has added "(Seoighe?)" before De Búrca. The informant, whoever it was, was age twenty-one, a worker, living in An Charraig Láir, born and raised there. He heard this story from Seán Ó Muldhia, age fifty, who lived in An Baile Ard. Translated by Kenneth E. Nilsen.

Once upon a time there was a man, and he got married, and within a year a son was born. It was written on the son's side that he would kill his father and marry his mother when he grew to be a man. That scared his father a great deal, and he made a box for him, and he put plenty to eat and drink in the box. He also put his son in it and threw it into the sea.

The box traveled along until it landed at some other island. A man found the box and took it home and opened it. He found the child inside. He raised the child until he was a young man, and then he left him. "I may as well go and earn my living in some other place," the young man said.

He traveled along until he came back to Ireland, and he got a job working for a farmer. He looked after cattle for the farmer. Another farmer had an apple orchard near the farm where he was working. The nice apples in the orchard tempted him greatly. One day he went to the orchard, and he climbed up a tree, and he put a few stones in his pocket. He had not been up in the tree for long when the farmer came with a gun. When he saw the boy in the tree, he raised his gun to shoot him. The boy in the tree took a stone out of his pocket, threw it at the man, and killed him. He went by that way quite often, and he used to go in to visit the widow. He hadn't been going there for long before he and the widow married. No one ever found out who killed the other man. But he and the widow were going to sleep, and she saw it written on his side that he would kill his father and marry his mother when he grew up. "Oh," she said, "you are my son." And then she told him the story. He left and said that he would not stay in the house any longer.

He brought chains and a lock, and he went out to an island, and he tied himself up. He put the chains around himself and put a lock on them. Then he threw the key into the sea. People used to go to the island, but no one managed to cut the chains or open them. People used to bring food to him, and at first he would not eat anything, but then when he got hungry, he ate it. People used to go fishing out on the lake there, and a priest went out fishing one day. He caught a fish, and when they opened the fish, they found the key in it. Then they opened the chains, and the boy was taken home and sent to college. He was in college for a while and became a priest. He was given a parish, and who should come to him for confession one day but his mother. When his mother confessed to him, he knew well who she was. When she had finished confessing, he told her that he was her son.

When she heard that, she took fright, and she fell down dead. When he saw her dead, he himself took fright, and he did not live long after that time. That is the end of my story. The blessing of God on the souls of the dead.

IR6 A MAN WHO KILLED HIS FATHER AND WAS
MARRIED TO HIS MOTHER

Source: Irish Folklore Collections, Dublin, MS. Vol. 248, pp. 202-16.
Collected in County Galway, Barony of An Ros, Parish of An Ros
(Clonbur) Pádraic C. Ó'Cadhain (Patrick O'Coyne) wrote down the
story from the recitation of Tomás Herward (Tomb Cheattaigh)
(Thomas Herward), age sixty-three, a farmer, living in the the townland
of Baile Árd, Clonbur, born and raised in the same place. He heard the
story thirty years earlier from Seán Cannon, itinerant peddler, age sixty.
Translated by Kenneth E. Nilsen.

A long time ago there was a poor scholar, and he knew a lot about
this world, and he used to travel about and spend one night in each
house. There was one farmer in particular in whose house he often
stayed, and he came there this night. He was so friendly with the farmer
that he did not have to ask for lodging, but he would just go in. And
he came in this night, and he sat on a chair beside the fire. He had not
been there for long when a woman came from another room, said hello
to him, and told him that there was no suitable place for him that night
because the woman of the house was ill. He apologized and explained
that he had been unaware of that. He got up and walked out. There was
a shortcut through the farmer's land. He was walking along the path
and met the farmer. They greeted each other in a friendly way, and the
farmer asked him why he had passed by his house as opposed to any
other night that he had gone by. The poor scholar told him what the
doctor who was attending his wife had said. The farmer said that the
doctor and his wife would be in one room and that the poor scholar
and he could stay in the kitchen. The poor scholar turned and went
back with him.

When they were near the door, there was a haystack in the field there,
and the poor scholar said that the night was fine and that they should
sit at the base of the haystack for a while. The farmer told him to do
that, and they had not been sitting there long when the poor scholar
told him to go inside and tell the doctor to delay the child for two minutes if he had not already been born. The farmer went in and told the
doctor to delay the child for two minutes, that is, if he had not been
born already. The doctor said that that was a thing that he could not do,
because the child had already been born. The farmer went out and told
the poor scholar. He told him there was no harm in it: only God could
say. The farmer and he went in when everything was ready, and they
spent the night talking to each other by the hearth fire until it was time
for them to go to sleep. When the poor scholar got up in the morning,
he was going to say goodbye and take his leave, but the farmer would
not let him leave until the baptismal celebration was over. The poor

scholar sat down and stayed that night until the celebration was over
and everything settled. The next day he said good-bye and walked out,
and the farmer walked out with him.

When they were parting from each other, the farmer asked him why
he had wanted to delay the child for two minutes. And the poor scholar
told him not to pay the matter any heed, that there was no harm in it!
The farmer told him that he hoped that he would not leave him in dis-
tress, considering what good friends they were. Well, the poor scholar
said that it would have saved a lot of trouble for the child if his arrival
could have been delayed for two minutes.

"It is written on his right side," he says, "that he will kill his father
and will be married to his mother."

The farmer went home grieving greatly, and when the child grew up
so that he was able to sit in his father's lap . . . whenever the mother
was busy doing anything she would place the child on the father's knees
. . . the father would put him aside, and when the mother noticed that
he set him aside she asked him what he had against this child as opposed
to any other child they had had and none of them was living but this
one. The farmer told her to look at his right side when he was taking his
clothes off or putting them on, and then she would know his reason. She
told him that she would not wait for that but that she would strip him
that very moment. When she had stripped him and had seen him, she
asked the father whether they would smother him or drown him. The
father told her that they would not do either of them, but that they
would take good care of him for three or four more years. When he was
old enough to eat his porridge,[1] his father had a cradle made for him.
It had a hood on it and a lock and key. He set up a pot of porridge [?]
for him and a spoon and placed him into the cradle. He locked it up
and threw it into the sea.

It proceeded until it came to the Eastern World. One fine morning
there was a king there standing on his pier, and he saw the box coming
toward him, and it was the color of gold. He thought it was the box of
a ship captain or a sailor, because at that time there were sailing ships,
many of which were shipwrecked and sunk. But he waited on the pier
until the box came in to him, and he thought he had found a treasure. He
lifted the box, took the lock off, and when he opened it, the child was
there, perspiring as he ate his porridge. He took him with him and
brought him into his own house to his wife, and she became exceedingly
angry. She told him that she thought that she was young enough and
good enough for him and that he should not have to do such a thing

---

1. *Puitin;* translation doubtful.

with anyone else. He said that it was not like that at all and that she should come out and he would show her how he had found the child. She walked out with him and when he showed her the cradle and how it was arranged, she became quiet and reasonable. He raised him and sent him to school along with his own children.

At that time the pastime they had after school was playing ball. The boy could play any two of the king's children. The boy always thought that the king was his father until one day he had an argument with the king's children. Then they told him how he had been found. He took off in a rage and went in and told the king what his brothers had said. He asked the king if it was true, and the king said it was true, that he had been found and that he would show him the vessel in which he had arrived. When he showed it to him, he said that he would not stop until he found out how he had gotten there. The king told him he would give him a ship anytime he wished, one that was better than the one he had when he came, and as soon as it landed, if he turned the boat around, it would come home by itself. He did not stop until he landed at his father's pier, and when he turned the ship around in the direction from which it had come, it took off, and that is when he realized that it was enchanted.

He was a fine affable, well-built man, and he went into the house of his father's steward, and he asked for lodging. The steward said that his place was not suitable for such a gentleman. He replied that any place that was good enough for the steward was good enough for him. He gave him lodging, and he thought he would only stay that night, but he was in no hurry to leave. One night when he had been there for a week and they had just eaten their supper, he asked the steward what kind of man lived in the big house. The steward told him that he was the nicest man that could be found, but that he goes out for a walk every night and that he would shoot any one he found in his garden.

"By cripes," he said to himself, "I will go there tonight, and he will not shoot me."

He went out to the garden and put a couple of stones in his pocket. He climbed up a tree. The farmer came out, walked around the garden, and saw something up in the tree. He pointed the gun to shoot, but just as he was ready to shoot, the other man threw a stone at him and killed him. He came down from the tree and went to the steward's house and acted as if nothing had happened. When the farmer's wife thought that her husband had been gone for a long time, she went out looking for him, and she found him dead at the bottom of the tree. She called for the steward, and this fellow went along with the steward and acted as if nothing had happened. They brought him into the house, and he worked there along with the steward while the farmer was being waked and until he was buried.

He was in no hurry to leave. The farmer had not been dead for a long time when, one morning, the steward was out walking, and he met the farmer's wife. She asked him what sort of a man his lodger was. The steward told her that he was the politest man he had ever seen. "Well," she said, "I cannot manage the affairs," she said, "by myself, and you should talk to him." "Indeed," he said, "I thought of that, but I thought it was too soon to mention it to you." "Well," she said, "if I do it at all, it is better for me to do it in time. I cannot run the place by myself."

When the steward came in, he told the lodger the story, and he said that he would not let the opportunity slip by since he had nothing else. They were married, and when the wedding was over that night, they went to sleep. She went to bed before him. At that time the old people had a habit of going to sleep without a shirt on. God must have caused it, because when he went to bed, he had his right side turned toward her. She saw the writing on his right side, and she knew that he was her son. She started to sigh and moan.

"It did not take long for you to regret it," he said.

"Oh, that is not it," she said.

"It is easy to tell from your moaning," he said, "I did not go to ask for you, but you sent word to me."

"Yes, I know," she said, "but you are my son."

"How could I be your son?" he said.

"I will show you," she said, "wait till I get a mirror for you."

She got up, and she brought him a mirror. "Now," she said, "put it in front of the writing that is on your right side." He did.

"Oh, it is true, mother," he said. They got up then, and they spent the night in sorrow.

Well, as soon as he saw that it was getting light out: "Now, mother," he said, "put on the worst suit of clothes you can find, and I will do the same thing, and we will go to two crossroads in such and such a place, and I will give you your choice, and whichever one you leave behind I will take, and we will never meet each other again."

They went off until they came to the two crossroads. She took one of them and he took the one she left behind, and thus they separated. He kept going along until he came to the seashore, to a place where there was a blacksmith. Johnny the Smith was what he was called. He ordered them to make such and such a chain with a lock and key. "You have to come with me now," he said, "and leave me on that island." The name of the island was the Island of Wilderness. "I will not go," said the smith. "No one who went there has ever returned." "I guarantee that you will come back," he said, "but leave me on the island."

The smith went with him and left him on the island. He made the smith tie him up with the chain from the top of his head to the bottom of his foot and lock it with the key.

"Do not come back for me," he said, "for seven years and a day."

"By cripes," he said, "I will never come back if I can get away safely."

As soon as he turned the key in the keyhole, the man who was tied up fell asleep. Life went on and time passed until the seven years were up. Well, there was a bishop, just as we have one in Galway or over in Tuam, and the way they got in was by election. And they were arguing together, some of them trying to elect this one and the rest of them trying to elect someone else.

A blessed spirit came above them from Heaven and he told them not to go any deeper into the matter because neither of the two would be the bishop there, but rather the man who had been tied up in chains on the Island of Wilderness for seven years. So, he told them to go and get him.

Two priests left, and they did not stop but they proceeded constantly until they came to the house of Johnny the Smith. They told him to get ready so they could go to the Island of Wilderness to get the man who had been tied up in chains for seven years.

"Ah," said Johnny, "I have no business there, hardly anyone who had gone there has come back, and it is hardly likely that the man who went there seven years ago is still there."

"He is," said the priest, "he is there and we have to go get him." They took off and came to the Island of Wilderness, and he was there, still looking as fine as any man you have ever seen. He was asleep, and as soon as they turned the key in the lock, he woke up. He asked Johnny why he had come before the seven years and a day had passed.

"That much time has passed," the priest said, "and three days more than that."

"Oh, it has not," he said, "I have been here only since last night. What do you want to see me about?"

"You have to be bishop in such and such a place," they said.

He was very happy then. He went with them and became bishop. Well, you know that when a new bishop comes to a place, everyone comes to him to confess his sins. He had not been listening for long when his mother came to him.

"You are my mother," he said.

"That cannot be, son," she said.

"Yes, you are," he said.

He got up then and explained to them all he had gone through from beginning to end.

"Well now, my good people," he said, "I will be with you only until twelve o'clock tomorrow." He told them that the woman was his mother.

"I have a good congregation today but I hope I will have twice as many tomorrow because I will be saying goodbye to you."

The clock of Heaven struck twelve. He and his mother turned into two white doves. He gave them a view of Hell and of Heaven. Whoever believed him would go to heaven, and whoever did not believe would have to earn his way. He and his mother went to heaven as two white doves, holy and free from worldly sins. The blessing of God on the souls of the dead.

Slavic

SC1 ST. SIMEON

Source: Vuk Stefanović Karadžić, *Srpske narodne pjesme*, vol. 2, 2d
state ed. (Belgrade, 1895), no. 13 (pp. 58-64). Translated by Albert B.
Lord. In this volume details concerning Karadžić's source for this song
are not given. On his methods as a collector, see Duncan Wilson, *The
Life and Times of Vuk Stefanović Karadžić: 1787-1864* (Oxford,
1970), pp. 314-33. Note that Karadžić had no qualms about editing the
material collected by him or supplied to him by his collecting agents
(p. 319).

   In his lecture on this song, which included a translation of the "St.
Simeon" (SC2) of my collection, Claude Fauriel called it one of the
most popular of Serb legends and pointed out its apparent connection
with Stevan Namanja, the founder of the Serb monarchy. Having ab-
dicated the throne in his old age, he retired to the monastery of Hilendar, which he had founded, and became a monk, taking the name
Simeon. His eldest son, Sava, who appears as the patriarch in "St. Simeon" (SC2), also retired to Hilendar and died there, with the title,
Protopapas, or Patriarch, of Serbia (Miodrag Ibrovac, *Claude Fauriel
et la fortune européenne des poésies populaires grecque et serbe* [Paris,
1966], p. 504.)

E arly in the morning, an old monk,
      Went to the cold Danube.
      To draw water from the Danube,
      To wash himself and to pray to God.
The old man was led by chance
To find a lead chest
Thrown by the waves on the shore.
He thought that there was treasure hidden in it;
Took it away to the monastery.
But when he opened the chest of lead
He did not find treasure hidden inside

170

But a boy child
A young child of seven days.

He took the child out of the chest
And christened him in his monastery;
Gave him a fine name,
Named him most beautifully: Simeon the Foundling.
The monk did not want to give the boy to a nurse;
Raised him himself in the monastery,
Nourished him on honey and sugar.
When the boy reached one year,
He was like any other child of three;
But when he was three years old,
He was like any other child of seven;
But when he was seven years,
He was like any other of twelve,
And when he was twelve,
He was like any other of twenty years.
Simeon the Foundling learned to read marvelously.
He feared no other student nor the abbot.

One morning (it was on the holy Sabbath)
All went out from the monastery school,
To amuse themselves in games,
To jump and throw stones.
Simeon the Foundling jumped farther than all of them,
Jumped farther and threw stones farther.
The monastery students grew angry with him,
Said to the boy Simeon:
"Simeon, you are a foundling.
You have neither family nor tribe,
Do not even know what family you are from.
In the chest, on the bank of the river,
The old abbot found you."
This was troublesome to Simeon the Foundling,
And he went into his monk's cell,
Took in his hand the holy Gospel,
Read in it, and wept tears.

The father abbot came to find him,
And he asked Simeon the Foundling:
"Tell me what the matter is, my son Simeon,
That your eyes overflow with tears.
Tell me what is lacking to you in my monastery."

Simeon the Foundling answered him:
"Sir, father abbot,
The students are mocking me
Because I do not know of what family I am,
Because you found me on the riverbank.
Father abbot, listen to me.
If you believe in the true God,
Give me your white horse from the stable,
Let me go out into the wide world,
That I may seek the one to whom I belong,
Whether I am of a lowly family
Or if I am of a lordly one.
Let me go, or I shall jump into the quiet Danube!"

    The old abbot was sad at heart.
He loved Simeon like his own son;
But he had shining clothes cut for him,
Gave him a thousand ducats
And his white horse from the stable.
So Simeon went out into the wide world.

    Simeon wandered nine years,
Searched everywhere for his family and his tribe.
How could he have found them,
When he did not know how to ask anyone?
When the tenth year began
It came to Simeon the Foundling
To return to his monastery,
And he turned back the white horse.
One morning he rose early
Beneath the city of white Buda.
Foundling Simeon had grown up.
He was handsomer than a maiden;
Had taken good care of his white horse.
He was prancing across the plain of Buda
Singing from his white throat.
The queen of Buda saw him,
And when she saw him,
She called to her trim slave girl:

    "Quickly go down, trim slave girl!
Stop the white horse of that hero,
Tell him: the queen calls you,
Has something to tell you."

Quickly went the trim slave girl,
And took Simeon's horse,
Softly she spoke to Simeon:
"O, hero! The queen calls you,
Has something to tell you."
Simeon turned the white horse back
Into the courtyard beneath the white tower,
Gave the white horse to the trim slave girl,
Went up the steps of the white tower.

When he reached the lady queen,
He doffed his hat, bowed to the ground;
Gave greeting: "God help you!"
And the queen received his greeting;
Sat him down at the table already laid.
They brought him wine and brandy,
And every fine delicacy.
Simeon sat and drank the ruddy wine.
The fair queen could not restrain herself
But ever did she look at Foundling Simeon
And when night began to fall,
She said to Simeon the Foundling:
"Take your clothes off, unknown hero.
You must spend the night with the queen
And love the queen of Buda."
The wine had deceived Simeon.
He took off his clothes and lay with the queen,
Kissing the face of the queen.

But when the dawn of the next day broke,
Then the wine left Simeon,
He saw what had happened,
And he was troubled.
And he sprang to his nimble feet, prepared himself;
Went to his horse.
The queen tried to stop him,
For sweet coffee and brandy.
Simeon would not be stopped.
And he mounted his horse.
He went down across the plain of Buda.
But suddenly he remembered
That he had left his Holy Gospel
With the queen in the white tower.
He turned back his spirited horse,

Stopped the horse in the courtyard,
Went to the white tower.

The lordly young queen was sitting
In the window of her tower,
Reading the Holy Gospel
Weeping tears down her white face.
Simeon said to her:
"Give me, queen, that Holy Gospel."
And the lady queen answered:
"Simeon! May you long be sorrowful!
Evil was the hour when you sought out your family,
More evil the hour when you came to Buda.
And spent the night with the lady queen,
And kissed the face of the queen,
And made love with your own mother!"
When Simeon the Foundling heard this,
He wept tears from his white face.
He took the Holy Gospel,
Now kissed the hand of the queen,
Then went to his white horse,
Mounted and went to his monastery.

When he was opposite the monastery,
The abbot saw him
And recognized his own white horse and on it Simeon,
And he came out to meet him.
From the white horse dismounted Simeon;
He bowed to the black earth,
He kissed the father's hands and the hem of his robe.
And the father abbot said to him:
"Where have you been, Simeon the Foundling?
Where have you been all this time?"
Simeon the Foundling said to him:
"Father abbot, do not ask me.
Evil the hour when I sought out my family,
More evil the hour when I came to Buda."
And Simeon confessed all to him.

But when the abbot had heard this,
He took him by his white hand,
Opened the accursed prison,
Where water lay knee-deep,
And there were snakes and scorpions in the water.

He threw Simeon into the prison,
Closed the door of the accursed prison,
Threw the keys in the quiet Danube,
And the old man spoke quietly:
"When the keys have come forth from the Danube,
May Simeon be absolved of his sin."

Thus nine years passed,
But when the tenth began,
Fishermen caught a fish;
They found the keys in the fish.
They showed it to the old man,
Then he bethought himself of Simeon,
And he took the keys to the prison,
Opened the accursed prison.
There was no more water in the prison,
Neither snakes nor scorpions crawled about,
In the prison, the sun was shining,
Simeon was sitting at a golden table.
He held the Gospels in his hand.

SC2 ST. SIMEON

Source: Vuk Stefanović Karadžić, *Srpske narodne pjesme*, vol. 2, 2d
state ed. (Belgrade, 1895), no. 14 (pp. 64–69). See the headnote to "St.
Simeon" (SC1), above. Translated by Albert B. Lord.

The Czar raised a young girl at Jania,
From infancy by his right side.
He did not raise her to give her to another,
But to take her for himself.
So the Czar desired, but not the girl.
Viziers and courtiers wooed her
But the Czar did not give her away.
He married her himself, by force.

Thereupon a short time passed,
A short time, only three years.
Among them a boy child was found
But the mother could not take care of him.
She wrapped up letters and shirts,
And put him into a heavy leaden casket
And threw him in the deep blue sea.
"O Sea, carry the iniquity from the land.
The one who nourishes the foundling will be as the one who bore him."

And, Sava, the patriarch, rose,
Rose to go hunting.
He hunted a summer day until noon
But he captured no game.
When he had returned to his house,
God granted and fortune brought it about
That he found a chest of lead
That the water had cast on the shore.
And in the chest a boy child.
He did not laugh, nor did he give his little hand.
He had not been blessed or baptized.
Sava took the boy child with him,
Carried him into the church of Vilendar.
There he baptized the child.
They gave him a fine name.
Fine name: Simeon the Foundling.

When the child was old enough to mount a horse
And to bear bright arms,
And had acquired book-learning,
Sava, the patriarch, said to him:
"Dear child, Simeon the Foundling,
I have raised you, boy,
Have raised but not begotten you.
I found you at the edge of the sea.
My son, take these letters and these shirts,
And go from town to town,
Go in quest of your father."

Simeon took the shirts and the letters,
And went from city to city.
He came to Jania.
The Czar of Jania had died,
Had died and was buried.
And the great Czarina remained alone
In her white castle.

And courtiers and viziers sought her hand.
Courtiers sought her, and the Czarina refused them.
She said:
"Choose amongst you sixty champions,
In beauty, that there be no one more beautiful,
In height, that there may be no one taller.
And I, from the top of the white walls,

Shall throw the apple of gold,
And of him who catches the apple of gold,
Of him shall I be the true love."

The sixty heroes assembled.
In beauty, no one was more beautiful;
In height, no one was taller.
They stood beneath the ramparts of the town,
And the great Czarina upon the ramparts.
And she threw the apple of gold.
Simeon the Foundling was there.
He caught the apple of gold
And married the Czarina.

Thereupon a short time passed,
A short time, only three weeks,
And Simeon the Foundling rose to go hunting,
To hunt the swift prey
And the lady Czarina remained alone,
She remained alone in the white castle.
When she shook out the bed,
She found the letters and the shirts.
"Dear God, be praised for all things.
But how gravely I have sinned against you!"

When the sun went to rest,
Simeon the Foundling returned from the hunt.
The lady Czarina walked out before him.
Tears rolled down her lordly face.
"Simeon the Foundling, my own child,
How gravely you have sinned against God!
You have married your own mother,
Without knowing it, my dear child."

When Simeon the Foundling heard this,
He wept tears down his lordly face.
He went to the church of Vilendar,
He threw himself upon the silken lap of Sava,
And began to weep great tears.
"O my father, O Patriarch Sava,
Let me tell you something.
I have gravely sinned against God.
Because I have married my own mother,
Without knowing it, Sava, my father.
Can you grant me absolution for that?"

Sava, the patriarch, answered him:
"O my child, Simeon the Foundling,
I can't absolve you of this.
Your own old mother is no jesting matter.
All the absolution that I can grant you
Is to build a tower of stone,
And to throw you into this tower of stone,
To throw its keys into the sea,
And when the keys emerge from the sea,
Then you will be absolved of your sin."
The patriarch, Sava,
Caused a tower of stone to be built.
He threw Simeon into the tower
And threw the keys into the dark blue sea.

Thereupon thirty years passed
And fishermen went out to sea.
They caught fish on the sea.
They caught one with golden fins.
They made a present of it to the patriarch, Sava.
When Sava had opened the fish,
He found the keys in it,
Sava had actually forgotten about it.
But he recognized them as soon as he saw them.
"Ay ay, by God all-highest!
I have forgotten Simeon.
Here are the keys of my Simeon."

Quickly he opened the door of the prison,
But Simeon had died,
Had died, and had become a saint.

The news spread in all directions.
Many priests gathered at the cloister.
They chanted three days and three nights.
They celebrated the holy vigils.
They chanted the great prayers.
They asked the saint whither he would go,
And the saint wanted to go to the church of Vilendar.
And so the saint rested
In the beautiful church of Vilendar.

A blessing on that Christian brother
Who kisses him, who makes offerings to him,
And looks upon him.

PL1 THE SON WHO KILLED HIS FATHER

Source: Stanisława Dabrowska, "Przypowiastki I Bajki Z Żabna," *Wisła: Miesiecznik Gieograficzny i Etnograficzny* 19 (1905), no. 10 (pp. 398–401). From the village of Zabno, in the district of Krasnostawsk, in the province of Lublin. No further details concerning the collection of the tale are given. Translated by Grażyna Slanda.

In a village a couple got married, and God was to give them children. When the day came, the father brought a woman to his wife, and he himself went out to the corridor and stood there. Suddenly he hears two voices. One voice, from the corridor asks: "So, is he already born?" And a second voice, from behind the window, answers: "No, not yet, but in a moment a son will be born, and when he grows up to be a strong man, he'll kill his father and marry his mother." So the father wondered about it and saddened. Then he opens the doors to the house and asks carefully what was born. They told him: a son. He is not glad that it is a son, but says nothing. Only after the baptism he tells his wife everything, and both think how to remedy this situation. And they agreed that they'd have a little coffin made for the baby and let it go with waters of the river. Because it's easier to remedy now than when he'll grow to be a strong man.

The father went to a carpenter and ordered a coffin, saying that the newborn child had died. They dressed up the baby, put it into the coffin. The father nailed the top, took it to the river, and let it go. Fishermen from other ports came there to catch fish. They cast nets and caught fish. They pulled up, and behold—a box like a little coffin. Curious, they opened it and found a sleeping baby. It amazed them. They thought the baby was dead; they fondled it, and it started crying. They took out the baby and let the coffin float away. One of these fishermen said: "God made me this gift, because I don't have any children, and now God gave me one. I'll take this child."

And he took this baby home, and told his wife: "God gave us great happiness; love this child better than if you suffered severe pains because of him."

A year later God gave them their own children. They had a son. In the third year they had a second son; in the fifth year, a third one, and so they enjoyed five sons [*sic*], and this one was their sixth. When this boy was seven years old, he was alert, strong, and he started helping out his foster father and his mother: he watched geese, pigs, cattle graze. Once, later on, the children somehow quarreled. So they started calling him names: "You are a foundling, a fosterling." And this boy couldn't understand why they called him so, and he complained to his father that the children call him so. And father tells him in answer: "Stupid child! Don't listen to any humbug. I am your father, and you are my son."

And so lots of time passed by. And when this boy became a big man, he learnt quite clearly that what the children explained in anger, that was true.

One day he says to his parents: "You know, my dear parents, what I have to make clear to you. You lived to enjoy your sons so they'll take over your farm. I'll give way."

"And why so?" says the father. "But we want to see you happy. We'll marry you, give you a farm so that you'll be a happy man."

"God reward you for that, you already gave me happiness and property," says the son. "Now I am big, strong, and healthy, you served me as example in farming; this is, mark my words, my property and my treasures."

"Well, too bad, as you wish. Go, if that's what you want, and God bless you," says the father.

So he packed his belongings, they kissed each other, and he left to look for work.

He goes from village to village and somehow doesn't get anything. Either the price is not right, or they say he's too big. And time passes by, until he comes to a village. Night approaches, so he asks a farmer for a place to sleep. The farmer didn't allow him to stay, and after supper asks him where he comes from, where he goes, and why. The country boy told him from where he comes and that he looks for a job. And this farmer says that his farmhand got married and that he can take his place.

And so they agreed and came to terms in half an hour.

The farmer had a big farm, and the boy was fit for farming, so he helped him out in everything.

Spring came, then the last weeks before the new harvest[1] and summer. And this farmer had an orchard that was very beautiful, and just this year the fruit grew plentifully. But what was the good, if a thief picked apples each night? The farmer built a cabin and watched for a few nights. But one night he fell asleep, and the thief stole apples again.

"You go to watch tonight," says the farmer to his helper, "and we have to get rid of this thief. Take a good stick, and when this thief appears, don't hurry, let him become busy and then be ready, jump out, hit his head, and kill him."

The farmer went to sleep, and the country boy took along a stick and went into the cabin.

"Poor world, hard world,[2] how he watches there," says the farmer to his wife. "I'll go to the orchard, move branches. Will he hear it or not?"

And he went to the orchard. The boy thought that it was a thief, he hit him once, and a few more times to make sure. . . . And it happened.

1. Implies hungry times or lack of grain.
2. A proverb.

The boy examined the thief to see if he was dead, and went to the farmhouse to tell the farmer what happened. But since the farmer wasn't there, he told everything to the landlady. And they wait for the farmer's coming to bury this thief. They wait and wait; no sign of the farmer, so they went alone to put everything in order.

And since it was terribly dark, they dug a pit and dragged the corpse into it. They came back home; the farmer wasn't there. Morning came, then noon, and not a word was heard about the farmer, not in the village either, so the landlady says:

"Didn't it happen that you killed the master instead of a thief? We'll dig him out and see."

At midnight they dug him out; undoubtedly the farmer. So the farmer's wife says to her dead husband: "You see, how it is to dig a pit for somebody else."

They covered everything, and told others that he went somewhere and got lost, and they took care of everything.

A year later this country boy would like to propose to this widow, but he hesitates because she is rich and he's poor, so she won't accept him. She thinks about the same thing, that she would like to marry him, but being already older in years, she thinks, he won't take her.

Then one time the landlady says to the country boy:

"I'll tell you this, that since you killed my husband and farmer, you should now marry me."

So, in three weeks, they got married, and in one year they had a son.

They lived together in perfect union, but once the wife says:

"We are married for four years and I don't know where you come from."

"God only knows from where I come. One farmer raised me for twenty-four years, and he found me on a river, in a little coffin."

So the landlady fell down on her knees and cried out:

"What God marks in heaven, can never be avoided on earth!"

And then the "wife" and "mother" tells her "husband" and "son" what happened and how his father heard voices when he was born.

PL2 FATED INCEST

Source: Stanisław Ciszewski, *Krakowiacy: Monografja Etnograficzna,* vol. 1 (Cracow, 1894), no. 58 (pp. 60–63). From the region of Szcz-odrkowice. No further information concerning the collection of the tale is given. Translated by Grażyna Slanda.

A traveler walked and he came to an inn. He came to this inn and asked for a place to sleep. But they did not want him there because a woman was sick. But he said that they [could] allow him to sleep even on this bench, where fiddlers play. So they let him. He accommodated himself and lays down. Meanwhile, as the woman was very ill, one [woman] asks another: "Well, will it come soon?"

But he looked from this bench, [saw] three white persons standing there. Each holds a candle, and one of them says: "If," she says, "a son will be born he will be a thief, in many ways." And the second one says: "If a girl will be born, she will be such a rogue." And the third one says: "If a son will be born, he will be a damn good craftsman, he will know something [cejco] and cabinetmaking and something [cejco]. And then, when he will grow up to older years, so he will kill his father and marry his mother."

When in the morning this traveler got up, he tells people who stayed [i.e., the women] with this woman, that he saw these persons, and they told him he [the newborn child] would have a hair on his head and seventy-five ells long it will be.

So when in the morning this traveler got up, he told these people. Later on, when he [the child] grew to full years, his parents took this son and dismissed him to go away, and themselves, they sold their farm and went far away! And they bought enough land. Later on, after a few years, this son came back to the place, where his parents lived; this place was already plowed and seeded. So he asks: "Hey, farmer, when went this innkeeper who was at this inn?" But they told him later that they did not hear about them, where they turned, in what direction. And so he goes on. Night came. And he entered again an inn and asks for lodging. They took him in, and he starts talking: "If I found good work I would take it and work eagerly and look after a farm." So this innkeeper told him to go near the forest: there lives a rich landlord who needs a helper. And he got up in the morning and went there. He came to this farmer and asks him about work. The farmer took him into his service gladly. And tells him: You will do nothing else but watch my bees, because they steal them. And gave him a double-barreled gun and said: "At midnight, if you see anybody near the bees, shoot him on my responsibility."

Midnight came; something happens to the farmer; he got up in a shirt and shorts; went among bees. The other fired and killed the master.

He runs to the room, to the landlady, and says that he killed a thief. The landlady rushes out, looks, and this is her husband. So then he stayed three years in the service of the landlady and looked after things very well. And after three years he married her.

Once upon a time, one lovely day, they went for a walk to the garden and what happens, his head itches suddenly. And he says to her, to this landlady: "Darling, see what I have on my head." And she started to look and she saw this hair on his head, which was seventy-five ells long, and then she meditated hard and tells him: "You were my son and now you are my husband."

After all that, he left and went far away, until he reached a sea. He came near the sea; a fisherman sits there. And he says to the fisherman: "My dear, didn't you hear about any desert [deserted place] for me, so I could rest and nobody would bother me?" And the fisherman tells him: "I know very well, there is a chapel in the middle of the sea." He took a boat and took him there. When he [fisherman] took him there, so he [boy] ordered him to lock the chapel and made him swear, this fisherman, that he would throw the key into the sea and wouldn't tell anybody about him. So many years later, his mother and wife packed and went en route. "I will go and confess to the Holy Father himself."

As she started, so she came to the Holy Father. And later, the Holy Father, close to his death, had a dream that there is such a one at sea, in the chapel; after his [the Holy Father's] death he will take his place. And he sent clergymen in search of such a one, but they looked for some time and couldn't find him. When the Holy Father was in very bad health, he again sent his clergymen out. And those clergymen found this fisherman who threw the key into the water and tell him: "Fisherman, if you could give us something to eat." But he says that he has nothing for them, and they tell him: "Maybe you will catch a fish for us." And he went fishing, caught two fish, and started preparing them for a meal.

He cut the fish open, and a key was inside this fish, and these clergymen ask him: "What key is it?" And he tells them, and from this joy, they didn't want to wait for the meal; they took a boat and went to him, to this chapel. And they took him to the Holy Father and he replaced him. When he took the place of the Holy Father, so again his mother-wife confessed to him and declared how it was from the beginning, and so after this confession they died together.

BL1 PAUL OF CAESAREA

Source: V. I. Lamanskij, "Neporěšennyj vopros" Bolgarskoe narěčie i pis'mennost' v" xvi–xvii věkax" [An unsolved problem: the Bulgarian dialect and writing in the sixteenth and seventeenth centuries], Pt. 2, in *Žurnal" Ministerstva narodnago prosvěščenija* (Journal of the Ministry of Public Instruction) 144 (St. Petersburg, July 1869): 112–14. Translated by Robert Pardyjak. Lamanskij found this tale in a manuscript in the public library of Ljubljana in northern Yugoslavia. This Bulgarian manuscript contained, in addition to the tale translated here, a discussion of the Day of Judgment (pp. 1–45), the life of St. Petka Ternovskij (pp. 96–103), and the sermon of John Chrysostom on evil wives (p. 108). Lamanskij believed that the manuscript had been written by a Bulgarian in the first half of the seventeenth century (see vol. 143 of the same journal, June 1869). He considered the attribution of the tale of Paul to John Chrysostom a later addition, but he believed, because of the subject matter of the tale, that it was a translation from the Greek.

St. Novaković published a Serb version of the tale of Paul in "Die Oedipus-Sage in der südslavischen Volksdichtung," *Archiv für slavische Philologie* 11 (1888): 324–26. The Serb version is exactly the same as the Bulgarian.

Sermon of our holy father John Chrysostom on spiritual repentance.

How much the apostles rejoice in heaven over one sinner who repents rather than over a righteous man. Listen to me, blessed Christians, and I will tell you a miracle, which took place.

There was a certain king of all Caesarea whose name was Anthon. He begot a son and a daughter, and then king Anthon and his queen died, and his son and his daughter remained and ruled their father's land. Another king wanted the sister and half of the land, and another king wanted her brother as his son-in-law and half of the land. The brother and sister came to an agreement and said: "What will we do if one takes the sister and half of the land?" Then their father's kingdom would be divided. So the brother took his sister, and they ruled their father's kingdom, and they gave birth to a son. And they said: "It is not proper for us to keep this child because it is from a brother and a sister." So they made a box and wrote a document and put it into the box with the child and said that this was the child of a brother and sister. They put it by the sea; let him who finds it know what he is. Then his father died, but his mother remained and ruled the kingdom. And then that box was taken by the wind and carried to the land of Herod, and it was found by a certain monk whose name was Ermola. He preserved the document and raised the child, and he grew and became literate and a great hero before the land of Herod.

His mother understood that there was a young king in the other land but did not know that he was her son, so she sent a letter to him that she would take him as her husband. And he made a marriage agreement with his mother that he would take her as his queen and would be king of all Caesarea. His name was Paul. And he went to the monk Ermola so that he would bless him. Ermola said to him: "O, my son Paul, if you knew who you are and what you are and that it is not fitting that you walk on this earth, much less rule." And Paul said to him: "Why is it not fitting that I rule? I am wise. I am a hero. I am literate, and I know everything, good and bad." And Ermola took the document and gave it to him, and told him: "Read, so you will see what you are." Paul took the document, but did not want to read it, and so gave it to a youth, and mounted a horse, and went to Caesarea. Then he remembered the document that Ermola had given to him and went to a hidden place, read it, and saw what it said. He wept bitterly, beat himself much, and said: "O woe is me, woe is me, accursed one, that the earth tolerated me and did not swallow me alive. And yet I want to rule." And from that time he did not go near his mother at all, and the queen was amazed that he did not come to her in bed. But Paul, every evening, would go into his room and weep much. The queen stopped a youth and asked: "Why is the king troubled?" And the youth said: "He has a document, which the monk Ermola gave him, and he reads it and weeps." The queen said: "I will go and find out what the book says." They gave it to her, and she found out about it and said: "O, woe is me, woe is me, that I was deceived. I am sorry for my son; my sin with my brother was not enough—I wanted to be seduced by my son as well." She told all to her son, how it really was. At that hour the queen dressed in horsecloth and every day ate crumbs of bread with ashes. Paul went to John Chrysostom to tell him everything. When I, John, heard this lawlessness, my soul became small in me, and my hair rose up on my head, and my heart stopped. And I said: "Brother, let such a sin have confession or forgiveness." Then Paul raised his great voice, crying and saying: "O Lord Chrysostom, give me over to death." And I, John, knew a small island by the sea where the water flows around, and inside there was a marble tower, and I brought Paul there inside the tower and chained his arms and legs and locked him in the tower with iron keys. And Paul said to me: "When will you be by me again, holy lord?" And I threw the keys into the sea and said: "When those keys come out of the sea, I will be by you." And I went to my patriarchate.

Twelve years passed. One day, on the Annunciation of the most Holy Mother of God, I was brought fresh fish. I noticed one fish had keys, and I was amazed and did not think I would recognize them after so many years had passed. One night I recalled Paul. And on the next day I announced to the brethren and said: "Alive is the Lord, and alive is my soul, that I will go there and see him in that tower." I left and put in the keys, tried it, and opened it. And I saw Paul shining like the sun, and chrism was flowing from his face. And with such happiness he said to me: "Rejoice, good teacher." And I was blessed through him. I gave him the Eucharist, and then he gave his soul into the hands of God. Later his mother came, and she found salvation of her soul when she repented with all her heart. Have we heard, blessed Christians, what kind of sin the Lord forgives if a person repents with all his heart.

UK1 THE INCESTUOUS ONE (ST. ANDREW)

Source: Mikhail Dragomanov, *Malorusskiia narodnyĭa predaniĭa i razskazy* [Little Russian popular traditions and tales] (Kiev, 1876), no. 29 (pp. 130–31). Translated by Marco Carynnyk.

Once there were a man and a woman, and they had a son. They dreamt that when their son grew up, he would kill his father and live with his mother, and then kill his mother too. They got up and began telling each other their dream. "Let's cut open his stomach, put him in a barrel, and send him out to sea," they said. They proceeded to do so. He drifted and drifted until sailors heard him. "What's that?" they asked. "A child crying in a barrel?" They caught the barrel, took him out, sewed his stomach together, and reared him.

When he grew up, he said good-bye to the sailors and went out to earn his living. He came to his father, who didn't recognize him. He hired himself out to guard his father's orchard, with the agreement that if someone came to the orchard, he would call out three times, and if there was no answer, the third time he would fire. After he had been working for a while, the master said to himself, "I think I'll go see if he's doing what I told him." When he came to the orchard, the son called out once. The father was silent. He called out again—the father was silent. He called out a third time—the father was silent, so the son shot him. When he came and looked at the body, he saw that it was his master. Then he ran to the house, married the mistress, and began to live with her.

One Sunday when he was putting on his shirt she saw his scar. "What's that you have there?"

"When I was little, sailors found me in the ocean with my stomach cut open and sewed it up."

"I'm your mother!"

He immediately killed her and went away. After walking about a good deal, he came to a priest and asked for absolution.

"What are your sins?"

He told the priest.

"No, I can't absolve you!"

He killed the priest and went to another one. The second one told him the same thing, so he killed him as well and went to a third priest.

"Here's a piece of charred apple tree. Plant it on that mountain and water it morning and night with water you have brought on your hands and knees in your mouth. If the wood takes root and puts forth apples, blow on it. If the apples fall down your sins are forgiven."

When he was twenty-five years old apples grew on the tree. He blew on the tree, and all the apples except two fell off. He went to the priest again.

"Now come with me, and I'll throw you in a well."

He put him in a well, locked the iron lid, covered it with earth, and threw the keys in the ocean. Thirty years later the priest's fishermen caught a pike, cut it open, and found the keys inside. They brought the keys to the priest. "O yes," said the priest, "I have a holy man." They went to the well and opened it, but he had died, and a candle was burning over him. Then all his sins were forgiven, and he became a saint.

UK2 MARY OF EGYPT

Source: P. P. Čubinskij, *Trudy Ètnografičesko-statističeskoj èkspedicii v" zapadno-russkijkraj* [Works of the Ethnographic-statistical Expedition to the Western-Russian Territory], Jugo-zapadnyj otdel" [South-western division], (St. Petersburg, 1872), 1:182–83. Translated by Robert Pardyjak.

This is what is sung in church at worship: "Most Holy Mother Mary, pray to God for us," and "Most Holy Father Andrew, pray to God for us," but Mary was the mother of Andrew and later became his wife also. This is how it happened: Mary did not love her husband, but loved another, so she went and poisoned her husband. At that time Andrew was small, and her lover said to her: "Kill your child, and I will take you."

She went and cut open Andrew's belly and thought that he would live no more. In order that no one would find it out, she quickly put him into a box and put it on the river. The box sailed off and came to a foreign land where the daughter of a gardener somehow caught the box, brought it home, and sewed up Andrew's belly. And he grew up there. And the gardener watched him work in the garden and wanted to marry him to his daughter who had found him. This is what happened one day:

Andrew went hunting in the forest, and when he went chasing after a hare, he got lost. He ran and ran about the forest even into the night, but nevertheless did not find the way. But he came upon a forest that is only heaven and earth. He walked and walked, and fell asleep. The next day he got up and went in the direction in which he could see. He walked and walked until he came to the edge of the forest and was amazed that there was some village here; this was the village where he was born. He went into the village and spent the night with a certain woman, not knowing that this was his village, and the next day he appeared before the commune. The commune added him to their community, and he was hired by his mother. But he did not know that she was his mother, and she did not know that he was her son. Her lover, when she set Andrew afloat, said:

"As you did not have pity on your child, you will put me to death."

And he did not want to take her. And so she lived. And when she hired Andrew, she immediately fell in love with him, for he was very handsome. And she said to him:

"You will be my husband."

He agreed. And they got married.

[Some lines have been omitted in the Ukrainian text.]

Andrew said to her:

"I was told that they found me on a river in a box, that my belly was cut open, and they sewed me up."

Mary then cried out:

"Oh, my God, you are my son!"

And she told him what she did. Andrew immediately said that he should be put into the old well where there was no water. And he lived there fifteen years, eating nothing; Mary went to the desert and died there, having eaten nothing for seven years. When they went to the well where Andrew was living, he was sitting as though alive over communion bread with his arms folded and his eyes closed—he was dead! And they called him "of Crete" for he hid in the well for fifteen years without bread![1] And they called Mary "Egyptian" because she lived in Egypt in the desert for seven years and died there and was buried by lions.

OR1 ANDREJ

Source: N. Kostomarov, *Pamjatniki Starinnoj Russkoj Literatury* [Monuments of old Russian literature] (St. Petersburg, 1860; reprinted, The Hague, 1970), pp. 415–17. Kostomarov says of this tale only that it is from a collection belonging to Professor F. I. Buslaev. He also gives a variant (pp. 418–23) from "a 17th c. manuscript procured by Gagel from Novgorod." Translated by Robert Pardyjak.

There was a city, and in that city there was a certain merchant whose name was Pulivač. He went out of his dwelling, and this merchant heard birds, called doves; two of them were talking among themselves: "Our master will have gladness: his wife will bear him a son, and they will give him the name Andrej, and this child will kill his father and will take his mother as his wife, and he will defile 300 nuns." And there was a monastery 30 poprišta [20 km.] from that city. The merchant hearing this marveled at what the birds had said. But the merchant told his midwife: Order him to be killed. And when the time came for his birth, the midwife feared God's judgment and does not have the child killed according to the orders of her master. And she told the mother of the child, and

1. There is an etymological pun on the verb root *kryt.* "to hide."

the mother ordered him taken to the priest for baptism, and they gave
him the name Andrej. And his mother ordered that his belly be cut
across with a knife, and ordered a band tied to a board and sent out to
sea. And the midwife did this as his mother ordered. By the command
of God the waves of the sea rose up and brought him to a convent called
Kupina [Blackthorn], 30 poprišta from the town, leaving him at the
convent and leaving the board by the shore, across from the monastery.
And a nun went out of the convent to draw water and saw a male child
lying on the board scarcely breathing, his voice scarcely audible. The
nun, seeing him, immediately told the Mother Superior. The Mother
Superior ordered that the summoning board be beaten. And all the
nuns assembled—300 of them in number—and went to look at the child,
and they saw his belly cut open. And the Mother Superior said to her
nuns: "What a wonderful miracle, sisters! Whence did the sea bring this
child to our convent?" They did not understand. And all the nuns cried
and invoked the name of God and the Most Holy Mother of God. This
was the convent of the Unburnable Blackthorns of the Most Holy
Mother of God. And they said to the Mother Superior: "We do not
know, Reverend Mother, this child, and we will not let it perish." And
the Mother Superior said: "If God wills it, it will be so." And the
Mother Superior took him and ordered that his belly be sewn up and
fed him goats' milk. And they took care of him until he was nine
years old, and they gave him to a certain nun to learn reading and writing, and they began to send him with the sisters. The youth was fifteen
years old when the devil, the hater of Christians, that old plotter, put
an evil thought in his head, and the youth began to defile the nuns one
by one, sometimes by force, other times with love in secret, and he even
committed fornication with the Mother Superior. The Mother Superior,
seeing her sin, assembled all her 300 sisters and began to repent her sin
before them, the evil sin she committed with this youth. And the nuns
said: "We despise that sin." And the Mother Superior bowed to the
sisters to the floor, and the sisters said to the Mother Superior: "The
youth defiled all of us, too, sometimes by force, other times with consent!" And they began to cry. And the Mother Superior said to them:
"I shall tell you how the youth raped me: he deceived me with his
many parables of people in the past falling into sin: the tax collectors,
persecutors, fornicatresses and fornicators, and all the righteous from
the beginning of time. He said: We shall be saved through repentance,
tears, and alms. Hearing these words of his, my body weakened, my
heart took fire, I hesitated in my mind, and thus I fell into great sin.
Forgive me, my sisters!" And they fell to the ground for many hours;
lying for many hours on the ground, they also begged her forgiveness,
and they accepted each others' forgiveness with tears. And thus they

began fasting and prayer and almsgiving, and they sent the youth from the convent and closed the gates to the convent tight so that no man would enter the convent. The youth Andrej went to the city of Crete. He recognized neither his father nor his mother and was hired to guard his father's vineyard. And he gave him the order: "If you see anyone going into the vineyard, during the day or night, shoot him to death." And so the youth guarded his master's vineyard and fulfilled his orders. And his master said: "I will go to my vineyard and test my guard." He came to the gates of the vineyard at midnight, and the youth, seeing him, took his bow and shot his father to death, expecting that a thief had come. The youth saw that it was his master, and he became afraid. He went and hid himself under an apple tree and told his mistress. The mistress, crying a little, buried him. After some time had passed, the youth desired to take his mistress as his wife. The marriage having been performed, he rejoiced, and lying down in bed to go to sleep, his wife grabbed his belly, and on his belly was a scar. And his mistress said: "How is it that you have this scar?" And he told her in order what had happened to him since childhood: how his father ordered that he be killed, how his mother ordered that his belly be cut with a knife, how he sailed on the sea on a board and arrived at the convent, how the Mother Superior and the sisters raised him on goats' milk, how he sinned with them, how they chased him from the monastery, and how he came to the city of Crete. "And now I took you, my mistress, as my wife." She cried out in a loud voice and said crying: "I am not a wife to you; I am your mother. You, dear son Andrej, shot your father in my vineyard!" And Andrej immediately jumped up from his bed and said: "O woe to me accursed one, that I sinned against the law worse than all men." His mother sent him to the city of Crete to look for his spiritual father to confess to him all his sins. But the priest did not forgive him his many sins. And he, Andrej, beat this spiritual father of his to death with the church lectern and secretly left the church alone. He went to another spiritual father, confessed to him also all the sins he had committed from his childhood to the present day, including fornication and incest. The priest did not forgive him, but said to Andrej: "It is not fitting for us to take such sins on our soul." And Andrej spoke, saying: "Christ came into the world to call sinners to repentance, while you, priest, do not want to forgive me my sins. It is said in the Gospel: "What you condemn on earth shall be condemned in heaven; what you forgive on earth, shall be forgiven in heaven." But the preist said: "I do not want to carry such a sin on myself, for a person who committed the sin will not get such forgiveness." And Andrej killed this priest also and dragged him out of the church with his belt. Similarly, he went to a third priest and confessed all his sins to him. He too did not forgive him his many sins. Andrej beat the third priest to death as well with the church lock. And Andrej said to himself: "I will go to the city of Crete; there is a bishop there. He will accept me for repentance for he is sagacious and God-fearing and will forgive me. If he does not forgive me, I will go to a distant land to the tsar's camp and raise a great army and burn the city of Crete and take the people into slavery and kill the bishop." God is good and a lover of man, not wanting death for sinners and expecting their repentance. And Andrej came to the city of Crete and went to the bishop. The bishop received him and ordered that Andrej's mother be found. The bishop, seeing Andrej with strengthened courage, that he wanted to be chosen a vessel of God, began to question him in private. Andrej confessed his sins to the bishop in order, committed from his youth to his old age. And the bishop feared the judgment of God and death and sent him for his mother. And Andrej came with his mother to the bishop. The bishop, instructing them spiritually and at length, released them. And the bishop ordered a cell dug out three sazhens[1] deep and one half sazhen on each side. The bishop summoned him and his mother and sent him for ink and paper. And when Andrej went into the cell, the bishop ordered him covered with an iron chain and sealed in the cell, and gave him a sentence of thirty years. And when the cell will be filled with earth and there will be earth on the top of the cell, then he will be forgiven his sins. And the bishop cut through the mother's nostrils and closed them with a lock and ordered the key to the lock thrown in the sea. The bishop ordered their wealth distributed among the poor. The bishop ordered Andrej's mother to walk the earth praising our Lord God and Savior Jesus Christ, asking mercy for her sins. And the bishop said: "She will be forgiven when the key to that lock again comes out of the sea." Andrej, having passed the time in the cell in prayer to God about his transgressions and in bringing his soul to many lamentations, and having mourned over himself, he sang the hymn that is sung on the Thursday of the fifth week of Lent. And the thirtieth year was reached. And merchants came from many countries, and the woman with the lock on her nostrils came. The merchants asked her: "How is it that you have this lock on your nostrils?" And she told them all. And at that time the bishop ordered that a fish be brought for the meal and its belly cut open. The key fell out of the fish, and they showed the key to the bishop. The bishop ordered that Andrej's mother be summoned. He ordered that the key be put to the lock, and the lock came off her nose. The bishop ordered Andrej's mother tonsured into the nun's order, and the bishop went to the cell to Andrej with the entire gathering. Andrej was sitting on the top of the cell finish-

---

1. One sazhen = 2.13 meters.

ing the writing of the ninth hymn of the great canon. And then the bishop praised God and Our Lord Jesus Christ that Andrej was vouch-safed to accept forgiveness of his sins, and the bishop tonsured Andrej into monkhood. The bishop brought the canon that Andrej had com-posed into the church and read it aloud to all the people, and ordered all the people to bow to the earth on each verse, and thus the bishop greatly praised God, Our Lord Jesus Christ. The bishop summoned An-drej and said: "My child! Forgive me in this life and in the next and spend, my child and brother, three days in my monastery, and on the fourth day come and bury my sinful body." And the bishop fell ill on the third day and went to the Lord. Andrej buried the bishop in the Church of the Savior. God deigned that Andrej be in the city of Crete as bishop for thirty years. He lived pleasing to God and righteously, mollifying God through fasting, prayer, alms, and tears. He built many churches and brought many people to salvation, and was kind to all people. And he entered into eternal life in Christ Jesus, Our Lord; glory to him now and forever, world without end, Amen.

RS1 LEGEND OF THE COMMITTER OF INCEST

Source: Nigolaj Kostomarov, "Legenda o krovosmesitele," Istoriceskija monogratti i izsledovanija, 2d ed. (St. Petersburg, 1872), 1:295–308. Kostomarov says that he heard versions of this legend in several pro-vinces (p. 308). Translated by Robert Pardyjak.

In the old days people were more pious. Many hermits lived in forests. When our land was still ruled by princes, there was a monastery in the wilderness. One of the monks made himself a cell in a ravine in the forest.

Not certain where this was but according to the legend it was near the Danube.

Although he tried to remain removed from mankind, he was not successful: many heard about him and came to visit him to get advice and forgiveness. He refused no one.

Once a young man came and said he killed his father and had sex with his mother. Very calmly the monk told him to describe what hap-pened.

There was a pagan land to the north. Its young prince married the young daughter of a neighboring prince, with whose land they had al-ways been enemies. The prince's mother was a Christian, but not the father, so she avoided him. When the son was born, the father called a magician, who told him the son would kill his father and have sex with his mother. The prince ordered him thrown to wild animals, but the mother made a vessel, put the boy in, put in a Bible, and put it in the

Danube. It reached a monastery in a distant land. When a monk went out for water to the well, he opened the vessel. He baptized the boy and raised him for the quiet life of the monastery. He learned to read and sing better and faster than the other boys. They became jealous and treated him badly. They even said that his spiritual father was his real father; he asked him about it and learned of his origin. When he was eighteen, he could stand it no longer and went to his master and said he wanted the Bible that was found with him and that he would go look for his parents. The monk tried to talk him out of it, but let him go.

He left and saw a boat on the Danube going to the lands upstream with goods; he got a job on it as a rower. The other rowers were Christians who knew little about their religion, so when they saw his Bible, they started to ask him about various things. The master saw they were working badly and scolded them, but when he learned what they were talking about, he told the young man that with such gifts he shouldn't be doing such hard work and so invited him to sit with them. The merchant told him that they were taking Greek goods to a Christian prince on the Danube, who would receive him well.

Four days later they arrived, and the merchant took him to the prince. He did not tell the truth to the prince when he asked who he was; he told him he had been brought up in a monastery and was now preaching.

The prince told him about a pagan principality to the north whose prince was fierce and immoral. In the center of the city is a wooden idol that they worship and to which they make human sacrifices, especially Christians. The number of Christians there is increasing and so is the persecution. Recently he has even begun to imprison our people who go there to trade, trying to make them worship their idol. Convince him to let my people go—or declare war in my name.

He sailed off with a retinue. When they arrived, he saw many people bound and frightened. "Among them are our people." They were shedding their blood for their pagan holiday.

As if inspired by God, the young man began to criticize their beliefs. He cut off the idol's head with his sword. Then all the people, who were Christians but were afraid of the prince, praised the true God. Then the enraged prince rode in and ordered his people to seize the young man. Only a few went for him.

The young man said that if their helpless destroyed idol wasn't evidence enough, he—a young and inexperienced man—would do battle with the prince. He stabbed him in the chest. The young man stepped on him. The prince begged for mercy, but he cut off his head.

Then a woman, who was not young, approached. She said that he had killed her husband, who had caused her all kinds of grief for twenty years. They asked the one who had saved them to be their new prince and take the princess as his wife. He accepted and they were married.

After the seven-day wedding feast, she asked him who he was, and he told her the story. When he showed her the Bible, she fainted. When she came to, she told him that he had killed his father and married his mother. She told him to go to the forest so the wild beasts could eat him up as his father had ordered. She said she would give herself to the Danube, "which saved him for your and my grief."

He tried to stop her, but she went out and told all to the people and jumped into the river's waves. The people came after him like waves of the sea to kill him, but he escaped to the forest to fulfill his father's order. A bear came up but was frightened and ran away.

After several days in the forest, he came to a village and ate. He learned that pagans had again taken control in his city. He thought about how all his actions had turned out badly, but he resisted the temptation to kill himself: God will forgive all sins. He didn't intend to do what he did. He went to a church, but the priest sent him away. He went to another church in another land, but the same thing happened. For three years he tried to get forgiveness but couldn't. Then he went to the hermit.

The hermit explained how he had erred: he left the monastery and his Heavenly Father to look for his parents. He killed the prince when he begged for mercy. Worst of all, why did he marry when his master had joined him in childhood with Christ?

For penance he told him to build a wooden building, cover it with a high mound of dirt, leaving only a small entrance. "Work and remember that a narrow entrance and a narrow path lead to life." He gave him tools and told him to return when he finished. The hermit gave him communion bread and water and "the great canon of Andrew of Crete, which is read by all repenting believers" on certain days of Lent. He was told how to use it and to do it until he returned. The hermit locked him in and threw the keys into the Danube.

Ten years later the Father Superior of the monastery died, and the brethren asked the hermit to be their new leader. He reluctantly accepted. He governed well for twenty years and when he was one hundred he felt that God was calling him, so he called the brethren, admonished them, and died. They buried him and arranged a feast. A fish was caught, and when they cut it open, they found the keys. When they tried to open the lock, it wouldn't open, since the key was rusty. They dug around the door and lifted it away. A light and a pleasant odor came out. They saw the sinner inside finishing the canon; the bread and water had not been touched. The man had a youthful face. They went to the temple, and he took part in the services and then died. He still prays in heaven for the country that gave him peace.

RS2 ABOUT THE MERCHANT'S SON (ST. ANDREW)

Source: A. M. Smirnov, *"Sbornik˝ velikorusskix˝ skazok˝ arxiva Russkago geografičeskago obščestva,"* in *Zapiski Russkago geografičeskago obščestva po otděleniju ètnografii* 44 (1917), no. 186 (pp. 526–28). Written down from the narration of the peasant Il'ja Bagrov, eighty-three years old, in 1914, in Smolensk province, Belyj district, village of Kamenee. Translated by Robert Pardyjak.

There survived a young son of a merchant. He grew up and married. They lived together in harmony. His wife got pregnant by him. It began to live and move, and her belly began to grow. She went to the garden to walk, and the child cried out in her womb: "I will marry my mother and shoot my father with a gun." They began to grieve, that this would come to something unheard of. At the end of her pregnancy, she did in fact bear a son. And they began to decide what to do with him, if this were to truly happen. They said to one another: "What are we to do? We will not baptize him but will ourselves give him the name Andrej Kritskij[1] (who *cried out* in the womb.)"[2] They washed and dressed him and decided by themselves to cut open his tummy, took a board, surrounded him with pillows, and put him on the river: "Do not prevent him from sailing where he knows" [*sic*]. And he sailed a day, or two, perhaps three, and reached shore. On the shore stood a convent. Laundresses from the convent were washing clothes. They saw this wonder, the child, stopped the board, looked, and the child is still alive. They told their Mother Superior, who ordered that he be brought to her room, sewed up his belly with silk thread, found a doctor, nursed him to health. And the baby still lives. The Mother Superior appointed a nanny to take care of him and teach him. She took care of him, taught him; they began to study reading and writing. He grew to understand his studies very well. When he grew older, he began to make merry and to play around with the nuns. The nuns began to complain to the Mother Superior. "What can be done now? We have fed him and now we can let him leave here; he can find bread for himself now." They let him leave that place. He thanked them for their hospitality and set out for the city. He was a good-looking young man and knew how to read and write well and was taken as an apprentice to a mer-

1. Andrew of Crete.
2. A folk etymology for Kritskij, based on the verb *kricat'*, "to cry out."

chant in his store. He worked so much, was nice, and the merchant and all the workers grew to like him. He worked so well he grew tired of being an apprentice. He left that city and went to another city. A merchant hires him as a shop-assistant and tries to get a certificate from him showing who he is and where he is from. "I do not know who my parents are. I am from such-and-such a monastery. I was raised in the monastery." And he hired him. And they became very fond of each other—with both the merchant and his wife—and the merchant decided to test him, to find out whether he was reliable. "Go," he says, "and spend the night in the garden on guard duty." He gave him a gun. "Whoever you may see, if you ask three times and he does not answer, shoot!"

He walks about and guards carefully. The merchant wanted to check his assistant. He went into the garden, and the other asks, "Who goes there?" Silence. He asks again, "Who goes there?" He is again silent. He asked the third time, and the merchant wanted to say, "It is I," but the assistant took aim—bang! And he killed the merchant! Well, they tried him. They held an investigation and said, "You can be kept as bailiff to pay him." The merchant's wife hired him as a bailiff. She lived and lived, and they fell in love. "Why should we live like this! Let's get married. Why should we sin before God this way!" They went and got married. Well, they went to bed in the bedroom. His scar was still visible where his belly had been sewn up. She rubbed her hand across his belly and found it. "What is this?" she asked. "I don't know myself what it is. It seems that nuns found me on the river, sewed me up, and raised me. And then from there I came to you as a shop assistant, having been brought up in a monastery." She then acknowledged that she had not forgotten the song that he had cried out in the womb. And she admitted to all the most holy ones that what her child had cried out in the womb had indeed come to pass. For this transgression they were given the following sentence: Two pits were to be dug like wells. They put one into one well, put the other into the other well, and then locked them up behind iron doors, "When these wells are overgrown and you come out, then God will forgive you." The keys were thrown into the sea, "When these keys are found, then God will forgive them." After the passage of several years (the tale says "soon," but the matter does not proceed "quickly"),[3] fishermen were catching fish and caught a pike. They began to clean the pike and found the keys in it. They began searching according to the inventory where these keys were from. It was recalled that a man and his wife had been put into the wells until

3. The narrator's comment.

forgiven by God. Thirty years had passed since then. The wells were opened, and they came out, and the pits had overgrown.—Now it is said that there is no God; but evidently He existed then, for He kept them alive thirty years without any food!

RS3 JUDAS

Source: A. M. Smirnov, *"Sbornik" velikorusskix" skazok" arxiva Rus-skago geografičeskago obščestva,"* in *Zapiski Russkago geografičeskago obščestva po otděleniju ètnografii* 44 (1917), no. 21 (p. 129). Collected in the Senkursk district of Arxangel'sk province. Translated by Robert Pardyjak.

Judas was born of Reuben and his mother, Cigaria. She was pregnant and had a dream that someone said: "You will bear an evil son; he will be the destruction of the entire world." She ordered that his belly be ripped open, that he be nailed into a barrel and set out to sea. And this was done. He was shut up in a barrel and set off to sea. The barrel reached Skariot Island.

On Skariot Island there was a convent. The nuns went for a walk and found the barrel. They opened it and found the child with the ripped-open belly. They told the Mother Superior about it. She ordered that he be brought to her and that his belly be sewn up. They began to feed him. They gave him the name Judas. Judas grew up and began to do things for spite. They drove him out. He went to a landowner and was hired to guard his gardens. People began to come to the gardens to steal. His father came, and he killed him. He married his mother: she took him into her house. They went to sleep. Then she began to tell him that it happened in such and such a way. Judas understood; he looked at his belly and saw a scar. He fled from his mother.

And here he joined Christ as an apostle.

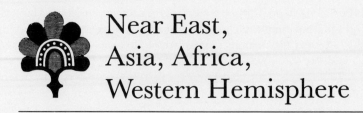

Near East, Asia, Africa, Western Hemisphere

TK1 THE SULTAN'S SON

Source: Collection of Professor P. N. Boratav. Set down in 1948 by Mehmet Yilmaz, a student at the institute of the village of Gölköy, born in 1932 in the village of Karafasil, district of Azdavay, province of Kastamonu. The indications of ellipses (. . . .) are as in the copy Professor Boratav sent me. Translated by Emil Tekin.

Once upon a time, when there was a sifter in the hay, when camels were town criers, when fleas were barbers, there was a sultan. This sultan never had a child. He prayed to God all the time, and his wife became pregnant, and they were both very happy because of this.

One night, the sultan had a dream. His son killed him and then married his mother. In the morning, he told this to his wife. She could not believe it, but she dreamt the same thing. Then the baby was born. They gave it to the servant. "Go and put this on a mountain." The servant took the child, and after a long walk he reached a plateau, and then he gave the child to a shepherd.

In this area there was a sultan who was childless. The shepherd took the child to the sultan. The sultan gave him five gold pieces as a reward. They took good care of the child and hired a special servant for it. They loved the child so much that if they stayed away from it for a day, it seemed like a year. In this place the child grew to eighteen or twenty years. . . . Sometimes he went hunting and horseback riding.

At this time he had a dream: he marries his mother and kills his father. . . . He became very upset at this. It might come true. He takes his bow and arrow and mace and departs. He goes and goes. He reaches a country. He saw a crowd. He entered the crowd. In this country they

198

kill every stranger. When they saw him, they questioned him. They began to fight with very, very great fury. Thereupon, he took his mace and hit his father on the head with it and killed him. After he had killed, he opened a way through the crowd with his sword and escaped. . . .

Time passed. After a while the widow had no one to make sultan, and she decided to get married. She made an announcement of her conditions. In this land there was a wolf. He ate everything, human or not. Nobody had the power to kill him. "Whoever kills the wolf and brings it to me, I will marry him." But whoever tried could not kill the wolf.

The boy, who was well known to be a keen hunter, shot the wolf, and the woman married him. A month passed, a day passed. The new sultan and his wife were living happily together. But at this time in this country everyone had mange and was dying. Whatever they tried, they could not find a cure. Wise old people started to say: "It seems to us that a son and mother have committed adultery." This news reached the sultan. His wife said: "I had a son by my first husband. When I was carrying him, I had a dream: this son will kill his father and marry his mother. And when he was born, we sent him to the mountain. The sultan had the same dream too." After this conversation, there was no doubt: they understood they were mother and son. He knew now he had killed his father. Both of them were ashamed.

In the morning the palace people and the vizier saw them in their room, that they had poisoned themselves. They understood they were mother and son. . . .

AR?2(HE) THE RABBI AND HIS SON

Source: Israel Folktale Archives (Haifa), 9171. Recorded by Herzel and Balfour Hakak (Jerus) from their grandfather, Murad (Iraq). The date is not given, but presumably falls in the period 1955–62: see Heda Jason, "Types of Jewish-Oriental Oral Tales," *Fabula* 7 (1965): 116. The translation is from Hebrew; presumably the original language was the Iraqi-Arabic dialect: see Jason, "Types," pp. 129–30. Translated by Marc Saperstein.

Once there was a rabbi who was a wise counselor in the king's court. He was an expert in incantations and amulets and in the secrets of mystical literature.[1] But it was an act of Satan: he had no son. The rabbi served the king, and he constantly comforted him. Through his incantations, many barren women were saved and cured, but his own wife was always sad, and her soul found no peace. All her life she hoped for a son whom she could carry in her arms, whom she could caress and em-

1. Literally, Kabbalah and Zohar.

brace with love, but all her hopes were in vain. The woman besought her husband: "Seek the help of God, that I too may have a son."

But her husband had a heart like stone. He did not grant her request, but said: "I have no need for a son."

In this way he would answer her with a quiet look, without explaining his enigmatic words. But the sobs and the entreaties of the woman helped her: one day her husband consented to her request, and in the course of time she became pregnant. The woman's spirit soared; she was filled with joy that, after all, she was saved from the shame of barrenness. Each day her joy increased as she felt the fetus growing in her belly and taking on skin, sinews, and life. But the woman did not know what was wrong with her husband recently. While she was entirely blooming with bliss, he took on an appearance of sadness, sorrow, and gloom. It was hard for her to understand what had happened to her husband that caused him such sadness. She asked him about it, but he refused to answer, saying: "Why should I end your joy and your happiness with sad and depressing matters?"

The woman implored him for a long time until he consented to tell her the answer: "It was not for nothing that I refused so long to save you from the shame of your barrenness. I knew that I would cause you unimaginable suffering, but all that I did was done out of love."

The woman was astounded, but out of the respect she was accustomed to show for her husband, she remained silent and allowed him to continue with his measured words. "A son will be born to us. This was made known to me by the divine presence [Shekhinah]. A son so handsome and strong that no one will want to stop looking at him. But it was inexorably stated and decreed long ago that this son of ours will do something evil and cruel. He will murder someone from his own family."

The woman was stupified and confused. She was unable to say anything, and so she remained silent. Both were silent, silent and sad.

From the time the child was born, the woman looked at him with fear and love. His sight was difficult to bear because of the thought that some time he would lift up his hand and kill a man. But despite this she was unable to keep from loving him. Her disposition was troubled, and her face showed fear because of the imminent future.

One day, as the sun was going down, the mother came to loathe the infant because of her great fear of what was in store for her. What did she do? She took the child with her, wrapped him in a blanket of wool, went to a cliff, and tossed him into the stormy waters of the sea. But the child was lucky; a fisherman passed by in his boat, and he saw a baby with beautiful eyes lifted by the waves and not sinking. The fisherman marveled; he drew close to the infant, lifted him from the sea on his shoulders, took him to his home, and brought him to his wife. The woman had been longing for a baby boy for some time, for she had only girls, and she was very happy about the gift from heaven. She nursed him, and the food was pleasant to the infant.

Thus the boy grew up and became strong in the house of the fisherman. Day after day he became more famous because of the heroic deeds he performed, and his reputation as a courageous man whose strength exceeded the strength of several healthy and well-fed horses spread throughout the land.

The king also came to hear about the mighty youth, and he commanded that he be brought before him. The king's runners hurried to the house of the fisherman, and the youth was taken to the king.

He bowed his knee before the king and said: "May his splendid Highness be praised and blessed." The youth was apprehensive, for he did not know what the king wanted with him. His voice trembled as he spoke, and his eyes were full of terror. With great fear he approached and kissed the king's feet.

But the king looked upon him with esteem and said: "It is my desire to appoint you to the position of *jilad bashi*.[2]

The youth's heart filled with pride, but in his desire to win the king's heart and to acquire his favor, he said in a low tone: "It will be a great honor for me to serve his royal Highness and to stand at his right hand." Then he bent his back slightly and lowered his eyes. Thus he began with his new position.

Every day he would cruelly cut off men's heads with the king's sharp sword. His blood grew cold, and he became a hard and evil man. Even the fisherman was terrified of his deeds when he saw that the youth no longer came to visit him, for he had forgotten all the kindness the fisherman had done for him. The sage in the king's court would see the *jilad bashi* every day, but he did not know that it was his son.

One day, ministers of the king falsely accused the sage of having cursed the king in a sermon he gave in the synagogue. The king grew angry and decreed a punishment of death upon him. The sage tried to combine Holy Names and to discover what was his sin, but he was not answered from heaven. The *jilad bashi* carried out the king's decree and cut off the head of the sage, without knowing that it was his father.

After the execution, the king commanded his hangman to marry the sage's widow, for he had left no descendants. At night after the wedding, when the youth wanted to come to his wife, she suddenly saw the image of her husband. She was terrified. The youth again tried to come

2. The executioner who carries out the commands and decrees of the king.

to her, and again she saw her husband's image and was terrified. When this had occurred several times, she requested him to wait until the following night.

That night her husband appeared to her in a dream and said to her: "This youth, who is now your husband, is our son. Take care that you do not sin." Then the rabbi told his widow that he had sinned and was punished because he had used combinations of Holy Names for vile purposes. Therefore he had not been answered from heaven before his death, and they had not revealed to him that the *jilad bashi* was his son.

The woman was alarmed and deeply troubled. She told the entire matter to the youth, who was so terrified that his entire body trembled. Then he fled from the city, with only the clothes on his back. This was in order to atone for his sins through exile.

When fourteen years had passed, they informed him that his sin had been atoned for, and that his mother had died, and then he returned to the city. What did he do during those fourteen years? He studied a great deal and became a learned sage. Some years later he was appointed as rabbi, and after that—as sage and advisor to the king. No one knew that he was the former *jilad bashi*.

Indeed, the man changed his name, and his heart also changed. He actually became another man.

AR?3(HE) THE MAN WHO KILLED HIS FATHER AND MARRIED HIS MOTHER

Source: Israel Folktale Archives (Haifa), 87. Recorded by Hada Yazon from Yafet Yehuda Shevili of Yemen. Translated by Marc Saperstein. The date of recording is not given, but presumably falls in the period 1955-62: see Jason, "Tales" (under AR?2(HE), above), p. 116. The original language was presumably the Yemenite-Arabic dialect (see ibid., p. 128). Jason comments that the Yemenite Jews "are to a high degree literate and familiar with the Hebrew traditional medieval literature" (p. 128).

Once there was a man and a woman. They were extremely rich, but they had no children. The man wept a lot because he had no luck. Once a seer came to him, and he asked the seer, "Do you know our fortune?"

The seer replied, "Your fate is to be without children. But if you really want it, you may have a son, but he will kill you, marry his mother, and eat his son."

"If that is so," the man answered, "I do not need children."

But after several days, he desired a son nevertheless, come what may. Fate decreed, and his wife conceived. When she gave birth to her son, the man told her about the words of the seer, and both of them decided to cast the child into the forest so that he would not become a cause of sorrow.

That day, an old woman came to the forest to gather wood, and she heard the child crying. She pitied him and took him home. The child grew to maturity and went out to seek work. He reached the city in which his parents lived. His father had orchards, and he took the youth as a watchman. He said, "I will give you a gun; guard near the gate of the orchard. If anyone comes after twelve midnight, shout first; if he does not answer, shoot him."

The youth worked several days. One night the owner of the orchard was unable to sleep. He went to see what the new workman was doing. When the youth shouted, he did not hear and did not answer. The youth shot and killed his father. In the morning, he opened the gate and saw that he had killed the owner. He wept.

People came and asked, "Why did you kill him?"

He told them about his work and about the owner's instruction. The people decided that he was not guilty, and he remained as a watchman. The wife of the owner, the mother of the youth, was a very young woman, and people decided that the two should be married.

The mother and the son got married. The woman gave birth to a child, and when the child was two years old, a misfortune occurred. He fell into a barrel of arrack. They searched for the child throughout the city, but did not find him. The arrack dissolved the child's flesh, and his father drank it without noticing anything.

One day, the mother went over to the barrel to bring some arrack to her husband, and she saw the bones of the child. "Woe!" cried the woman to her husband, "you are my son!"

"How do you know that?" said the astounded son.

"You killed your father, you married your mother, and you have eaten your son," answered the woman, and she told him the entire story.

"Truly, the old woman who raised me told me that she found me in the forest," replied the boy.

AR?4(HE) THE FARMER'S SON

Source: Israel Folktale Archives (Haifa), 4729. Recorded by Elisheva Shenfeld from Shoshana Parvi (?), born in Yemen. On date, original language, etc., see AR?3(HE), above. Translated by Marc Saperstein.

There was a man, who had no children. Once when he was walking to work in his cornfields, as was his custom, a sorcerer appeared before him. "A child will be born to you"—the man turned to him—"but the child will kill you and marry his mother."

When he finished these words, the sorcerer quickly disappeared, and the man returned to his house. At suppertime, he told his wife what the sorcerer had revealed to him. The woman became pregnant, and when the time came, she gave birth to a son.

"The words of the sorcerer were undoubtedly true," she said to herself. She took the infant and brought him to a field far from the house. There she took out a knife from her pocket, and with it opened up the child's belly. The woman returned to her house and told her husband that she had killed the infant who endangered the lives of them both by his very existence.

But the infant did not die. A shepherd passed by the place where the mother had left him; he took some of the child's excrement, and with it he plastered the wound, and then bound up the belly. He took the child to his house, took care of him until he returned to health, fed him, and clothed him after his recovery. The years passed and the child grew up. One day the shepherd said to him. "I am going out now; if I do not return within three days, you must go away from here to earn your own bread."

The shepherd left the house and did not return within three days. The boy went away in order to find a source of livelihood. He went from place to place, taking alms and working at different jobs. In his wanderings, he reached the house of his parents. As they did not recognize him, they gave him something to eat and to drink. They asked him, "Who are your parents?"

"I have no father or mother," he replied.

"If that is so, remain with us, for we have no children."

The boy readily agreed to this proposal, and he remained in their house. One day the man said to the boy, "You are now a young man, and you are strong enough to defend the house against thieves. In the near future, I will have to go away, sometimes for several days, and it will undoubtedly occur that I will return at night. If you hear the password from me [you will know] that it is I who am returning home. But if it should happen that they do not reply with this password, you can be sure that thieves have come."

Several days later, the man went away on business and returned in the middle of the night. He called out the password, and the youth opened the door for him. Two weeks passed; the man left his home a second time and returned at midnight. The youth heard the sounds of a man's steps approaching; he ran to the window and called. Since he did not hear the password, he went out from the house and killed the man. Only the next day did he realize that he had killed the man who had given him refuge in his home, and in fact was also his father.

The youth and the wife mourned many days. Several weeks after the period of mourning ended, they agreed to get married. The woman did not want to remain alone, and the youth had grown accustomed to the house, and he also was familiar with the affairs of her former husband.

After a while, a child was born to them. Both rejoiced in their little son; they cared for him with love and saw to it that he would lack nothing. On his sixth birthday, they prepared a great celebration and invited the women of the village to help them in their preparations. They placed a large pot of soup on the fire, and they did not notice that the little child went off by himself and played among the women who were busy preparing the spices. The boy went near the large pot, peered into it, lost his balance, and fell into the boiling soup.

At sunset the women went back to their houses, and the man returned from his business. The couple sat down at the table to eat their supper, and the woman approached the large pot to give some soup from it to her husband. But with her ladle she drew out a head. She dipped the ladle again, and drew out a foot.

A cry burst from her throat, "Where is the boy?" The man arose in terror, and both of them searched for their small son. They looked through every corner of the house, but the child was not there. Both knew that he had fallen into the pot of boiling soup. At that moment, the woman remembered the words of the sorcerer, uttered so many years before, and a dreadful thought entered her mind. She turned to her husband. "You have never told me from whence you came to us. Please, tell me this now."

"I grew up on a certain mountain in the home of a shepherd who found me nearby when I was still an infant, terribly injured."

When the woman heard these words of his she fainted. After she returned to consciousness, she said, "Indeed, the words of the sorcerer were right. For a long time I was unable to give birth, and one day my husband returned from the field and told me about his meeting a sorcerer who prophesied that we would have a child who would kill his father and marry his mother. You are the child. I tried to kill you and left you injured in the place where the shepherd found you."

The man heard this; he got up and left the house.

AR?5(HE) THE BOY WHO KILLED HIS MOTHER

Source: Israel Folktale Archives (Haifa), 6410. Recorded by Gila as from her father's grandmother, Hannah David, from Iraq. On date and original language, see AR?2(HE), above. Translated by Marc Saperstein.

There was once a woman who had seven daughters. She conceived. They took her to the hospital, and her husband stood by the door waiting to hear the news. A breeze fluttered by his face. The man was a great sage [a rabbi], and he knew that it was an angel. The rabbi asked, "What have you written on his forehead?"

The angel answered, "He will kill his mother."

The rabbi said to himself, "There is no need for such a child."

Women, children, men—on the face of all the man could see the news that his wife had given birth to a son after seven daughters. He got up and went to a carpenter and asked him to make a small case. The carpenter made the case and gave it to him. He took his son and wrapped him with all kinds of linens. The mother wept; he said to her, "There is no need for such a child—he will kill you."

She was comforted. They set the case afloat on the sea. It floated and floated endlessly, floated calmly on the surface of the water. On the other shore of the sea was a woman washing clothing. She saw the case approaching and took it, placing it on the shore, and then continuing her work. When she finished, she took the case to her house and showed it to her husband. He said to her, "What have you brought?"

She said, "There might be something inside." She thought that there might be silver or gold.

She and her husband began to open the case, and they saw that there was a small child inside. They decided to raise him. So they did, until he was fifteen years old. He quarreled with his foster mother, and she said to him, "Why are you quarreling with me, do you think I am your mother?"

He said to her, "Then who are you?"

She said, "I am a woman who saw you inside a case floating on the surface of the water."

He said, "Good-bye; if you are not my mother, I will go." He went here and there through the world, passing mountains and hills and tiny brooks until he came to a certain house, which was the house of his first father. The parents began to weep and said, "If our son had remained until now, he would be as big as you."

He said, "Why, what happened to your son?"

They answered, "We left him on the sea."

"If that is so, I am your son, for they took me from the sea."

They decided to make a party. The party was magnificent. He was with them for about two years, when suddenly he quarreled with his mother and said, "I want to marry the daughter of the millionaire."

They said to him, "We are poor; marry someone poor, for they won't want you." At that time, he gave his mother something, and she was killed. Thus whatever is written on the forehead of a child cannot be erased.

UL1 SIKHALÓL AND HIS MOTHER

Source: William A Lessa, *Tales from Ulithi Atoll: A Comparative Study in Oceanic Folklore,* University of California Publications: Folklore Studies 13 (Berkeley and Los Angeles, 1961), pp. 49–50. The tale was collected by Lessa on Ulithi in the late 1940s. "The atoll lies in the western Carolines, about 10° north of the equator. It is about 380 miles southwest of Guam, 850 miles east of the Philippines, and 900 miles north of New Guinea. . . . In 1949 there were 421 inhabitants . . . " (p. 7). Lessa heard the tale from Melchethal, who first heard it early in the century on Mogmog, another island in the Carolines, from an old man called Thau. "Thereafter, he heard it several times from other men and women, on both Mogmog and Sorlen. The story is told without any apparent emotion, either of approbation or condemnation" (p. 49).

Orthography and pronunciation: *ó* as the *a* in all; *ú* as in sun. "The consonants have about the same values as those in English, with the following qualifications: *g* is close to the *g* in go; *kh* is a voiceless palatal fricative; . . . *r* is trilled. . . . Accent is usually on the last syllable" (p. 7).

A very beautiful young woman by the name of Lisòr was married to a chief by the name of Sokhsùrum. She became pregnant, and the child was born prematurely at seven months. The infant was still covered by the amniotic membrane, and the mother did not know there was a baby inside. She put the membrane in a coconut spathe and set it adrift in the ocean.

On the east end of the island, separated from the main village, there lived about ten people. One of them was Rasim, a man who had a large stone trap for catching fish. The spathe with the baby drifted against the sides of the trap, and one day when Rasim went out to see if he had caught any fish, he saw the infant lying on the coconut bract. He lifted it up and took it home. He then performed some magic so that it would grow up. Every day he would repeat the magic, at the same time giving the infant nourishment. This went on for many days, and in a month the baby had grown to be a young man. Rasim had guessed the identity of the child from the beginning, for he knew that a girl from the village had been pregnant and had had a premature baby at the same time he had found the infant on the spathe.

Rasim made a small canoe for the youth, whose name was Sikhalòl. One day, Sikhalòl went sailing on the reef with some youths from another village. Their canoe passed by the menstrual house, where his mother happened to be confined because she was menstruating. Lisòr saw her son and said to herself, "Who is this handsome youth?" She waded out into the water and caught hold of the canoe, which was being pushed near shore by the wind while the boys swam playfully after it. Sikhalòl told her to give him back his canoe. She told him to come over to her, as she wanted to tell him something. He replied, "I cannot come ashore as I do not have on a loincloth." Lisòr walked over near to him, still holding his canoe, and said, "Come and see me tonight and we shall spoon." The youth told her he did not know where she slept, and Lisòr told him she was staying in the menstrual house. Sikhalòl said he would come. Then he sailed away with the other boys who were with him.

Sikhalòl waited for darkness to fall. When nighttime arrived he went to see the beautiful young woman in the menstrual house. They made love. About four in the morning he returned to his house. These visits were repeated for several days in succession. After the tenth day, the chief, Sokhsùrum, went to see his wife at the menstrual house to find out why she was staying there so long. She did not want to return with him, so she lied and said her period had not yet ended. The truth was that she wanted to continue making love with the handsome youth.

Sikhalòl's foster father, Rasim, suspected that the youth was visiting a girl each night, so he asked him if he had a sweetheart in the village. Sikhalòl replied that he had. Rasim asked him where the woman lived, and he answered that she lived in the menstrual house and was the wife of the chief. Rasim told him he was making a great mistake, for the woman was his own mother. Then he related the story of how he had removed him from the sea and raised him.

When Sikhalòl went the next night to see Lisòr, he revealed to her that he was her son—the child she had set adrift on the sea. He said they had better stop their love-making. But his mother did not care and said they should continue, and so they did. When Sikhalòl returned home in the morning, he had a talk with his foster father, telling him he had spoken to his mother but that she did not care and wanted to go on making love. Rasim replied, "All right. I don't care, either." Sikhalòl returned to his mother the next night and many nights thereafter, making love to her for three more months. On one of these occasions he happened to scratch her with his fingers on the side of her face.

The chief had meanwhile become very impatient with Lisòr, and one day he went to see her and demanded that she leave the menstrual house, saying she was lying to him since she had been there for four months. She refused to leave, whereupon Sokhsùrum became angry, so she returned with him.

Lisòr's face still bore the scratches that she had got from Sikhalòl. She was afraid her husband might see them and guess their origin, so in order to conceal them she kept her hair, which was long, close to the sides of her face. But Sokhsùrum knew she had the scratches and had made up his mind how she had got them; therefore one day he suddenly pulled back her hair away from her face and exposed them. He demanded, "Have you been making love to someone else?" Lisòr replied, "No!"—

but he did not believe her. He took a conch shell and blew it. All the men of the village assembled to see what was the matter. The chief told them to step up one by one and put their fingers near his wife's face so that he could see which ones fitted the marks. As each man did so, Sokhsùrum held an ax poised to strike him down if he were the guilty one. When they had all submitted to the test, he realized that none of them was responsible for the scratches.

The next day he sent word for the handful of men in the nearby village where Rasim and Sikhalòl lived to come to see him. Rasim told the men to go one at a time and return. While they were doing so, he told his foster son that he was going to teach him to wrestle, and Sikhalòl learned how to protect himself. When all the other men had completed their tests, Rasim himself went and then returned. Now only his foster son was left and all the people in the little village surmised that he was the guilty one. Thinking he was about to be killed, they decorated him with turmeric, armbands and anklets of young coconut palm leaves, and a sweet basil wreath, and dressed him in a new hibiscus-banana fiber loincloth. Then they accompanied him to see the chief.

As the group approached the chief's house, Lisòr looked at Sikhalòl and began to cry. The other people sat down near the house. Sokhsùrum called over to the youth to come and put his fingers alongside his wife's face. He told him as he held up the ax that he would kill him if he were guilty. When the youth put his fingers near the scratches, Sokhsùrum saw that he was the guilty one. He began to swing the ax on Sikhalòl, but the youth knew how to defend himself, for his foster father had taught him. He seized the ax and with it cut off the head of the chief—his real father.

Sikhalòl then took Lisòr back to his village, and they lived together from then on.

PO1 THE BOY AND THE CHIEF

Source: John L. Fischer, "A Ponapean Oedipus Tale," *Journal of American Folklore* 79 (1966): 112-13. Ponape is in the Caroline Islands. Fischer states that the story comes from "a manuscript history of Ponape written by a native of the state of Matolenim, probably sometime in the 1920's or 1930's. The author, Silten, . . . died about 1940. A sister's son, Lorens, . . . married Silten's widow and thus also came into possession of the manuscript. I copied the manuscript through the courtesy of Lorens in February, 1951, and also obtained his assistance in explaining unclear parts" (p. 111). Such manuscript histories belong to a number of Ponapean families. "Although technically the text is written rather than oral, it may be regarded very properly as a self-recorded oral text" (p. 111).

As for places mentioned in the tale, Nan Matol, now unoccupied, was the seat of a dynasty whose rulers bore the title Lord of Teleur. Nan

Matol consists of about a hundred artificial islands. Both Pahn Kedira and Peimet, the places where the king and his sister live respectively, are such islands. Isoh-Kelekel is believed to have deposed the dynasty of the Lords of Teleur.

Another version of "The Boy and the Chief" was published by John L. Fischer, Saul Riesenberg, and M. G. Whiting in *The Book of Luelen* (Canberra, 1977). In his doctoral dissertation, "Language and Folktale in Truk and Ponape: A Study in Cultural Integration" (Harvard University, 1955), Fischer gives the text of a similar Trukese tale (pp. 289–306) and an analysis of structural similarities (pp. 284–88).

Isoh-Kelekel was a Commander[1] and his wife became pregnant. And the Commander went to Tamwaroi[2] and left word with his wife: "If you bear a son then kill him." The Commander thought that his wife was not with him in his conquest of Ponape; that she was like the High One of the Land,[3] who was on the side of Ponape: that the two had forgotten the face of Thunder.[4] "But if it is a girl then let her live."

And the woman bore a boy. No sooner did the boy fall out than he ran off. And the Queen said to the boy: "Come back here so I may cut off your umbilical cord." The boy just bent over and bit it off and threw it away.

There was a man who lived at Kerengke whose title was Lord of the Masters of the Sea of Roahlaeng. He was a relative of the Queen. He brought a food offering to Pahn Kedira.[5] And the Queen gave him her son. And he took him to the place named Kerengke.

One day he [the boy] made a fish spear and he went out spearing fish in the shallow waters of the channel. The ruler had returned and was drunk with kava, and lying on the platform over the outrigger booms under a shade. The canoe was being paddled out in Senipehn Channel. Those accompanying the ruler spoke to each other: "What boy is that who spears fish so well?" The ruler then decided that his wife had given birth, for no one used to stand before him. And he said to them: "You all beckon him, and watch how he comes."

The boy then thrust his spear and it hit two sengiseng fish, and both were on the one spear. He then lifted up his spear and walked toward the canoe. And he climbed up on the outrigger float and ran up a little ladder that stood by the posts connecting the float and the boom; and walked in on the outrigger boom.

And the ruler just reached out for him and lifted him over himself and set him down on the central platform over the canoe hull. He then

1. The English word is used.
2. This and other places, unless noted, are in the state of Matolenim.
3. Lepen Moar, a Matolenim noble.
4. A god associated with Isoh-Kelekel's clan.
5. Site of the Commander's palace in Nan Matol.

said to those who were accompanying him: "Paddle on."

They got to Pahn Kedira. The boy got off the canoe, and walked up into the feast house, and leaped up on the chief's platform, and sat down in the doorway which is named the Breadfruit Doorway, Side of the Mouth of the Enclosure.[6]

The ruler then went to his palace and saw that his wife was no longer pregnant. And he decided that the boy was his. He said nothing more to the Queen but he sent for his retainers to come for he would give the boy a feast.

The fires for the boy's feast were lit. And the boy took his fish spear and came on, spearing fish as he proceeded; and approached the islet of Peimet,[7] where Li-kapar[8] lived. And Li-kapar beckoned to the boy to bring her one of the fish. He stopped there. He was the woman's brother's child. The two then got under the blanket together, and this is what constituted "giving birth of Matolenim."[9] The real name of the boy was Nahn Lepenien; and that of the drink for his feast was "Aged Kava."

He did not go on and the cup was carried to Peimet. Li-kapar said to Nahn Lepenien: "Get up and go out and watch the cup coming. Then perform the spell 'Turning the Corners' and 'Walking Cup.'" The woman then recited to him "Turning the Corners" and "Walking Cup."[10] And the cup came on around and the man performed "Turning the Corners" over it, and afterwards "Walking Cup." He then took the cup and lifted it and offered it to the woman. The woman said: "You drink it. And then go away, for it has grown weak."

Nahn Lepenien left and went on across [to his father's feast house], and he went up onto the chiefs' platform, and he sat down in the Breadfruit Doorway, on the Side of the Mouth of the Enclosure. And he said: "First squeezing. This one is for the King; the second for me." This was the beginning of titles being called after the Side of the Mouth of the Enclosure; the first time that the Side of the Mouth of the Enclosure had been appointed. The ruler's son was made evident. He deigned to pay Nahn Lepenien for the fish with the title of Nahniken, the first Nahniken.[11] It was bestowed on the Side of the Mouth of the Enclosure in Ponape.

The ruler's sister became pregnant unto the Nahniken and bore a son.

6. Ponapean: wa-bn mei-mei, peli-en ew-en-did; translation uncertain—a small doorway used exclusively by those of highest rank.

7. Also in the capital of Nan Matol.

8. The king's sister.

9. A euphemism for a kind of incest.

10. Thus teaching him valuable esoteric lore.

11. A sort of "talking chief" or "prime minister" title.

He no sooner fell than he ran off. The woman said: "Child, come here that I may cut off your umbilical cord." And he just bent over and bit it off and threw it away.

The Nahniken was ashamed and grew angry and went off downwind. The ruler's sister's son followed after him and caught up with him at the Bay of the Nahmwarekis. They got to a reef named Poun Intok. And the Nahniken deigned to bestow on him the title of Nahnmwareki.[12] And he said to him, "Child, you return and be Nahmwareki of Matolenim, and I shall go be Nahnmwareki of U." They then went in opposite directions, Matolenim paddling with the great end of the canoe first, and U paddling with the lesser end of the canoe first.

Nahn Lepenien went to the state of U. And he deigned to prepare a palace for himself. He raced the rain in building the house and finished before it. He married two women of the Lipitahn clan. The name of one was Likeilap and the name of the other was Likendinias.

There is no time to talk about his family.

AR2(GM) THE BOY THROWN IN THE NILE

Source: Samia Jahn, "Themen aus der griechischen Mythologie und der orientalischen Literatur in volkstümlicher Neugestaltung in nördlichen und zentralen Sudan," *Fabula* 16 (1975): 65-66. Jahn tape-recorded the tale at the village of Abu Hara on the Blue Nile (Gezira). The village is a religious center of the Qadriya, one of the most widespread Sufi sects in the Sudan. The storyteller was a woman. On the Nile Maidens, see Jahn, pp. 70-73. Translated by Gerald Proietti.

After a pious "Bismillah" [in the name of Allah] the storyteller began her tale:

There was a poor woman who was with child and found herself compelled to get water from the Nile. She went down to the river, but while she was lingering at the Nile her womb was suddenly convulsed with the throes of childbirth, and she knew not what she should do. Then the Maidens of the Nile came and helped her in the delivery. They helped her to bring forth a son, and laid him in her arms. Then they went forth. When they were now on their way, the seven Maidens of the Nile spoke among themselves and asked one of their sisters: "Now you have let the woman carry her son away. Did you know in truth what has been ordained for him?" She said to them: "I know nothing at all about him." Thereupon they spoke to her: "Go there and inspect him." She inspected him. When she had observed him thoroughly, she saw that the boy, when he became big and grew to manhood, would slay his father and

12. King.

marry his mother. When she had seen this, she gave the child back.[1] When she arrived home, her husband said to her: "Where is the infant?" She answered him: "The infant died, and I have thrown him into the Nile." Then they lived on as before.

The boy floated near a sultan of the water sprites in the Nile. The sultan found him, reared him, and when he had grown big, made him his son.

One day a war broke out in the land of his mother and father. When the youth arrived in the place where the war prevailed, he encountered his father in combat. He slew him, took his mother as booty, and delivered the captured people over to his family. When some time had passed, he said to his father, the sultan: "I wish to marry." The sultan said to him: "To whom shall I marry you?" He answered: "Marry me to the woman whom I took as booty in the war." The sultan said: "But is she not an older woman?" He spoke: "Only her shall you give me in marriage." Thereupon he gave her to him to be his wife. After they had performed the wedding and had made her redolent with the smoke of fragrant wood, anointed and sprinkled her with perfume, and put on her new robes, they brought her into his bedchamber. As soon as he went unto her, however, milk gushed forth from her breasts and made his eyes blind. So did it happen each day in succession.

Then he went to his father and told him of it. He reported to his father: "On each occasion as I go to the woman, it comes to pass thus and so." The sultan said to him: "Let the scholars come, the Fekkis, who are experienced in the Koran and in the traditions, who are old and wise men." They went forth and brought them. Then they said to them: "We have given that woman for a wife to this youth. Each time that he goes unto her, milk flows from her breasts and makes him blind." They questioned the woman. They asked her and said: "O Woman, we ask you in the name of him who created you. What has befallen you?" She answered them: "By Allah, an unwonted thing befell me. I am a poor woman, and my husband was likewise poor. One time when I felt the first pangs of labor I had no water. I went down to the Nile to get water. There my womb was suddenly convulsed with violent pains. The Maidens of the Nile rose up out of the Nile, assisted me with the birth, and laid my son in my arms. Just as I was about to go away, the seven Maidens came up to me. They addressed one of their number and said to her: 'Inspect this infant. Have you seen whither the road of his life leads?' She said: 'No.' Thereupon they spoke to her: 'Inspect him.' She

---

1. A line has fallen out of the German text. The line would have gone like this: The woman, hearing this prophecy, carried the infant off, threw him into the Nile, and went home.

came, uncovered his face, and said to them: 'I have inspected him. When he becomes big and has become a man, he will slay his father and marry his mother.' Thereupon I carried him off and threw him into the Nile.''

Then the youth understood that the woman was his mother, and from then on lived with her in harmony and joy according to the command of Allah.

ZL1 USIKULUMI KAHLOKOHLOKO

Source: Henry Callaway, *Nursery Tales, Traditions, and Histories of the Zulus* (London, 1868), pp. 41–47. On the method of collection, see p. i. The informant is not identified, but was probably a woman (p. 1). The title of this tale means, "Usikulumi, the son of Uthlokothloko" (p. 41, n. 40). Usikulumi means orator or great speaker. "Uthlokothloko may be either his father's name, or . . . a surname given to himself intended to characterize his power as a great speaker," because of the name's resemblance to the Zulu for "finch" (p. 41, n. 40). In the source, the Zulu and the English translation are printed in parallel columns. Callaway's notes have not been included here.

It is said there was a certain king; he begat many sons. But he did not like to have sons; for he used to say it would come to pass, when his sons grew up, that they would depose him from his royal power. There were old women appointed to kill the sons of that king; so when a male child was born, he was taken to the old women, that they might kill him; and so they killed him. They did so to all the male children the king had.

He happened on a time to beget another son; his mother took him to the old women, concealing him in her bosom. She made presents to the old women, and besought them earnestly not to kill him, but to take him to his maternal uncle, for it was a son she loved exceedingly. The mother, then, besought the old women very much, and told them to suckle the child. They suckled him, and took him to his uncle, and left him there with his uncle.

It came to pass when he had become a young man that he liked to herd the cattle at his uncle's, and followed the boys of his uncle's kraal; they respected and honoured him. It came to pass, when they were herding, he said to the boys, "Collect large stones, and let us heat them." They collected them, and made a heap. He said, "Choose also a fine calf, and let us kill it." They selected it from the herd they were watching. He told them to skin it; they skinned it, and roasted its flesh joyfully. The boys said, "What do you mean by this?" He said, "I know what I mean."

It happened one day when they were herding, the officers of his father were on a journey, being sent by him; they said, "Who are you?" He did not tell them. They took him, without doubting, saying, "This child is like our king." They went with him, and took him to his father.

When they came to his father, they said to him, "If we tell you good news, what will you give us?" His father said to the officers, "I will give you cattle of such a colour, or of such a colour, or of such a colour." The officers refused, saying, "No; we do not like these." There was a selected herd of black oxen, at which they hinted. He said, "What do you wish?" The officers said, "The herd of black oxen." He gave them. And so they told him, saying, "It happened in our journeying that we saw a child which is like one of yours." So then the father saw that it was indeed his son, and said, "Of which wife is he the child?" They who knew that she concealed the child said, "The daughter of So-and-So, your wife, your Majesty."

He assembled the nation, being very angry, and told them to take his son to a distance. The nation assembled; his mother and sister also came. The king told them to take away his son, and to go and put him in the great forest. For it was known there was in that forest a great many-headed monster which ate men.

They set out for that place. Many did not reach it; they became tired, and turned back again. The mother and sister and the king's son went, those three. The mother said, "I cannot leave him in the open country; I will go and place him where he is ordered to go." They went to the great forest; they arrived, and entered the forest, and placed him on a great rock which was in the midst of the forest. He sat down on it. They left him, and went back. He remained alone on the top of the rock.

It came to pass one day that the many-headed monster came, it coming out of the water. That monster possessed everything. It took the young man; it did not kill him; it took him, and gave him food, until he became great. It came to pass when he had become great, and no longer wanted anything, having also a large nation subject to him, which the many-headed monster had given him (for that monster possessed all things, and food and men), he wished to visit his father. He went with a great nation, he being now a king.

He went to his uncle; but his uncle did not know him. He went into the house; but neither did his uncle's people know him. His officer went to ask a bullock of the uncle; he said, "Usikulumi, the son of Uthlokothloko, says, give him a fine bullock, that he may eat." When the uncle heard the name of Usikulumi, the son of Uthlokothloko, he started, and said, "Who?" The officer replied, "The king." The uncle went out to see him. He saw it was Usikulumi, the son of Uthlokothloko, indeed. He rejoiced greatly, and said, "Yi, yi, yi!" sounding an alarm for joy, and said, "Usikulumi, the son of Uthlokothloko, has come!"

The whole tribe of his uncle was assembled. His uncle gave him a part of a herd of oxen for his great joy, and said, "There are your oxen." A great feast was made; they eat and rejoiced because they saw him, for they did not know that they should ever see him again.

He passed onward, and went to his father's. They saw that it was Usikulumi, the son of Uthlokothloko. They told his father, saying, "Behold your son, whom you cast away in the great forest." He was troubled exceedingly. He collected the whole nation, and told them to take their weapons. All his people assembled. The father said, "Let Usikulumi, the son of Utholokothloko, be killed." Usikulumi heard it; and went outside. The whole nation assembled. His father commanded him to be stabbed with a spear. He stood in an open space, and said, "Hurl your spears at me to the utmost." He said this because he was confident he should not die; although they hurled their spears at him a long time, even till the sun set, he should not die. He merely stood, until the sun set. They hurled their spears at him without having power to kill him. For he had the power of not dying; for that monster strengthened him, for it knew that he was going to his people, and that his father did not want his son; it knew, by its own wisdom, that they would kill Usikulumi, the son of Uthlokothloko, and gave him strength.

They were unable to pierce him with their spears. He said, "Are you worsted?" They said, "We are now worsted." He took a spear, and stabbed them all, and they all died. He took possession of the cattle; and departed with his army from that country with all the cattle. His mother too went with him and his sister, he being now a king.

ML1(FR) THE TWO BROTHERS WHO MARRIED TWO OLD WOMEN

Source: Gabriel Ferrand, *Contes Populaires Malgaches* (Paris, 1893), pp. 93-101. The text was dictated to Ferrand by one of the Betsimar-aka tribe. Translated by Dorothy Dilts Swartz.

There were, it is said, two brothers who, having married two old women, had not yet had children by them. They made the following agreement one day: "If your wife becomes pregnant," said the older to the younger, "I promise to furnish all that will be necessary for her during her pregnancy until the day of her delivery. We shall call the infant Ratananomby."[1] "I will do the same for your wife," replied the younger brother; "and your infant will bear the name of Ratongotromby."[2] They

---

1. Author's note: Ox hand.
2. Author's note: Ox foot.

promised then to throw the infant into a pond, if it should be a son, for fear that he might harm them when he grew up.

A short time later, the wife of the older became pregnant. The younger brother furnished her, as he had promised, all the viands she desired. She was delivered of a daughter who was named: Ratananomby.[3] The younger brother bought an ox and a pig, which people ate on the occasion of the birth of the infant.

The following year, the wife of the younger was delivered of a boy. In accord with the previous agreement between the two brothers, the male child was to be thrown into the pond. The father was anguished to have consented to such an agreement, but he was obliged to comply with it. The younger brother and his wife put their son in a box and gave it to a servant that it might be thrown into the water. However, they ordered their servant to make a mark on the infant so that one might recognize him if he happened to survive.

The servant threw the infant into a pond far from the village, and the parents went into mourning for him. Quite near the pond lived a rich and childless woman. Emerging by chance from her house, she saw with astonishment a floating box. She had it fetched by one of her servants, opened it, and found there the newly born infant. "It is a being God has sent me," she said. She embraced him and took good care of him so that the infant might be grateful to her later when he had become a man.

He grew up. One day, he said to his adopted mother, "I have a father and mother who live far from here; allow me to go to pay them a visit." "How many servants do you wish to accompany you?" replied the woman. "Three will suffice for me," said the young man.

And they departed. Along the road, the young man stumbled on a small tree and fell to the ground. "Pull me up," said the shrub; "I will accompany you to the home of your parents." Astonished, the young man obeyed. While he continued his journey, the shrub, which he had gathered, said to him, "There is an evil village that we are going soon to reach. If we must take a meal there, the master of the house in which we stay, will say, "Here is some rice that has been prepared for you. Eat it while I go outside for an airing." There will also be rice in a pot. It is that which we shall eat; and we shall put in its place that which has been offered us." The young man promised to follow the advice of the shrub.

He arrived a little later in a village inhabited by sorcerers. These were delighted to see strangers, for they planned to poison them and share their spoils among themselves. The master of the house to which the traveler and his servants had come offered them rice and added, "Eat

3. Later the *son* of the *younger* brother is called Ratanonomby.

this while I go to take an airing in the garden," and he went out. The foundling and his servants ate the rice that was in a pot and put in its place that which had been presented to them.

After the guests' meal was finished, the master of the house reentered and began to eat the rice that was in the pot, believing it to be what he had left there. This rice was poisoned, and the master of the house died of the poison that he had intended for his guests. Upon the suggestion of the shrub, the young man possessed himself of all the goods of the sorcerers.

At some distance from there, our voyagers encountered a cottage, at the edge of the road, where there lodged a brigand who harmed all those who entered his home. Since the village that was the goal of his journey was still far in the East, the young man entered with his servants into the home of the brigand. The latest wife of this brigand was in his cottage; his first wife lived in a nearby village. When the brigand saw strangers enter the cottage, he came before them. He ordered his wife to prepare hot water and a good bed where they could rest from their exertions; then he went out. The woman said then to the strangers, "Leave this house, I beg of you; my husband, whose cruelty you don't know, will kill you if you remain." "We are not afraid," replied the travellers. The shrub added to the young man, "Tonight, place me above the door; and when the brigand returns and speaks to you, do not reply; but allow me to do so in your place."

As soon as the brigand returned, he asked news of the stranger. "I am doing well," replied the shrub, which was above the door. And the brigand replied, "Woman, heat some water for your guest." "Very well," replied the shrub. The master of the house went away to the home of his first wife to prepare the assassination of the strangers. After having had supper, he returned to the house and demanded, "Are our guests sleeping well?" "Yes," replied the tree. "Let us alone, we are sleeping well."

Meanwhile, the young man strongly urged the latest wife of the brigand to grant him her favors. She refused. "If my husband hears you," she replied, "your life will only be in more danger therefore." "It makes little difference to me," replied the young man. "Don't be at all afraid on my account." Upon this reassurance, the wife yielded to the desires of her guest.

A little later, the robber arrived. "Do the strangers sleep well?" he asked. "Very well," replied the shrub. The robber returned to the village to prepare death for his guests, whom he was to assassinate at midnight. He took a little nap while awaiting that hour, but he slept so well that he didn't wake up until full daylight and could only verify the departure of the young man and his servants. His wife had even followed the strangers. Furious not only at not having been able to accomplish his criminal plan but also at the carrying off of his wife, he began to set about pursuing them.

As they went along the way, the shrub said to the young man, "When the robber who is pursuing us rejoins us, let him alone, don't say anything, but kill him." Soon the robber overtook them. He cried to his guest, "Why have you taken away my wife?" Ratananomby, without saying anything, killed him with one blow.

They finally arrived at the home of the parents of the young man. Entering the cottage of the servants, they saw that they wore mourning. "Why are you in mourning?" asked Ratananomby. "We are clothed in blue,"[4] replied the servants, "and our hair is not combed because we have lost our master." "Tell the parents of your master that I am coming to pay them a visit." The servants repeated these words to the father and the mother, who commanded the visitors to be admitted. Entering the courtyard of the house, Ratananomby took a *valiha*[5] that he found there by chance and began to play. "Don't play," said the master of the house, "because we are in mourning." "Let me do so," replied the young man. "I will give you the funeral coin."[6] The man and the woman accepted. Ratananomby accompanied himself with the *valiha* and sang,

"Alas! a fatal promise
    Caused me to be abandoned.
It is two brothers who did that,
    By promising to kill the son who might be born;
Because they believed this child
    When grown would kill his father and mother.
It is I who am that infant!
    I am Ratananomby;
Still alive although they had wished
    To make me perish."

The father and the mother, astonished at these words, asked, "Are you really Ratananomby, our child; for you do resemble us?" "I assure you of it," replied the young man. And his father and mother threw themselves at his feet. Then the slave who had cast Ratananomby as an infant into the pond after having made a mark on him added, "Take off your hat, master." The young man obeyed and showed, upon uncovering

4. Author's note: Blue is the color of mourning in Madagascar. At the death of a parent, women disarrange their hair and keep it disheveled during the duration of the mourning.

5. Author's note: A musical instrument made of bamboo.

6. Author's note: It is the custom to offer a piastre or a piece of silver of inferior worth to friends who have just lost one of their parents.

himself, a scar on his ear. It was the mark the slave had made upon him. That gave the parents formal proof that the young man was their child.

The joyous father and mother tore up their garments of mourning, dressed themselves in new ones, and ordered some oxen to be killed, some sheep and pigs, in order to celebrate the return of their son. Music and drumming announced the rejoicing in the village. The older brother, father of Ratongotromby, hearing this noise, asked what was happening at the home of his younger brother. "The son of your brother," they replied to him, "who had been thrown in the pond, is still living and has just arrived at the home of his father." "My brother has deceived me," said the elder, "in saying his son was drowned. He had, on the contrary, given him to one of his servants to be brought up in secret, and he wishes it now to be believed that he was found again by accident. I cannot accept that; according to our promise, our male infants ought to have been killed; hence it is necessary that he die." And he went toward the house of his brother. At that very moment, Ratananomby was saying to his parents, "Let me leave, because my uncle is going to be angry to find me alive." "We prefer you to him," replied the father and mother. "Remain."

The elder brother arrived meanwhile. "Why didn't you perform the promise we made together?" he said. "Father," said Ratananomby, "if my uncle desires my death only to inherit your goods, give them to him. I am rich, so rich that it would be impossible to spend all my fortune." The elder brother tried then to kill Ratananomby. He did not defend himself at first; then he responded to his uncle's attack with only one blow, which laid him out dead. The elder brother was buried with great pomp at the expense of his nephew.

Hence the following proverb: Each one receives the reward or the punishment of his acts.

FC1 HE KILLED HIS FATHER AND MARRIED HIS MOTHER

Source: Elsie Clews Parsons, *Folk-lore of the Antilles, French and English*, pt. 2, Memoirs of the American Folk-lore Society, vol. 24 (New York 1936), no. 111 (pp. 205–6). The tale, in French Creole, comes from Guadaloupe. The informant was Cérge Pontoparia, age seventeen. "His grandfather was a 'Congo' " (p. xii). Translated by Jean-Claude St. Louis.

A mother had two sons, Eugene the Great and Eugene the Bohemian. Those two sons signed a marriage contract but never got married. One day Eugene the Great left Eugene the Bohemian to spend three months in a boat. There, he found a beautiful girl and fell in love with her. He went back to tell his brother about his adventure. He told him: "I found a beautiful girl who is going to marry me. The marriage contract we signed is lost." Then Eugene the Bohemian told Eugene the Great: "The first child you have, make sure you kill him, because he can be a real problem for you." Then he said: "I will!" He got married and had a baby boy. He also had a servant. He bought her a knife and asked her to take the baby with her and kill him in the forest. The maid thought that was too much for her. Instead, she bought a chicken, killed it, and left the child in the forest without killing him. She returned to the house with the bloody knife. She said, "Mr. Eugene, I killed him." Then Mr. Eugene said, "Well! I am going to give you a raise. You were making twenty-five francs, now you are going to make fifty francs."

There was an old charcoal maker who was making charcoal in the forest. He heard a baby cry. He walked straight in the direction of the voice and found a deer who was nurturing the child. He then took the child home with him. Without knowing anything about the baby's history, he called him Eugene the Found.

As the child was growing older, he started to talk. The old man was very rich and told the boy that he was so rich that he had a lot of money saved in a white silver box. This would make the child walk faster while he is on duty. He would also have the chance to meet his father, Eugene the Great, without knowing that he is his father. In fact, he saw him on a carriage that was being pulled by two horses. As he was going to pass in front of the carriage, his father barred him from passing without knowing that was his child. The boy decided to go downtown and saw a very beautiful girl. He went back and told the old man, "Anytime I go downtown there is always a man who bars my way." He took a gun and went downtown with it. The man again came to bar his way. This time he pulled his gun, fired one shot, and killed Eugene the Great. Then the carriage returned to depose the dead man on the doorstep of his wife's house. His wife lamented and buried him. The boy went downtown and saw a very beautiful woman and fell in love with her without knowing that she was his mother. He then decided to talk to her, and she, in turn, fell in love with him. They got married without knowing that they were mother and son. As he was taking a walk downtown, he saw Eugene the Bohemian. Then Eugene the Bohemian told him, "The man that you killed on the carriage was your father, and the woman you married and with whom you have a child is your mother. Your father's name was Eugene the Great. My name is Eugene the Bohemian, and your name is Eugene the Found." The boy left very sad. He came home at noon, dinner time, his wife said, "What's the matter with you?" And he started to cry. He said while he was crying, "My mother, my wife, and my children, all of you who are here, are my brother, my sister, and my mother."

Then his mother said, "Are you joking, Eugene?" He replied, "I killed my father, Eugene the Great, on the carriage, and you are my mother. I have four children with my mother. When I was a child, my father sent his servant to kill me in the forest. By chance, the servant did not kill me, and instead she bought a chicken, killed it to let him think that she killed me, and brought the bloody knife to him. My father thanked her by giving her a raise. It was the old charcoal maker who took me and raised me. My name is Eugene the Found. By this we know that a man should not marry a widow. So I took a gun, I, Eugene the Found, killed myself, and my mother killed herself. The children are left to cry. My cousin, Eugene the Bohemian, took the children and raised them." Here it is, it is forbidden for a young man to marry a widow.

SP2 TWO PUERTO-RICAN RIDDLES*

Source: J. Alden Mason, "Porto-Rican Folklore: Riddles," ed. A. M. Espinosa, *JAF* 29 (1916) no. 762 a and b (p. 499). Translated by Susan T. Edmunds. Most of the material in this collection came from schoolchildren. Sources for the individual items are not given. The two riddles translated here belong to a group of riddles provided with short explanatory anecdotes or folktales. Mason collected a fuller version of the explanation to riddle *a*. A translation of this fuller version follows the riddles.

(a) Take, lady, this branch
     from the hands of this child.
     He is your son, he is your grandson,
     The brother of your husband.

[A child was born and when he was very small he was sent to study outside of the city. His father died, his mother remarried, the child changed his name, he came to where his mother was; she fell in love with him, they got married, and had a son. When this child was born they put the branch in one hand.]

(b) Take, lady, this rose
     Which this child gives you.
     He is your son, he is your grandson,
     And the brother of your husband.

[A woman had a son and abandoned him. After some years the son returned, and not recognizing his mother, he married her. She gave birth to a child that, one day, when he could not yet walk, gave his mother a rose and said to her this verse.]

SP3 THE ABANDONED SON

Source: J. Alden Mason, "Porto-Rican Folklore: Folk Tales," ed. A. M. Espinosa, *JAF* 37 (1924), no. 13 (pp. 304–5). Translated by Susan T. Edmunds. A brief introduction to this division of Mason's collection is given by Espinosa in *JAF* 34 (1921): 143. Sources for the individual tales are not given. "The Abandoned Son" is a fuller version of the explanation to the first of the preceding riddles.

There was once a woman who had a son, and because society had not rejected her, she gave orders that he be cast in a river in a basket; and she went on living very happily. In the basket she put a letter commending him to whoever found him.

A fisherman picked him up, reared him to manhood. One day the young man went to the city, passed by a house, saw a woman on the balcony and fell in love with her, and the woman fell in love with him also.

On the following day at the same time, the man passed by once again and she was on the balcony and let fall a handkerchief so that the youth would pick it up and come up to bring it to her. So it went, they became acquainted, fell in love, and decided to marry.

At the end of nine months she had a child, and when he was six months old, when both were sitting in the parlor, and she with the child in her arms, the child jumped up walking, went to the balcony, took a branch of a plant that was there, and came and said to his mother, "Take lady this branch from the hands of this child, he is your son, he is your grandson, the brother of your husband." When the child had said this he fell dead.

They could not explain what phenomenon this was because her history remained hidden. Then he asked for explanations and she gave them. They sent to find the man who had brought him up and he explained how he had found him, telling them of the letter that was in the basket. Then they recognized that a mother had married her son, and on seeing the crime they had committed, they relinquished their lives.

Let this serve as an example for some women.

Bibliographies

There are four bibliographies. The first is on the Oedipus legend in antiquity. For the most part, I list only works that study the ancient legend from a mythological or folkloristic point of view and exclude literary criticism on Sophocles' Oedipus tragedies, Euripides' *Phoenician Women,* and Aeschylus's *Seven Against Thebes.* The second bibliography lists works on the survival of the Oedipus legend in the Middle Ages and on the medieval legends and folktales analogous to the ancient Oedipus legend. The third bibliography lists works on modern folktales analogous to the ancient Oedipus legend. None of these bibliographies lists psychoanalytical studies of Oedipus stories in any period. For these, see Lowell Edmunds and Richard Ingber, "Psychoanalytical Writings on the Oedipus Legend: A Bibliography," *American Imago* 34 (1977): 374–86. The fourth bibliography lists the published sources of the analogues, and the sigla of the analogues are given after the bibliographical references.

BIBLIOGRAPHY 1: THE ANCIENT OEDIPUS LEGEND

Akoun, André, Françoise Morin, and Jacques Mousseau. "The Father of Structural Anthropology—A Conversation with Claude Lévi-Strauss," *Psychology Today* 5, no. 12 (1972): 36 ff.

Albright, W. F. *Yaweh and the Gods of Canaan,* pp. 81–82. London, 1968.

Bachofen, J. J. *Der Mythus von Orient und Occident: Eine Metaphysik der alten Welt,* pp. 259–71. Ed. Manfred Schroeter. Munich, 1926.

Baldry, H. C. "The Dramatization of the Theban Legend," *Greece and Rome,* 2d ser., 3 (1956): 24–37.

Bethe, E. *Thebanische Heldenlieder.* Leipzig, 1891.

Binder, Gerhard. *Die Aussetzung des Königskindes: Kyros und Romulus.* Beiträge zur klassischen Philologie, 10. Meisenheim am Glan, 1964.

Bréal, Michel. *Le Mythe de Oedipe.* Paris, 1863.

Brillante, C. "La Leggende Tebane e l'Archeologia," *Studi Micenei ed Egeo-Anatolici* 21: *Incunabula Graeca* 72 (Rome, 1980): 309-40.

Brisson, Luc. *Le mythe de Tirésias: Essai d'analyse structurale.* Leiden, 1976.

Buxton, R. G. A. "Blindness and Limits: Sophocles and the Logic of Myth," *Journal of Hellenic Studies* 100 (1980): 22-37.

Comparetti, Domenico. *Edipo e la Mitologia Comparata.* Pisa, 1867.

Daly, L. W. "Oedipus." In *Real-Encyclopädie der classischen Altertumswissenschaft,* edited by A. Pauly, G. Wissowa, et al. (1893-), 34th half vol. (1937), cols. 2103-17; suppl. vol. 7 (1940), cols. 769-86.

de Kock, E. L. "The Sophoklean Oidipus and Its Antecedents," *Acta Classica* 4 (1961): 7-28.

————. "The Peisandros Scholion—Its Sources, Unity, and Relationship to Euripides' *Chrysippos,*" *Acta Classica* 5 (1962): 15-37.

Delcourt, Marie. *Oedipe ou la légende du conquérant.* Liège, 1944.

Deubner, Ludwig. *Oedipusprobleme.* Abhandlungen der preussischen Akademie der Wissenschaften. Philosophisch-historische Klasse, 4. Berlin, 1942.

Devereux, G. "The Self-Blinding of Oidipous in Sophokles: Oidipous Tyrannos," *Journal of Hellenic Studies* 93 (1973): 36-49.

Dirlmeier, F. *Der Mythos von König Oedipus.* 2d ed. N.p., 1964.

Edmunds, L. "The Cults and the Legend of Oedipus," *HSCP* 85 (1981): 221-38.

————. *The Sphinx in the Oedipus Legend,* Beiträge zur klassischen Philologie 127. Königstein/Ts., 1981. The main section, with revisions, is reprinted in Edmunds and Dundes, pp. 147-73 (Bibliography 3).

Gostoli, Antonietta. "Some Aspects of Theban Myth in the Lille Stesichorus," *Greek, Roman, and Byzantine Studies* 19 (1978): 23-27.

Höfer, O. "Oidipus." In *Ausführliches Lexikon der griechischen und römischen Mythologie,* edited by W. H. Roscher. Leipzig, 1897-1909. Vol. 3, cols. 700-746.

Huxley, G. L. *Greek Epic Poetry from Eumelos to Panyassis.* Cambridge, Mass., 1969. Pp. 39-50.

Kirchoff, K. "Der Kampf der Sieben vor Theben und König Oidipus." Ph.D. diss., Münster, 1917.

Lambert, W. G., and Peter Walcot. "A New Babylonian Theogony and Hesiod," *Kadmos* 4 (1965): 64-72.

Legras, L. *Les légendes thebaines dans l'épopée et la tragédie grecques.* Paris, 1905.

Lesky, A. "Sphinx." In *Real-Encyclopädie der classischen Altertums-wissenschaft,* edited by A. Pauly, G. Wissowa, et al. (1893-), 2d ser., 6th half vol. (1929), cols. 1703-26.

Lévêque, P. "Oedipe le conquérant," *Dialogues d'histoire ancienne* 7 (1981): 127.

Lévi-Strauss, Claude. "The Structural Study of Myth," *Journal of American Folklore* 68 (1955): 428-44. Reprinted in *Structural Anthropology,* pp. 202-28. New York, 1967. Also reprinted in *The Structuralists from Marx to Lévi-Strauss,* edited by R. and F. DeGeorge, pp. 169-94. New York, 1972.

Luria, S. "ΤΟΝ ΣΟΥ ΥΙΟΝ ΦΡΙΞΟΝ (Die Oidipus-sage und Verwandtes)." In *Raccolta di Scritti in Onore di Felice Ramorino,* Publicazioni della Università Cattolica del Sacro Cuore, 4th ser.: Scienze Filologiche, vol. 7 (1927): 289-314.

Littleton, C. Scott. "The 'Kingship in Heaven' Theme." In *Myth and Law among the Indo-Europeans,* edited by Jaan Puhvel, pp. 83-121. Berkeley and Los Angeles, 1970.

Margani, Margherita. *Il Mito di Edipo.* Syracuse, 1927.

McCartney, E. S. "Greek and Roman Lore of Animal-Nursed Infants," *Papers of the Michigan Academy of Science, Arts and Letters* 4 (1925): 15-42.

Moreau, Alain. "A propos d'Oedipe: La liaison entre trois crimes—parricide, inceste, et cannibalisme." In *Études de littérature ancienne,* pp. 97ff. Paris, 1979.

Moret, J.-M. "Un ancêtre du phylactère: Le pilier inscrit des vases italiotes," *Rev. Arch.* (1979): fasc. 1, pp. 1-34, and fasc. 2, pp. 235-58.

Niebler, Klaus. "Die Oidipussage in der attischen Tragödie." Ph.D. diss., Hamburg University, 1960.

Nilsson, M. P. "Der Oidipusmythos," *Göttingische gelehrte Anzeigen* 184 (1922): 36-46. Reprinted in *Opuscula Selecta,* vol. 1 (Lund, 1951), pp. 335-48.

Pellizer, Ezio. *Favole d'identità, favole di paura: Storie di caccia e altri racconti della Grecia antica.* Rome, 1982.

Porzig, Walter, "Das Rätsel der Sphinx," *Lexis* 3 (1953): 236-39. Reprinted in *Indogermanische Dichtersprache,* edited by Rüdiger Schmitt, Wege der Forschung 165, pp. 172-76. Darmstadt, 1968.

Pötscher, Walter. "Die Oidipus-Gestalt," *Eranos* 71 (1973): 12-44.

Robert, Carl. *Oidipus: Geschichte eines poetischen Stoffs im griechischen Altertum.* 2 vols. Berlin, 1915.

Rose, H. J. *Modern Methods in Classical Mythology.* St. Andrews, 1930.

Röhrich, Lutz. *Sage.* 2d ed. Stuttgart, 1971.

Rudhardt, Jean. "De l'inceste à la mythologie grecque," *Revue française de psychanalyse* 4 (1982): 731-63.

Schachter, A. "The Theban Wars," *Phoenix* 21 (1976): 1-10.

Schröder, F. R. "Hera," *Gymnasium* 63 (1956): 72-77.

Small, J. P. *Studies Related to the Theban Cycle on Late Etruscan Urns.* Rome, 1981.

v. Vacano, O. W. and B. v. Freytag gen. Löringhoff. *Talamone: Il Mito dei Sette a Tebe,* Catalogo della Mostra, Florence, Museo Archeologico, Feb. 14-Oct. 3, 1982. Florence, 1982.

Vernant, J. P. "From Oedipus to Periander: Lameness, Tyranny, Incest in Legend and History," *Arethusa* 15 (1982): 19-38.

———. "Oedipe." In *Dictionnaire des mythologies.* Paris, 1981.

Vian, Francis. *Les Origines de Thèbes: Cadmos et les Spartes.* Paris, 1963.

Wehrli, Fritz, "Oidipus," *Museum Helveticum* 14 (1957): 108-17. Reprinted in *Theoria und Humanitas,* pp. 60-71. Zurich and Munich, 1972.

West, M. L. "Epic Cycle." In *The Oxford Classical Dictionary.* 2d ed. Oxford, 1970.

BIBLIOGRAPHY 2: MEDIEVAL
ANALOGUES TO THE OEDIPUS LEGEND

Baum, P. F. "The Medieval Legend of Judas Iscariot," *Publications of the Modern Language Association of America* 31 (= N.S. 24) (1916): 481-632.

Constans, Léopold. *La légende d'Oedipe.* Paris, 1881.

de Gaiffier, B. "L' 'Historia Apocrypha' dans la Légende dorée," *Analecta Bollandiana* 91 (1973): 265-72.

Delehaye, Hippolyte. *The Legends of the Saints,* trans. V. M. Crawford. Notre Dame, Ind., 1961.

Dorn, Erhard. *Der sündige Heilige in der Legende des Mittelalters.* Medium Aevum 10. Munich, 1967.

Edmunds, L. "Oedipus in the Middle Ages," *Antike und Abendland* 25 (1976): 140-55.

———. "A Note on Boccaccio's Sources for the Story of Oedipus in *De Casibus illustrium virorum* and in the *Genealogie,*" *Aevum* 66 (1982): 248-52.

Köhler, Reinhold. "Zur Legende von Gregorius auf dem Steine," *Germania* 15 (1870): 284-91. Reprinted in *Kleinere Schriften zur erzählende Dichtung des Mittelalters* (Berlin, 1900) 173-84. (For another work by Köhler, see Bibliography 3.)

Krappe, A. H. "Über die Sagen von Geschwisterehe im Mittelalter," *Archiv für das Studium der neueren Sprachen* 167 (1935): 161–76.

Lehman, Paul. "Judas Iscariot in der lateinischer Legenden-Überlieferung des Mittelalters," *Studi Medievali,* NS 3 (1930): 289–346. Reprinted in *Erforschung des Mittelalters,* 2: 229–85. Stuttgart, 1959.

Loomis, R. S. *Celtic Myth and Arthurian Romance.* New York, 1927. Ch. 33.

Mann, Thomas. "Bemerkungen zu dem Roman 'Der Erwählte.'" In *Gesammelte Werke,* 11: 687–91. 2d ed. Frankfurt, 1974.

Martins, Mário. "O Mito de Édipo na Idade Média Portuguesa," *Euphrosyne,* NS 7 (1975–76): 73–101.

Ohly, Friedrich. *Der Verflüchte und der Erwählte: Vom Leben mit der Schuld.* Vorträge G 207. Rheinisch-Westfälische Akademie der Wissenschaft, 1976.

Rosenfeld, Hellmut. *Legende.* 2d ed. Stuttgart, 1964.

Seelisch, Adolf. "Die Gregoriuslegende," *Zeitschrift für deutsche Philologie* 19 (1887): 385–421.

Spaarnay, H. "Der Enkel des Königs Armenios und die Gregorsage." In *Zur Sprache und Literatur des Mittelalters,* pp. 247–62. Groningen, 1962.

Zuntz, Günther. "Oedipus and Gregorius," *Antike und Abendland* 4 (1954): 191–203. Reprinted in *Hartmann von Aue,* edited by Hugo Kuhn and Cristoph Chormeau, pp. 87–107. Wege der Forschung 359. Darmstadt, 1973. Also reprinted in *Sophokles,* edited by Hans Diller, pp. 348–69. Wege der Forschung 95. Darmstadt, 1967.

BIBLIOGRAPHY 3: MODERN
ANALOGUES TO THE OEDIPUS LEGEND

Aarne, Anntti and Stith Thompson, *The Types of the Folktale,* 2nd ed. Folklore Fellows Communications 184. Helsinki, 1961.

Brewster, Paul G. *The Incest Theme in Folksong.* Folklore Fellows Communications 212. Helsinki, 1972.

Campbell, Joseph. *The Hero with a Thousand Faces.* New York, 1949.

Carroll, M. P. "Lévi-Strauss on the Oedipus Myth: A Reconsideration," *American Anthropologist* 80 (1978): 805–14.

Cosquin, Emmanuel. *Le lait de la mère et le coffre flottant.* Paris, 1908.

Diederichs, Victor. "Russische Verwandte der Legende von Gregor auf dem Stein und der Sage von Judas Ischariot," *Russische Revue* 17 (1880): 119–46.

d'Penha, G. F. "Folklore in Salsette," *The Indian Antiquary* 21 (1892): 45–47.

Edmunds, L. and Alan Dundes, eds. *Oedipus: A Folklore Casebook.* New York, 1983.

Fortes, Meyer. *Oedipus and Job in West African Religion.* Cambridge, 1959.

Frazer, J. G. Folk-lore in the Old Testament, vol. 2. London, 1918. Pp. 437-54.

Frenzel, Elizabeth, "Oedipus." In *Stoffe der Welt-Literatur,* pp. 554-58. Stuttgart, 1970.

Girard, René. "De l'expérience romanesque au mythe oedipien," *Critique* 222 (Nov. 1965): 899-924.

——. "Symétrie et dissymétrie dans le mythe d'Oedipe," *Critique* 249 (Feb. 1968): 99-135.

——. "Une analyse d'Oedipe Roi," In *Critique sociologique et critique psychanalytique,* pp. 127-63 (with discussion). Éditions de l'Institut de Sociologie de l'Université de Bruxelles, 1970.

Holley, N. M. "The Floating Chest," *Journal of Hellenic Studies* 69 (1949): 39-47.

Ishida, Eiichiro. "The Mother-Son Complex in East Asiatic Religion and Folklore." In *Die Wiener Schule der Völkerkunde: Festschrift zum 25 jährigen Bestand,* pp. 411-19. Vienna, 1955.

Jensen, P. "Aussetzungsgeschichten," In *Reallexikon der Assyriologie,* edited by E. Ebeling and B. Meissner, 1: 322-24. Berlin and Leipzig, 1932.

Karpati, Mirella. "Un mito edipico nella tradizione zingari," *Lacio Drom* 12 (1976): 5-9. Translation in Edmunds and Dundes, pp. 23-27 (see above).

Karve, Irawati. "A Marathi Version of the Oedipus Story," *Man* 50 (1950): 71-72.

Käster, Otto. "Über die Schuld des König Oedipus." In *Beiträge zur geistigen Überlieferung,* pp. 167-83. Godesburg, 1947.

Köhler, Reinhold. "Leggenda di un sant' uomo bruciato e rigenerato," *Archivio per lo studio delle tradizioni popolari* 2 (1883): 117-20. Reprinted in *Kleinere Schriften zur erzählende Dichtung des Mittelalters,* 2: 241-44. Berlin, 1900. (For another work by Köhler, see Bibliography 2.)

Kluckhohn, Clyde. "Recurrent Themes in Myths and Mythmaking." In *Myth and Mythmaking,* edited by Henry A. Murray, pp. 46-60. Boston, 1968.

Krappe, A. H. "La légende d'Oedipe êst-elle un conte bleu?" *Neuphilologische Mitteilungen* 43 (1933): 11-29. Translation in Edmunds and Dundes, pp. 122-32 (see above).

Krauss, Friedrich S. "Die Ödipussage in südslawischer Volksüberlieferung," *Imago* 21 (1935): 358-67. Translation in Edmunds and Dundes, pp. 10-22 (see above).

Laistner, Ludwig. *Das Rätsel der Sphinx.* 2 vols. Berlin, 1889.

Lessa, W. A. *Tales from Ulithi Atoll: A Comparative Study in Oceanic Folklore.* University of California Publications: Folklore Studies 13. Berkeley and Los Angeles, 1961. Pp. 48-51, 172-214.

———. "Oedipus-Type Tales in Oceania," *Journal of American Folklore* 69 (1956): 63-73.

Lessmann, Heinrich. *Die Kyrossage in Europa.* Wissenschaftliche Beiläge zum Jahresbericht über die städtische Realschule zu Charlottenburg. Ostern, 1906.

Lévi-Strauss, Claude. *Anthropologie structurale deux.* Paris, 1973. Pp. 31-35.

Lüthi, Max. *Märchen.* 5th ed. Stuttgart, 1974.

Mitchell, Roger E. "The Oedipus Myth and Complex in Oceania with Special Reference to Truk," *Asian Folklore Studies* 27 (1968): 131-45.

Novaković, St. "Die Oedipus-Sage in der südslavischen Volksdichtung," *Archiv für slavische Philologie* 11 (1888): 321-26. (See headnote to BL1.)

Propp, Vladimir. "Edipo alla Luce del Folclore." In *Edipo alla Luce del Folclore,* edited by Clara S. Janovič, pp. 85-137. Turin, 1975. (A translation of "Edip v. svete fol'klora." *Učenye zapiski Leningradskogo gosudarstvennog universiteta,* Serija filologičeskich 72. 1944. Fasc. 9, pp. 138-75.) An English translation appears in Edmunds and Dundes, pp. 76-121 (see above).

Raglan, Lord. *The Hero: A Study in Tradition, Myth and Drama.* London, 1936.

Ramanujan, A. K. "The Indian 'Oedipus'." In *Indian Literature,* edited by Arabinda Poddar, pp. 127-37. Indian Institute of Advanced Study, vol. 16. Simla, 1972. A thoroughly revised and expanded version appears in Edmunds and Dundes, pp. 234-61 (see above).

Rank, Otto. *Das Inzest-Motif in Dichtung und Sage.* Leipzig and Vienna, 1926.

———. "The Myth of the Birth of the Hero." In *The Myth of the Birth of the Hero and Other Writings,* edited by Philip Freund, pp. 3-96. New York, 1964.

Redford, Donald B. "The Literary Motif of the Exposed Child," *Numen* 14 (1967): 209-28.

Sanders, N. K. "The Irrelevance of Incest to Oedipus," *Agenda* 7 (1969): 23-28.

Schenkeveld, D. M. *"Van Sophocles tot Claus: Toneelstukken over Koning Oedipus"* (inaugural address). University of Amsterdam, 1972.

Thorslev, Peter L., Jr., "Incest as Romantic Symbol," *Comparative Literature Studies* 2 (1965): 41-58.
Turner, Terence S. "Oedipus: Time and Structure in Narrative Form." In *Forms of Symbolic Action* (Proceedings of the 1969 Annual Spring Meeting of the American Ethnological Society), edited by Robert F. Spencer, pp. 26-68. Seattle, 1970.
von Hahn, J. G. *Sagwissenschaftliche Studien.* Jena, 1876. Pp. 340-44.

BIBLIOGRAPHY 4: PUBLISHED SOURCES OF THE ANALOGUES IN THE COLLECTION

Abraham of Vilna. *Rav Po'olim.* Warsaw, 1894. [HE1]
Amélineau, E. *Contes et romans de l'Égypte chrétienne.* vol. 1. Paris, 1888. [AR?1(FR)]
Baum, P. F. "The Medieval Legend of Judas Iscariot," *PMLA,* NS 24 (1916): 490-91. [LT1—also in Rand]
Callaway, Henry. *Nursery Tales, Traditions, and Histories of the Zulus.* London, 1868. [ZL1]
Caxton, William. *The Golden Legend or Lives of the Saints.* Vol. 3. London, 1900; reprinted, New York, 1973. [LT2]
Ciszewski, Stanisław. *Krakowiacy: Monografja Etnograficzna.* Vol. 1. Cracow, 1894. [PL2]
Čubinskij, P. P. *Trudy Ètnografičesko-statističeskoj èkspedicii v" zapadno-russkijkraj (Jugo-zapadnyj otdel").* Vol. 1. St. Petersburg, 1872. [UK2]
Dabrowska, Stanisława. "Przypowiastki I Bajki Z Żabna," *Wisła: Miesiecznik Gieograficzny i Etnograficzny* 19 (1905): 398-401. [PL1]
d'Ancona, Alessandro. *La Leggenda di Vergogna.* . . . Bologna, 1869. [IT2-3; IT3 also in Knust]
Dragomanov, Mikhail. *Malorrusskiia narodnyĩa predaniĩa i razskazy.* Kiev, 1876. [UK1]
Espinosa, Aurelio M. *Cuentos Populares Españoles.* Vol. 1. Madrid, 1946. [SP1]
Ferrand, Gabriel. *Contes populaires malgaches.* Paris, 1893. [ML1(FR)]
Fischer, John L. "A Ponapean Oedipus Tale," *Journal of American Folklore* 79 (1966): 112-13. [PO1] Another version appears in Fischer, Saul Riesenberg, and M. G. Whiting, *The Book of Luelen.* Canberra, 1977.
Gonzenbach, Laura. *Sicilianische Märchen aus dem Volksmund gesammelt.* Pt. 2. Leipzig, 1870. [IT1(GM)]
Hasluck, Margaret. "Oedipus Rex in Albania," *Folk-Lore* 40 (1949):

341–43. [AL1] Another translation appears in S. E. Mann, *A Short Albanian Grammar*. London, 1932.

Jacobus de Voragine: *see* Caxton, W.

Jacopo da Varaggio: *see* Caxton, W.

Jahn, Samia. "Themen aus der griechischen Mythologie und der orientalischen Literatur in volkstümlicher Neugestaltung in nördlichen und zentralen Sudan," *Fabula* 16 (1975): 65–66. [AR2(GR)]

Juhász, László, "Népmese: A jövendeőleis," *Magyar Nyvelvőr* 25 (1896): 572–74. [HU3]

Kálmány, Lajos. *Hagymányok: Mesék és Rokonnemüek*. Vol. 1. Vácz, 1914. [HU2]

Karadžić, Vuk Stefanović. *Srpske narodne pjesme*. 2d ed. Vol. 2. Belgrade, 1895. [SC1–2]

Knust, Hermann, "Italienische Märchen," *Jahrbuch für romänische und englische Literatur* 7(1886): 398–401. [IT3—also in d'Ancona]

Kostomarov, N. *Pamjatniki Starinnoj Russkoj Literatury*. St. Petersburg, 1860; reprinted, The Hague and Paris, 1970. [OR1]

——. "Legenda o krovosmesitele," *Istoriceskija monogratii i izseldovanija*. 2d ed. Vol. 1. St. Petersburg, 1872. [RS1]

Lamanskij, V. I. "Neporešennyj vopros˝ Bolgarskoe narečie i pis'mennost' v˝ xvi–xvii věkax," pt. 2. In *Žurnal˝ Ministerstva narodnago prosvěščenija*, pp. 112–14. St. Petersburg, July 1869. [BL1—a Serb version is in Novaković]

Lessa, William A. *Tales From Ulithi Atoll: A Comparative Study in Oceanic Folklore*. University of California Publications: Folklore Studies 13. Berkeley and Los Angeles, 1961. [UL1]

Mason, J. Alden. "Porto-Rican Folklore: Riddles," *Journal of American Folklore* 29 (1916): 499. [SP2]

——. "Porto-Rican Folklore: Folktales," *Journal of American Folklore* 37 (1924): 304–5. [SP3]

Megas, G. "Ho Ioudas eis tas Paradoseis tou Laou," *Epetēris tou Laographikou Archeiou* 3 (1941–42): 3–32. [GK1; GR1–3]

——. "Ho peri Oidipodos Mythos," *Epetēris tou Laographikou Archeiou* 3(1941–42):198–200. [KV1(GR)—a very similar version is in Papahagi]

Niedre, I. J., ed. *Latviešu Pasakas*. Vol. 2. Riga, 1948. [LA1]

Novaković, S. "Die Oedipus-Sage in der südslavischen Volksdichtung," *Archiv für slavische Philologie* 11 (1888): 324–26. [A Bulgarian version of Lamanskij, BL1]

Obert, Franz. "Rumänische Märchen und Sagen aus Siebenbürgen," *Archiv fur siebenbürgische Landeskunde* NF 42 (1924): 454–55. [RM1(GM)]

Papahagi, P. N. *Basme Aromâne*. Bucharest, 1905. (See headnote to KV1(GR).)

Parsons, Elsie Clews. *Folk-lore of the Antilles, French and English.* Pt. 2. Memoirs of the American Folk-lore Society, vol. 26, pt. 2. New York, 1936. [FC1]

Qissat 'Antara ibn Shaddad Al-'Absi. Vol. 1. Cairo, 1961. [AR1]

Qvigstad, J. *Lappiske Eventyr og Sagn.* Vol. 1. Oslo, 1927. [LP1(NG)]

Rand, E. K. "Mediaeval Lives of Judas Iscariot." In *Anniversary Papers by Colleagues and Pupils of George Lyman Kittredge,* pp. 305-16. Boston, 1913. [LT1—also in Baum]

Róna-Sklarek, Elisabet. *Ungarische Volksmärchen,* NF. Leipzig, 1909 [HU1(GM)]

Rudbeck, Erik. *Suomalaisen Kirjallisuuden Toimituksia.* Vol. 17 = *Suomen Kansan Satuja Ja Tarinoita.* Vol. 2. Helsinki, 1854. (See headnote to FI7.)

Salmelainen, Eero (pseud.): *see* Rudbeck

Schullerus, Pauline. "Rumänische Volksmärchen aus dem mittleren Harbachtale," *Archiv des Vereins für siebenbürgische Landeskunde,* NF 33 (1905): 531-34. [RM2(GM)]

Smirnov, A. M. "Sbornik″ velikorusskix″ skazok″ arxiva Russkago geografičeskago obščestva," *Zapiski Russkago geografičeskago obščestva po otděleniju ètnografii* 44 (1917): 129, 526-28. [RS2-3]

Swan, Charles. *Gesta Romanorum or Entertaining Moral Stories . . . ,* rev. and corr. Wynnard Hooper. London, 1877. [LT3]

Index of Sources

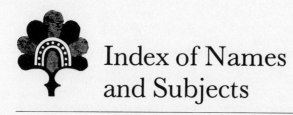

Index of Names
and Subjects